Perspectives on Research and Scholarship in Composition

Edited by
Ben W. McClelland and
Timothy R. Donovan

The Modern Language Association of America
New York 1985

Library of Congress Cataloging-in-Publication Data

Main entry under title:

Perspectives on research and scholarship in composition.

  Bibliography: p.
  Includes index.
  1. English Language—Rhetoric—Study and teaching—Research—Addresses, essays, lectures. 2. English language—Composition and exercises—Study and teaching—Research—Addresses, essays, lectures. I. McClelland, Ben W., 1943–
II. Donovan, Timothy R.
PE1404.P45   1985   808'.042'072   85-15401
ISBN 0-87352-144-7
ISBN 0-87352-145-5 (pbk.)

Published by The Modern Language Association of America
10 Astor Place, New York, New York 10003

Second printing, 1986
Third printing, 1987
Fourth printing, 1988
Fifth printing, 1990

Contents

Contents

Preface

At a national conference in the fall of 1982, an English department chairman greeted us at a reception by remarking that he used our collection of essays *Eight Approaches to Teaching Composition* in his teacher preparation classes. He jested that composition studies had changed so much in just the two years since the publication of *Eight Approaches* that perhaps we should publish another book, called *Eight More Approaches to Teaching Composition*. That joke led to serious discussion and the genesis of this book. If *Eight Approaches* had shed some light on changing composition pedagogy, a similar publication might be useful for composition research and scholarship. During the rest of that conference we walked through the hotel corridors from one panel meeting to the next, talking with prominent composition scholars, who confirmed the need for such a book. By the end of the conference the book was launched.

The traditional closing line here is, "And the rest is publishing history," but we need to add a few more lines. Over the months of writing, our contributors maintained a dialogue by meeting at national conferences, mailing around drafts, and conferring by telephone. The result, we believe, is a multi-authored book with a particularly fresh and coherent treatment of its subject.

Perspectives is a collection of a dozen original essays presenting the major research and scholarship in the sundry but related fields that are shaping the theory and practice of composition studies. Each chapter defines a special area of study, assesses its published literature from the perspective of the author's (or authors') expertise, and presents issues or questions that remain to be addressed. Conscious of several points of convergence and departure, the contributors make note of such junctures and forks in the road. In addition, the composite bibliography and the index indicate both the common points of reference for their work as well as the disparate roads they travel.

The first chapter presents a professional and historical context for the role of composition in the English department. It recalls the dissolution of "English" as the discipline of rhetoric and oratory and the emerging dominance of literary criticism. It also describes, however, the interest in the teaching of writing that is both the result and the cause of the new research and scholarship in composition described herein. The chapter asserts that this new work argues for a redefinition of English studies, partly under the leadership of the MLA.

The next five chapters address major philosophical issues in our field. Lil Brannon surveys and analyzes three major philosophies of composing: the empirical-experimental, the phenomenological, and the philosophical-historical. She explains each school's theoretical basis by summarizing how each addresses questions about the nature of the composing process and writing pedagogy. Although these schools are a long way from formulating a unified theory of writing and the development of writing abilities, Brannon's analysis of their positions offers a productive means for studying the issues.

As the parent discipline, rhetoric is central to contemporary composition studies. Two controversial questions concern the role classical rhetoric should play in defining composition studies and the exact nature of contemporary rhetoric as an academic field. Cy Knoblauch, in his chapter, continues the discussion of things philosophical as he argues that rhetoric "is *generically* the study of discourse or language use" and that it includes writing as a subdivision; and so he focuses on the epistemological issues by which rhetoric and writing are related. Classical rhetoric continues to have a major impact on writing theory, but modern rhetoric is experiencing its own renaissance. An awareness of both the history and the current developments of rhetoric enables composition teachers and researchers to understand the "tradition in which they work even as they make their own contributions to it."

The split between teaching literature and teaching composition is longstanding, but the recent theories about the relation of writer and reader to written texts have begun a rapprochement. John Clifford and John Schilb survey these theories, especially approaches that use writing to understand literature and vice versa. Several new composing and critical theories, such as reader-response criticism, initiate the exploration of the dialectic between reader and writer, text and context. William Strong demonstrates how linguistics, the third major branch in English studies, continues to provide insights on composing. Recent critiques of sentence combining have sent its advocates searching for a rationale that sets it in the context of the composing process. In addition, new developments in the study of textual cohesion have led to illuminating ways of examining student writing. For Strong the information from these studies allows composition teachers to translate "new linguistic insights into activities that reveal, by induction and indirection, what we want students to internalize and transfer to their prose. The challenge, in short, is to use [text analysis] to extend understandings of the writing process."

In the next chapter John Trimbur moves the discussion again into a wider context—the philosophy of education and the nature of knowledge—as he examines the origins, theory, and current practices of collaborative learning in the teaching of writing. This new methodology challenges the basic educational philosophy of the academy by changing the roles of teacher and learner and by modifying traditional ideas about the authority of knowledge. In the familiar hierarchical model of education, the teacher-authority delivers knowledge to students. In collaborative learning, knowledge is created socially by a group of peers through language that they create and authorize. Answers to the fundamental questions about education that collaborative learning theory raises "can enrich composition studies by developing a much fuller sense of social and cultural contexts of composing."

The next five chapters survey the kind of research being conducted in composition. Anne Ruggles Gere explores the relation between composition research and evolving philosophies of science. Based on positivism, much of this century's early research on composition focused on matters of formal correctness and occurrence of error and on textual analysis. Recent changes in scientific epistemology have resulted, she relates, in different research methodologies and different questions about the meaning of competence and the categorizing of writing, for example.

Lucy McCormick Calkins examines research design and methodology. Citing the limitations of positivist research methods, she also examines problems of definition and theoretical base within the ethnographic and descriptive case-study research traditions. She calls on these naturalistic researchers—among whom she numbers herself—to examine carefully the theory on which their work is based and to develop common definitions of terms. Finally, Calkins calls for research "to involve theory building and reexamination as well as method testing."

Andrea Lunsford introduces cognitive studies as an interdisciplinary field that seeks a general theory of cognition and communication. She reviews the theories of representative cognitive-developmental theorists, including Piaget and Vygotsky, and examines the work of contemporary researchers who are applying cognitive studies to reading and writing. Demonstrating that cognitive studies make an important contribution to the field of composition, Lunsford raises questions that hold implications for teaching and research. For instance, what constitutes cognitive development in the college years? how is it related to comunication skills? and what cognitive processes are basic to all types of writing?

In the next chapter Glynda Hull explores the topic of error and correction. Nearly a decade ago Mina Shaughnessy first pointed out, in *Errors and Expectations*, how writing teachers who focus on error hunting misread or ignore the meaning of errors. Despite a great deal of revealing research in this field, many teachers continue fruitlessly to mark errors. Hull analyzes the relevant research on error, the meaning of error to a writer's development, and the ways error analysis may be used to help students improve their writing.

Research on children's writing has progressed significantly since Britton, Graves, and others demonstrated young writers' competence at composing, primarily narratives. Thomas Newkirk and Nancie Atwell, in their chapter, extend and modify that research by showing that the most current work in the field reveals that children's abilities are much more complex and sophisticated than the earlier research found. Young children can, in fact, effectively compose in a variety of expository forms.

The collection's last two chapters survey and assess two rapidly expanding areas of composition studies. Michael Keene reviews technical communication in the context of an information economy. Defining the field as an area of rhetoric specializing in information intended for practical purposes, Keene describes the branches of technical communication within and without academia and analyzes its current pedagogy and research concerns. He concludes by considering the concerns technical communicators have with the concept of audience in a society where information is becoming a more and more valuable commodity.

Hugh Burns describes the current research in artificial intelligence, explaining that it may lead to some promising applications for composition studies. He maintains that, by modeling expert systems, the emerging computer technology will help researchers understand better both the cognitive processes in writing and the evolving educational technology called intelligent computer-assisted instruction.

Collectively, the authors describe research and scholarship that repudiate the ignominy that composition studies once suffered within English departments. Their work recognizes the significant evolution of both literary and composition studies, rejects the isolated positions of narrow specialists, and calls for a reexamination of the disciplinary boundaries of English studies. Each perspective contributes to the dialogue by delineating the diverse areas of research and scholarship in composition. The authors' perspectives contribute to a creative revision of English studies and call on us to reconsider our understanding of the field and of ourselves as professionals. Pushed by this theory and pulled by that set of data into a state of disequilibrium, we are challenged to look wholly anew at the learning and teaching of writing and thereby renew our commitment to one another's work and to our work with our students. What we said of the essays in *Eight Approaches* is true of these: "They simply invite us to reconsider our own teaching, our own enactment of theory and practice in the classroom. It is through such dialogue that everyone stands to gain—but most of all our students" (Donovan and McClelland xv).

We want to acknowledge the assistance of a number of people in completing this project. David L. Greene, dean of faculty at Rhode Island College, provided substantial personal and institutional support. The Rhode Island College Faculty Research Fund supported the project's beginning work with a grant. Paul O'Connell supported the idea and encouraged our work throughout. Frances Taylor and Natalie DiRissio provided professional typing services par excellence. Ellen F. Gardiner not only provided typing and proofreading services but also served generally as an editorial assistant, troubleshooting on many fronts. The book manuscript was submitted to the MLA both on computer diskettes for typesetting and on paper; the considerable computer-related problems that arose involved additional work for everyone, and we give thanks for their enduring patience. Computer personnel on many campuses lent expertise, including Peter Harman, director of the Computer Center at Rhode Island College. Special thanks go to Roslyn Schloss, assistant managing editor of MLA publications, who—with a keen eye, a sharpened pencil, and great patience—shaped the manuscript into a book that meets the academic community's expectations of high editorial standards. Finally, we want to thank Walter Achtert, the MLA's director of book publications and research programs, for his eager interest, seasoned advice, and sure guidance of this project to its completion.

Ben W. McClelland
Timothy R. Donovan
April, 1985

Where Are English Departments Going?

Ben W. McClelland and Timothy R. Donovan

Nearly twenty years ago William Riley Parker, secretary of the Modern Language Association, posed this question in the title of his address to the members of the Association of Departments of English: "Where Do English Departments Come From?" Even though the question came from a respected Milton scholar and commonsensical Hoosier, it must have sounded anachronistic and naive. After all, major figure and period courses in literature were flourishing, and English departments in general were busy meeting the quotidian demands of expansion in American higher education. Who cared, really, where we came from?

But while our eyes were riveted on the promising future, Parker reminded us of Cicero's admonition, "Not to know what happened before one was born is always to be a child" (Parker 339).

Undoubtedly, Parker surprised many and vexed a few with his answer:

> It was the teaching of freshman composition that quickly entrenched English departments in the college and university structure – so much so that no one seemed to mind when professors of English, once freed from this slave labor, became as remote from everyday affairs as the classicists had ever been. . . . Surprising as the idea may at first appear to you, there was, of course, no compelling reason at the outset why the teaching of *composition* should have been entrusted to teachers of the English language and literature. (347)

Entrusted in theory but relegated in practice, for the emergence of a literature curriculum during the latter half of the nineteenth century and the split from oratory at the beginning of the twentieth had redefined the study of "English" in the academy. Already seeming more concerned with language as the ornament rather than the origin of thought, rhetoric was soon reduced to and identified with freshman theme writing, dispersed, as Parker elegized, "to academic thinness" (349). Squeezed into a single course or two, it was often further distilled for beginners – students and instructors alike – into the so-called modes of discourse: description, narration, exposition, persuasion. Some English departments, dominated by scholars of New Criticism, often turned to reading and critiquing literature, excluding all other forms of writing. And too frequently a discipline with the heritage of Aristotle and Quintilian settled for drilling in rules and correcting mistakes. The medieval trivium (grammar, logic, rhetoric) had become, finally, trivial.

As secretary of the MLA for over a decade, Parker blamed this devolution in part on the "acquisitiveness and expediency" of departments of English that "cared much less about liberal education and their own integrity than . . . about their administrative power and prosperity" (350). But surely some of the blame lay in the confusion over what modern composition was—or might become—as a discipline. It was, after all, a subject in which few teachers had specialized. In fact, it was considered not much of a subject at all. Four years after Parker's speech was published, James Kinneavy introduced his influential book on discourse theory by noting the "present anarchy" of composition studies and by observing that:

> Composition is so clearly the stepchild of the English department that it is not a legitimate area of concern in graduate studies, is not even recognized as a subdivision of the discipline of English in a recent manifesto put out by the major professional association [MLA] of college English teachers [Thorpe], in some universities is not a valid area of scholarship for advancement in rank, and is generally the teaching province of graduate assistants or fringe members of the department. (*Theory* 1)

One of the earliest surveys of modern research in written composition (Braddock, Lloyd-Jones, and Schoer) corroborated this view, citing the relative scarcity of valuable scholarship in the field. Kinneavy called for such work, saying that "there are histories to be written, there are theories to be evaluated, there are many important questions to be raised and answered," even while acknowledging that the nascent field lacked a comprehensive disciplinary system that might receive "some general acceptance and which could serve as a framework for research, further speculation, innovation, even repudiation" (2).

When the profession's waxing moon waned during the next five years, Richard Ohmann, former editor of *College English*, asserted that it was time to reconsider how well we had done with the subject entrusted to us:

> Freshman English is our sore subject. Or at least it was until sorer subjects came along: enrollments began to decline, budgets to shrink, and Ph.D. candidates to go jobless. And even these troubles are in part epiphenomena of our troubles with freshman English. . . . [O]ur

inability to make sense of freshman English for ourselves and our colleagues has made hard times even harder. (133)

Ohmann went on to charge, "[T]he kind of acculturation [grammar usage, verbal decorum] practiced in [freshman English], with red pencil and *Harbrace Handbook*, is not the kind Matthew Arnold or the professional ideologues have envisioned" (229). Meanwhile, the American public, responding to falling SAT scores and concern over a perceived decline in literacy, asked for just that, urging the profession to go "back to basics" as though the basics practiced by English departments had at some time really been coherently defined and were worth the going back to.

But within the last decade, especially, the English department's stepchild has come of age as an academic field. Research in the entire composing process—from initial impetus to final presentation—has both expanded and deepened our understanding of writing. No longer is composing regarded merely as the transcribing of thought onto paper or the application of form to content. Now we regard it more properly as a complex, recursive interaction of thought and language. The modes of discourse, too, have been modified by new theories about genres, purpose and audience; composition has rediscovered its classical heritage; and it has formed research alliances with new disciplines as well. In short, while in isolation rhetoric has renewed itself.

That composition is emerging as a significant academic field can now be read in the record of its published research and scholarship. Every year for about the last ten years there has appeared at least one important collection of essays in composition studies, such as *Teaching Composition: 10 Bibliographic Essays* (1976), *Evaluating Writing: Describing, Measuring, Judging* (1977), *Research on Composing: Points of Departure* (1978), *Linguistics, Stylistics, and the Teaching of Composition* (1979), *Reinventing the Rhetorical Tradition* (1980), *The Writing Teacher's Sourcebook* (1981), *The Rhetorical Tradition and Modern Writing* (1982), *The Present State of Scholarship in Historical and Contemporary Rhetoric* (1983), and *Essays on Classical Rhetoric and Modern Discourse* (1984). Furthermore, there are some fifteen composition journals, from an assessment of which Robert Connors concludes, "Composition studies is a genuine discipline, no longer merely a hobby, or avocation, or punishment" ("Review" 349).

But as composition develops (with a concomitant jargon), the longstanding condescension of literary studies threatens to become mutual. Communication between the well-established professoriate and the newly enfranchised specialists can be tenuous, especially when political turf, academic status, and intellectual orientation seem to hang in the balance. Still, were composition or literature specialists to remain isolated, they would bring a plague on the common academic house. As Wayne Booth warned in the 1982 MLA presidential address:

> Too often, when people address the scandalous divorce of composi-
> tion and rhetoric from literature and criticism, they talk as if the harm
> all flowed one way, against the teaching of writing. We forget that
> scholarship itself, which for many of us is still the raison d'être of
> the MLA, is a major victim whenever it is torn from its roots: the
> effort to free minds into critical understanding. (320)

Leaders from across the profession now stress the common points of interest between contemporary literary and composition theories (see Booth's "The Common Aims"). Bruce T. Petersen, for example, proposes a unified theory of reading, interpretation, and composition. Nan Johnson suggests ways of discovering correspondences in our views of text creation and interpretation, calling on us to develop a "coherent professional identity . . . [by] creating a common philosophical, theoretical, and pedagogical language" (25). Louise Weatherbee Phelps's theories about text and process present another opportunity to discuss the points of convergence between writers, texts, and readers ("Dialectics"). Some writing programs are embracing not just literary analysis but the discourse of other humanities disciplines and the sciences and social sciences as well (Maimon, "Maps and Genres"; Art Young; Kinneavy, "Writing"). Thus, the profession is engaged in a conversation about how composition will be defined and how it will serve the academy, both within and without English departments.

The Modern Language Association's interest in stimulating productive discussion of the issues can be seen in recent articles in the *ADE Bulletin*. In addition, in 1983 the MLA established a Commission on Writing and Literature, charged with:

> improving communication between those who teach writing or liter-
> ature primarily; with developing programs, publications, and projects
> that will improve the teaching and study of both fields and our un-
> derstanding of the relation between them; with encouraging depart-
> ments to institute policies adequate to the range of programs they
> offer; and with identifying ways in which the MLA and ADE can
> support the teaching of writing and literature in the secondary
> schools. (Brod and Franklin iii)

The Association of Departments of English has also organized a coalition of professional associations charged with holding a symposium in the summer of 1987 designed along the model of the Dartmouth conference on the teaching of English two decades ago. The coalition's aims are no less ambitious than to initiate a new millennium in English studies.

We have learned a good deal more about who we are since Parker's history lesson in 1967. But the uncertainty today about the future of the profession indicates that we have still more to learn. It would be comforting if the corollary question to Parker's could be answered definitively: "Where Are English Departments Going?" Certainly, if the future of English departments is, like their past, tied closely to rhetoric and composition, at the very least a more varied curriculum lies ahead. Even more than that there may come an inclusive, comprehensive redefinition of "English" as well. William Riley Parker believed that "To live intellectually only in one's own time is as provincial and misleading as to live intellectually only in one's own culture" (339). We would add that bridging the intellectual division among the branches of English would be a way constructively to shape our own time and culture and that of the future, too.

Toward a Theory of Composition

Lil Brannon

People new to composition studies are often puzzled by the conversation among practitioners, scholars, and researchers who have staked claims in its area of inquiry. Composition draws together literary critics, psychologists, linguists, educators on all levels, rhetoricians, learning theorists, and philosophers in a common concern for composing in writing. Because those interested in composing come from varying disciplinary vantage points, they have, at times, conflicting theoretical commitments, and they value different, occasionally competing research methodologies. Amidst the seeming confusion that such diversity has caused, even many composition specialists question whether their work constitutes a "field" rather than merely a shared interest. To the extent that membership in a field presumes, as Janet Emig has noted, "a ready understanding and colloquial use of that discipline's (1) lexicon; (2) syntax and rhetoric; (3) definitions of evidence, including methods of inquiry; (4) its root metaphors and governing paradigms; and . . . (5) its tacit tradition" (*Web* 147), composition is predisciplinary, dependent on established intellectual perspectives to identify its directions and goals, its methodologies, its standard historical texts, and its conceptual heritage. But to the extent that composition studies is defined by a bounded subject matter, a preoccupation with certain root questions binding researchers and teachers together, there is increasing legitimacy in the suggestion that it is indeed emerging as a "field."

Particularly, composition studies is concerned with answering the following questions:

1. What is the nature of the composing process?
2. How does one develop from an inexperienced to a mature writer?
3. How can schools, particularly teachers of writing, assist the development of writers?

Of course, though I have listed these questions separately, researchers in the field do not necessarily see them as distinct and therefore do not always (or even typically) focus on answering one rather than another. Rather, because composition is so strongly linked to the teaching of writing, researchers often view the questions as interrelated and attempt to answer more than one in any given study. For example, in her important work on the revision processes of student writers and experienced adult writers, Nancy Sommers attempts, at least in part, to answer all three questions ("Revision Strategies"). The statements offered from experienced adult writers pertaining to their concepts of revision give us insight into the nature of the composing process. The statements of the student writers, to the extent that they diverge from the experienced adults, may show us how college freshmen are developmentally different from more experienced adults. Issues of development, because of their evident relation to curricular design and strategies of teaching, often interest researchers. So, to the extent that Sommers offers observations about how student writers' previous schooling limited their understanding of revision and to the extent that she makes recommendations about how to encourage revision in the classroom, she is answering the third question. The fact that much recent research addresses more than one of these questions does not mean that the questions are inextricable. But it does mean that we must consider carefully the emphases of a given researcher and the implications that an attempt to answer one question may have (or may be asserted to have) for answering the others.

Not only must we consider the research questions, but we must examine closely the research methodology as well. At present composition studies is dominated by three strands of research: the empirical-experimental, the phenomenological-ethnographic, and the philosophical-historical. They are complementary in some ways but competing in others. Each has contributed to a theory of composition, although the intellectual traditions underlying them and the theoretical commitments that shape them are quite different. The empirical-experimental perspective assumes that the methodology originally developed in the natural sciences can be applied to human behavior as well, specifically the intellectual and social act of composing in writing. The social sciences, including psychology and sociology, have depended on experimental method for a century or more. Composition has looked to it only recently, in a move, dating from the early 1960s, to become more carefully and deliberately analytical. Empirical-experimental researchers try to discover general principles in an attempt to organize phenomena within categories into which all cases, no matter their context, can be subsumed (see Gere's article in this collection). They observe and study some range of experience while assuming that they stand apart from and independent of it, seeking to classify it in terms of the objective characteristics that systematic inquiry reveals. By contrast, the phenomenological perspective, a still more recent development in composition research, assumes that context cannot be stripped from the experience under study and that the researcher cannot stand apart from what he or she observes. Phenomena, from this vantage point, are not dispassionately reducible to "objective" characteristics. Rather, the perception of characteristics arises from the researcher's way of looking and of making connections. Researchers in this area depend on the human science tradition for its research method of "naturalistic inquiry," observation, and "thick description" (Mishler; Geertz, *Interpretation*; and, in this volume, Calkins). The third perspective, the philosophical-historical, is perhaps the oldest of the three, and, like the other two perspectives, it depends on observation. But philosophical research attends to experience chiefly in order to assess the well-formedness and conceptual adequacy of statements intended to characterize it, while historical research attempts to connect earlier and later formulations as coherent developments. These researchers look for plausible lines of reasoning to describe the nature and purposes of composing and for characterizations of the assumptions and values that underlie different arguments. Typically, philosopher-historians look to other texts throughout history that may enhance or illuminate the arguments they offer (see Knoblauch's essay in this volume). Their methodology is much like that of the literary critic or the rhetorician (see North, *Dynamics of Inquiry*).

Over the last two decades, researchers from all three perspectives have made considerable progress toward answering the questions of the field. Any review of writing theory before this time shows the greater number of studies to be narrowly concerned with teaching alternatives, attempts to prove that one classroom strategy is superior to another, without examining first if any teacher intervention assists the development of writers or if any classroom method is congruent with a theory of composing (see Braddock et al.). Janet Emig's well-known 1971 study, *The Composing Processes of Twelfth Graders*, was one of the first to question whether the theory of composing implicit in textbooks and expounded in traditional classrooms bore relation to how children actually compose in writing. Since then, researchers and philosophers of composition have been concerned, for the most part, with theory, with an attempt to derive the general principles that underlie composing and to formulate an inclusive description of the nature and value of composing and the nature of learning to write. They have written primarily to an audience of teachers, practitioners whose motive is to bring theory, examined or not, to bear on classroom practice. The complexities of learning to write, coupled with the issues and problems associated with the teaching of writing, have, therefore, become the starting point for the development of a theory of composition. Of course, the questions that define the field remain unanswered and an articulated philosophy of composition remains to be written, so it is difficult to see how the discipline is emerging. Issues in the teaching of writing and in the development of writing abilities are often researched and discussed in very narrow terms, resulting in isolated clusters of ideas and practices with nothing to connect them. Yet I believe that by examining this research one can discover some unifying theoretical premises that are beginning to shape our field of study. I can only attempt here to be representative, and the organizing framework I offer is unavoidably based on my own values concerning the theory and teaching of writing. But composition studies cannot hope to become truly coherent without prior and persistent efforts to assert its coherence and to evaluate the success of different assertions. Consider, then, the first of the three questions that encompass my sense of the unity of the field, and the ways in which researchers have attempted to answer it.

What is the nature of the composing process?

Only during the last two decades have scholars, researchers, and teachers of writing come self-consciously to this question as something highly problematic and unresolved. Until recently, the field had tacitly assumed that the process of composing was simply the conscious application of the rules and procedures that people learned in school. Those rules and procedures had evolved from traditional rhetorical and literary critical analysis of valued texts written by acclaimed professional writers. For instance, a critical judgment that expert discourse was organized around a controlling idea, with more general statements preceding more specific ones, typically led to inferences about the "operations" of composing and finally to textbook prescriptions. Teachers, then, would have students construct thesis statements and outlines as the beginning points of composing so that a paper could become focused and organized. Students were asked to memorize and practice rules for good writing and were exhorted to "be specific" or "be sure to write clearly," as though what students could recognize in skilled prose they could readily emulate in their own. This model of composing based on operations inferred from the examination of finished texts dominated the field for years, principally because it sustained classical rhetorical prescriptions while also suiting the angle of vision of those primarily responsible for writing instruction, namely, teachers of literature schooled in the methods of criticism (Knoblauch and Brannon, *Rhetorical Traditions*). Unfortunately, these prescriptions, this product-centered, mechanistic view of composing, still dominate much of the teaching of writing today, if textbook sales can be considered a reliable indicator (Donald C. Stewart, "Composition Textbooks"). Many practitioners are introduced to the field through these textbooks, and because most still find their primary intellectual commitments outside composition studies, they do not question the assumptions about composing represented there. But scholars and researchers in composition today do question those assumptions as well as the concepts and practices that traditional textbooks have so long supported.

Composition studies as a serious field of inquiry emerged, perhaps, when researchers began to scrutinize the product-centered orientation to composing. Among the first was Richard Braddock, who, in a detailed examination of texts written by modern writers ("Frequency"), discovered that topic sentences, one of the chief traditional features of paragraph organization, appeared with very little frequency and almost never as the first sentences of paragraphs in nonfiction prose. Others quickly began to follow suit, examining teaching practices for the underlying assumptions about composing. What they soon discovered was the vast separation between actual composing activity and textbook statements about it, between what writers do and what teachers tell them they ought to do. What was needed, the researchers recognized, was an examined theory of composing based on solid philosophical premises confirmed and elaborated through rigorous observation (Cooper and Odell, *Research*; Sommers, "Need for Theory"). Concurrently, those interested in composition began to turn to people outside of literary study and rhetoric, specifically to psychologists and educators, not only for their theoretical models of learning but for their research methodologies as well.

Those pursuing the question "What is the nature of the composing process?" did not abandon totally their analyses of the texts that writers produced; rather they enriched those analyses with observations of writers engaged in the act of writing and with speculation about what composing is and why people engage in it. In other words, scholars and researchers became interested just as much, if not more, in the writer writing a particular piece as in the final version of a text. Interest, however, in the writer writing, or in the "process of composing" as it has come to be called, presented its own problems, perhaps the most difficult being one of definition: what, in fact, did "process" mean? Although scholars and researchers were looking to modern views of language, discourse, and mind to assist them in defining terms, even a modern perspective did not provide a clear and plausible definition of *process*. Thus, for several years the dominant view of composing was that the process was linear, proceeding from prewriting, to writing, to revision, and finally to editing (Rohman, "Pre-Writing"; Murray, "Internal Revision"). After much activity based on this model of composing (prewriting heuristics, revision strategies), researchers began to point out the insufficiency of the theory for describing the actual behaviors of writers. Writing, in fact, does not proceed in a neat and organized way, nor does it necessarily follow a set of fixed stages. Few, if any, writers plan a piece totally before they begin to write and leave all revision until they have an entire manuscript in front of them. Process, then, could not be defined as a set of separate operations happening in fixed stages in the production of a text and still account for the behaviors of most experienced writers.

The dominant theory today posits that writing is a recursive process, happening in no fixed sequence. Sondra Perl ("Understanding Composing") describes this process as movements forward (projective structuring), where writers attend to shaping thoughts as they move along, making their meaning clear for their intended readers, and as movements backward (retrospective structuring), where writers shuttle back and forth from what they wanted to say, to the words they have written, and back to their inward sense of their ideas. Writers rely on this sense to determine whether or not to continue writing or to revise. This "sense" Perl calls "felt sense," the nonlinguistic feelings by which a writer determines if what has been said is indeed what was intended. James Britton offers a similar theory, "shaping at the point of utterance," which he describes as "the moment by moment interpretive process by which we make sense of what is happening around us" (*Prospect* 139), the enactment of the pattern-forming propensity of the mind, where one draws on a storehouse of perceived events and, through the intention to share the perceptions, shapes them anew. Ann Berthoff calls this process "learning the uses of chaos," trusting the form-finding, form-creating processes of mind to make meaning through language (*Making*). Writing offers the unique opportunity both to create experience and to reflect on it, to see and see again (Emig, *Web*). Writing is a way of knowing, a process of discovering connections amid the chaos of sensation, shaping a coherence through acts of language. The value of writing lies principally in the meaning-making and reflecting activities that it makes possible.

Using this perspective as a foundation, researchers have sought to test, extend, and elaborate the theory by observing writers writing. What has evolved over the last two decades are portraits of writers of all levels and abilities engaged in the complex act of composing in writing. The information yielded from this research has been valuable, but it has also raised new questions: what shall we regard as "normative" when we speak of "writing"? are some activities "developmental" rather than "mature"? how typical are the portraits gathered so far? are some simply idiosyncratic? For example, Nancy Sommers ("Revision Strategies") discovered that the professional writers she talked to had a concept of revision that included a willingness to sabotage the coherence of their texts and reformulate ideas. These writers saw revision as a way of making their meaning clearer and therefore saw their texts as malleable. College freshmen, by contrast, defined revision as simply changing a word here and there. Revision was only polishing a text, finding the right word or editing for spelling or mechanics. Given the small number of writers she was studying, we cannot be certain whether either portrait is typical of the group of writers it claims to describe. In the Paris Review *Interviews*, for example, professional writers tell of revision practices that appear to be similar to those of the college freshmen in Sommer's study. When Donald Murray agreed to keep meticulous records of his composing process as part of a research project, he discovered that he revises texts less than he had first thought (Berkenkotter and Murray). Further, we can't be certain whether the college freshmen have concepts of revision typical of a certain developmental level (that is, whether they exhibit behaviors of writers of normal development for their age and experience) or if they are in some way deficient and their behaviors problematic. In the face of such difficulties, a coherent characterization of composing in writing remains elusive. But the models that researchers have provided us, to the extent that they look at experienced adult writers, are at least suggestive, offering a starting point for further observation. Several major studies that discuss the composing processes of experienced adult writers are worthy of comment.

These studies can be divided into those that are concerned with describing the entire composing process and those that are concerned with smaller segments of the process. Perhaps the most extensive model of composing has been offered by Flower and Hayes ("Cognitive Process Theory"), who have attempted to describe the activities of skilled adult writers through a method used successfully in cognitive psychology, namely, protocol analysis. They analyze transcripts of taped recordings of writers thinking out loud while attempting writing tasks assigned by the researchers. Flower and Hayes describe writing as a goal-directed activity made up of three major elements: the environment, which includes everything outside the writer (the writing assignment, the physical location, the growing text itself); long-term memory, in which the writer has accumulated a history of composing and the material with which he or she writes; and the writing process, which includes the basic activities of planning, translating, and reviewing, all controlled by an internal monitor. Composing in writing, to Flower and Hayes, involves the dynamic interaction of these three elements. Instead of seeing composing as linear, they see it as hierarchically organized, a complex network of goals and subgoals, routines and subroutines, which are driven by a writer's purpose, audience, and subject. Experienced writers have quite elaborate sets of goals to which they return throughout composing, moving from lower- to higher-order goals in no fixed sequence and recreating their goals in the light of what they learn through the effort to compose. A main thrust of Flower and Hayes's research has been to classify these goals in the service of characterizing the entire process.

Other researchers have concentrated on particular aspects of composing or on the demands of particular tasks, the writers' concept of audience and purpose, the writers' planning and invention, or the practical problems of writing in the workplace (see, e.g., Knoblauch; Berkenkotter, "Understanding"; Susan Miller, "How Writers Evaluate"; Selzer, "Composing Process"; or, for a review of research on "audience," Ede). No matter their angle of vision, these researchers all begin with the assumption that composing involves the dynamic interplay of many activities, one or two of which they select for close analysis. While a variety of such specialized emphases is reflected in the literature, studies on revision seem to be the most prevalent. Perhaps revision has got the most attention because this process is a microcosm of the entire act of composing. In "Revision Strategies" Nancy Sommers describes experienced adult writers as being motivated to revise when they perceive dissonance between what they have written and what they intend to say. Their texts in progress are only tentative, and these writers are willing to delete segments, add more material, substitute one section for another, and rearrange the entire text if they perceive that they have not discovered or expressed their meaning. Faigley and Witte were able to confirm Sommers's work ("Analyzing Revision"). Where Sommers developed case-study profiles of writers through interviews with them about the texts they were composing, Faigley and Witte developed a system of analysis to be used on texts to quantify kinds of changes. After having professional writers not only compose a text but also revise one written by someone else, they discovered that experienced adults revised by substituting new material for old, rearranging material, and changing words or phrases; and, more important, they were able through revision to bring a text closer to the rhetorical demands of a particular situation.

Although case-study evidence about many aspects of composing is mounting, a coherent characterization of the nature of composing in writing still eludes us. The problems of developing a theory are enormously complex principally because so much of the writing process either resists reliable observation or remains altogether inaccessible to it. Whenever we look at writers in order to study them, our acts of looking affect their behavior as well as the picture we get of their behavior. The advantage of protocol research, for instance, has been that it offers us a glimpse of what writers might be thinking when they write. But the disadvantage is that the process the researchers wish to describe is distorted by the procedures used to gain access to it. Case-study research is not exempt from the same criticism. Although the case-study method offers a close and in-depth examination of some aspect of composing or of some group of writers composing, the methodology that sets up the researchers' angle of vision simultaneously sets up a system of controls that distort what goes on in the act of composing. Phenomenological research, so far almost absent from the field, acknowledges the intrusion of the researcher into what is being observed and so to some extent accounts for this intrusion through its process of describing events. But while phenomenological research can describe composing as a social act governed by observable public constraints, it can never describe the unobservable internal acts of mind that constitute each individual's performance. Inevitably, therefore, researchers are forced to depend to a large extent on speculation in order to develop a theory that can guide observation while also evolving in response to it. No easy task, certainly, but one that must be accomplished before we can assuredly begin to appraise the abilities of particular (student) writers with reference to a norm of "skilled adult performance." What is an experienced adult writer supposed to be able to do? Are individual writers' performances always rough approximations of a single standard of maturity? Or is there more than one standard? Or does composing in writing develop through stages of growth with different standards characterizing the stages? The trouble is, the number of completed studies that examine mature writers is relatively small and the number of writers studied even smaller.

How do people develop from inexperienced to mature writers?

Before we can attempt to answer this question, it is important to consider a prior question difficult enough in its own right. What do we mean by "development"? We know through commonsense observation that writing produced by children has different features from writing produced by more mature people. Children's writing does not display the same syntactic sophistication, the same rhetorical sensitivity, the same command of material, the same intellectual penetration of a subject, the same world-view as that of an adult writer. So it seems that if a child's text is observably different from an adult's, development must occur. But what is developing and what do we mean by development? The work of Piaget, Vygotsky, and others suggests that the powers of mind develop in observable and progressive stages. Development of this type is the acquiring of certain abilities that were inaccessible to a person at an earlier stage. The work of language-acquisition researchers (Bissex, Donaldson), however, complicates our definition of development and offers us a different sense of what might be developing. These researchers show us that, from birth to about age five, children develop all the essential linguistic resources of English in a predictable sequence of steps, suggesting a concept similar to Piaget's or Vygotsky's. But after age five, children continue to "develop" a competence they already have through repeated application; that is, the child's uses of language grow and mature, just as a child's body, which is an organic entity, grows and matures with time and use. It is difficult to determine which kind of development—the acquiring of previously unavailable abilities or the maturing of "innate" capacities—properly applies to changes that writers undergo. It is also difficult, when we speak of writing development, to point out exactly what is developing and to determine—whether we look at writers or at writing—what the indices of writing development might be. We have all known persons whose writing was linguistically or rhetorically inadequate even though they had developed intellectual competence. And we all have known persons who have written linguistically adequate prose lacking in intellectual substance. Is one of these groups more developed than the other? Is conceptual subtlety an indicator of writing ability or is that ability more properly limited to control of the technical operations that typify writing as opposed to other intellectual activity? How do we know when a particular activity, for instance the tendency to revise first drafts extensively, constitutes a sign of development (as Nancy Sommers argues) and when it simply indicates one of several equally possible and equally mature behaviors (some skilled writers, after all, do far less revising of texts than others do)? Finally, what has failed to develop when we speak of writers as remedial? What should they be able to do that they are not yet doing, and when should they have been able to do it? Is an observed "deficiency" the result of intellectual immaturity, or the result of insufficient writing experience, or the result of a failure or an inability to acquire skills? Can the incapacity—whatever it may be—be remedied through instruction? Or is the writer simply not "ready" to do what is being asked? When does a writer start to become remedial?

Does it happen in the first grade or the third, the seventh grade or the thirteenth? How do we know when a writer fails to develop? What are the signposts? Although we know that some seventeen-year-olds are clumsy writers, others are highly skilled. Keats had produced a substantial body of work at an age when others have barely begun to control the medium. The fact is, we cannot as yet answer any of these questions satisfactorily, given the present state of research. We simply don't know what is developing when we speak of writing abilities developing or what stages, if any, constitute that development.

Added to the intrinsic difficulty of the questions is the limited and still embryonic research designed to answer them. The handful of studies completed so far have restricted themselves to describing a writer or a small number of writers over a short period of time, the longest being six years (Bissex), or to describing a group of writers at one age and comparing them to a group of writers at another (see Sommers, "Revision Strategies," or Susan Miller, "How Writers Evaluate"). These descriptive accounts may offer us a sense of the kinds of competencies that are manifest at certain maturational levels, but subject to the philosophical complications just mentioned. We can add other insights to these by piecing together studies that have attempted to describe the composing processes of different individuals: for example, Calkins's of a first-grade child (*Lessons*); Emig (*Composing Processes*) and Bridwell ("Revising Strategies") on twelfth graders; Sommers ("Revision Strategies"), Peitzman, and Onore on college freshmen; and Sommers ("Revision Strategies") and Flower ("Writer-Based Prose") on mature adults. By seeing each of these studies as an instance of a writer developing, we gain some insight (perhaps) into how a child might develop into a mature adult writer. Again, the difficulty of asserting from such studies that writers "develop" lies in the danger of moving from conclusions about individual writers with certain kinds of skills to an entirely different order of conclusion about when or how or even if those writers at earlier moments came to acquire such skills. If we overlook this difficulty for a moment, however, and emphasize instead the pictures of individual writers that recent research offers us, we can speculate about a possible course of writing development. The course would appear to progress from children's first scribbles as attempts to shape their world visually, through the discovery that their speech can be represented by means of symbols, through their use of written language to shape the world symbolically and reflect on their experiences of it, and culminating in an ability to use writing to discover and communicate meanings that accomplish both private and public intentions in different circumstances. Young children eventually learn the conventional aspects of writing through their interactions with print.

The development of writing abilities, therefore, seems to be connected with children's abilities to read and their willingness to use writing to make and share meaning (Frank Smith).

Despite our limited knowledge of the stages of development that writers may go through, a concept of "remedial writers" has evolved that assumes a priori the concept of development and looks to what writers' texts supposedly indicate about their lack of competence. The features of writers' texts are typically compared with teachers' estimates of what writers ought to be able to do in their classes. Those writers who meet teachers' expectations are considered competent. Those who do not are considered remedial or basic, in need of special attention and often additional instruction. Leaving aside the question of our ability at this time to determine what writers "should" be able to do at particular moments, the possible causes and cures of the "remedial" writer have preoccupied a number of researchers. Mina Shaughnessy was among the first to describe the features of basic (i.e., remedial) writers' prose and to offer suggestions about stimulating their development. Her most important contribution was her reappraisal of the concept of "error," regarding it in positive developmental terms, as an indicator of growth deriving from any writer's attempt to try new and more complex structures (*Errors*). Sondra Perl suggests that basic writers often prematurely edit their work, a concern for correctness overpowering the concern for making of meaning. Their fear of failure, their lack of experience in sustaining written expression, their focus on rules and formats for writing, all tend to inhibit their ability to compose and to grow as writers ("Composing Processes"). Mike Rose has found that the "inflexible rules and rigid plans" presumed by well-intentioned teachers to assist composing may actually inhibit writers who fear putting words on paper. He, Andrea Lunsford ("What We Know"), and others argue that writers develop when they are afforded opportunities to write, to read their work to trusted readers, to hear responses, and to revise their work to make their meanings clearer. These researchers make the case that a premature concern about correctness shifts the writer's attention away from developing ideas and may truncate the writing process. They suggest further that writers develop through exercising their competencies as composers, not through the learning of abstract principles of grammar, style, or structure. David Bartholomae argues that the difficulties of basic writers are even more complicated because these writers often read into their texts the meanings they intended to be there rather than the actual words on the page ("Study of Error"). These insights into basic writers' composing processes are interesting and may prove fruitful. Moreover the most recent arguments for assisting basic writers' development are, if nothing else, more humane than earlier emphases on relentless drilling. But what must continue to trouble us is our uncertainty about the nature of development and the difficulty of estimating writers' abilities in the absence of real knowledge about what writers are supposed to be able to do and how they come to be able to do it.

The reason researchers have been frustrated in their efforts to describe writing development has been partly because the student writing they require for their studies has been artificially constrained by the requirements and preoccupations of the school environment. Traditionally, schools have imposed their own model of development and have taught in accordance with it. The model assumes that writers acquire competence by mastering gradually more complicated skills, from the making of sentences to organizing paragraphs to developing essays. Typically teachers locate the "skills" that students need to master by recollecting the features of skilled adult prose and noting the extent to which student writing fails to manifest those features. Then the "skills" are arranged in ascending order of complexity through the school curriculum. Students have been compelled to "develop" their practice with reference to the artificial agenda of the school, usually through writing assignments tailored to a priori assumptions about growth. Hence a belief that growth includes learning to write topic sentences yields assignments that require them. Researchers have had difficulty approaching the question of development as long as the behaviors of the writers they have studied have been forced to conform so narrowly to these school assumptions and practices. Recently, however, new models of development have begun to oppose the traditional school model, evolving in the light of work in learning theory, sociolinguistics, and philosophy of language. As these newer theories have evolved they have begun to change both the assumptions about development and the means of assisting it that are enforced in schools. Generally, researchers and theorists agree that, instead of developing from correctness, to clarity, and finally to fluency—the priorities followed in schools—writing abilities develop in precisely the opposite way: from fluency, to clarity, to correctness (Mayher, Lester, and Pradl). An elaborate theoretical model of development is offered by James Moffett, who sees writers developing first by exploring the "drama" of what is happening now to an audience close to the writer and then by moving on to more and more complex intellectual tasks assuming readers progressively more distant from the writer.

Perhaps the most influential research study in the area of writing development, the first to give us a glimpse of the paucity of writing in the schools and one of the first to offer a new model of writing development, is James Britton et al., *The Development of Writing Abilities, 11–18*, a descriptive study of the writing produced in selected London schools. Although the expressed

purpose of the study was to investigate the stages by which children acquire competence in written discourse, the researchers could not describe
those stages, because the children were offered so few opportunities to compose outside of the restricted boundaries of school writing described above.
To Britton et al., the dominant motive for writing is self-expression; communicative and aesthetic abilities depend on the nurturing of the expressive capacity. Expressive writing is the logical starting point for the nurturing
of writing abilities because it has its foundations in talk. Writing to readers
who value the writer and the writer's ideas could provide a context for
growth, just as children learning to talk do so because the contexts are
supportive. Britton et al. theorize that as writers mature, they become more
able to differentiate their own worldview from that of others. Their texts,
therefore, manifest their ability to take into account the needs of readers
beyond themselves. Their writing then moves out along a continuum from
expressive toward "transactional" writing, which is the writing of the world
of work (expository or argumentative), or from expressive to poetic writing, which is the writing of literature (poems, short stories, novels, drama).

   Those theorists and researchers (among them Maimon, "Talking"; Martin et al.; Fulwiler and Young; and Wotring and Tierney) exploring the
uses of writing to learn across the curriculum have used Britton's model
when advocating conditions that might facilitate development. Like Britton they draw on learning theory offered by Bruner and concepts of language learning offered by Piaget and Vygotsky to posit that developing
writers need to write often to trusted readers, people who are more interested
in what the writers have to say than in the formal and technical lapses
that the discourse might manifest, and that writing abilities develop when
people are afforded opportunities to exercise their natural human competence to make and share meaning by writing in a variety of modes for their
own purposes to many different audiences. They support Britton et al. and
Applebee, who argue that the paucity of writing in the schools stifles the
creative imagination and allows little room for intellectual growth through
writing. Britton, for example, reported that the ability to abstract appears
to be a highly significant index of development for children ages eleven
to eighteen, that few students they studied reached the level of theorizing,
and that this result might be attributable to the lack of thinking opportunities offered students or to the wide variance in the rates teachers throughout the curriculum move students up the levels of abstraction. Research
in this area draws also from the work of William Perry, who offers a model
of intellectual and ethical development in the college years (*Forms*). Perry's
schema of development, based on a longitudinal study, posits that students
move from dependence on authority to a more relative stance as they grow

through their college experiences. He argues that a liberal arts education stimulates a student to grow in this way. Writing researchers have used Perry's categories in order to describe the substance of student writing (see Bizzell, "William Perry").

Along the course of this broad movement from self-expression to the full control of public discourse, certain features of texts appear to indicate evolving competence. One such feature is syntactic maturity. Developed by Kellogg Hunt and by John Mellon, who researched how young children and adults combine sentences, this measure gives us broad indicators of syntactic features that appear in child, young-adult, and adult writing. For example, children before the age of thirteen tend to use simple and coordinate structures where older children begin to rely on more complex structures. Apart from syntactic maturity, however, most of the technical and structural features of prose—facility with usage and the mechanics of written discourse as well as organizational facility—have been shown to be less reliable as developmental indicators than previously expected. Recent case-study research (Graves with elementary school children, *Writing*; and Onore, Peitzman, and Freedman and Pringle, "Writing in the College Years," with adults) suggests that when writers push toward intellectual complexity in their work, their texts may not demonstrate the formal and technical competence of their previous, less complex texts. In other words, writing abilities, even on the level of technical facility, do not grow ever better from draft to draft or from paper to paper. Rather, when writers grapple with ideas, they may lose some of the control over their writing that they previously enjoyed (Barritt and Kroll). Further, as writers take intellectual risks in their work, they may write more elaborated and complex sentences, which in themselves provide more opportunity for writers to lose technical control. Part of the difficulty of relying on textual features in making judgments about development is the complexity of evaluative reading (Williams, "On Defining Complexity"). It is simply very difficult to get groups of readers, however well-trained they are, to agree consistently about what constitutes good writing or to agree about the extent to which writing fails to meet some standard of maturity (Diederich; Cooper, *Nature*; Cooper and Odell; Gere, "Written Composition"). Nevertheless, these difficulties notwithstanding, some of the most important achievements in the field of composition studies must eventually pertain to the question of development. We cannot claim to know the capacities of particular writers at particular moments, cannot predict what writers "should" be able to do, cannot speak about "improvement," cannot begin to make assertions about the "remedial" writer, cannot hope to differentiate between beneficial and impertinent instruction without more knowledge about how writers develop, what enables them to do so, and what competencies they can be expected to demonstrate through the course of their growth.

How can schools, particularly teachers of writing, assist the development of writers?

Until recently, the teaching of writing had been governed more by tradition and personal preference than by theoretical or research knowledge and had not been regarded as a subject for reflection or reconsideration. Even today most textbooks are very much like their late nineteenth-century ancestors, offering a hodgepodge of concepts, formulas, and instructional methods drawn from different rhetorical traditions with little philosophical or historical awareness and little more than conventional wisdom to sustain the enterprise (Stewart, "Composition Textbooks"). Hundreds of so-called "rhetorics" (manuals of practice), handbooks, readers, and workbooks dominate the marketplace, far outnumbering research reports and theoretical studies, each new one very much like the one before it, each written with more regard for "what teachers want" or for the market challenge of competitors than for the state of research, and most written by individuals whose only credential is some previous experience as writing teachers. Therefore, unlike most academic fields, in which textbooks reflect the basic concepts that make up the discipline, composition studies has textbooks that, all too often, perpetuate outmoded concepts. The new teacher's introduction to writing instruction ordinarily comes from these books, not from rigorous academic training in composition studies, so that misinformation is perpetuated. And much of the literature on teaching, besides textbooks, does not help to reverse the trend, since so much of it is given over to statements from teachers about what "worked" in their classrooms and polemical comparisons pitting one method against another on the strength of some potent but not necessarily informed ideological commitment. The consequence has been that, although there is a large accumulation of prose devoted to writing instruction, there is very little to say about the largest part of it.

Slowly, however, the teaching itself is improving beyond the books intended to support it. Within the last decade, the gradual popularizing of new research has resulted in some movement away from textbook lore and toward practices more closely related to contemporary theory. Traditionally, writing instruction has been based on the assumption that, in order to write well, one must first learn to write correctly in a neat and ordered way. Therefore, classroom time was devoted to teaching the constituent parts of the sentence, then patterns for paragraphs, and finally organizational structures for essays. Students dutifully memorized the parts of speech and other technical information; they endured drilling in mechanics, punctuation, and usage; occasionally, they were provided with opportunities to write paragraphs, and even "themes," to the teacher's specifications. Such relentless drill and practice, focusing primarily on the correctness of finished products, was considered essential to a mastery of "the basics" that necessarily preceded fluent writing. This "building block" vantage point, and its exaggerated emphasis on correctness, has slowly given way to more sophisticated lines of argument. The central debate about teaching today concerns the proper role of teachers in assisting writers in the process of writing. But the debate presumes that writers grow only by engaging fully in that process, not by learning "the basics" in piecemeal fashion or by producing correct but perfunctory products. Assuming the necessity for practice at meaningful writing tasks, the questions are, how should the teacher intervene? what information, support, encouragement should the teacher provide? And these questions all derive from a larger one: is the teacher's function generally to give students something they need but do not as yet have (typically skills, strategies, and forms) or is it to enhance capacities that they already have but need additional practice to extend? Many writing teachers believe that students need "strategies" for composing, a repertory of invention heuristics and organizational structures, for instance, from which they can choose as they compose. They see the teacher's role as giving students such strategies and monitoring their practice of them. A growing number of teachers, however, believe that they do not primarily "give" writers things those writers lack; rather, they provide a classroom context in which students have a chance to exercise innate language capacities—talking, reading, and writing—in meaningful ways, finding motivation to grow through a variety of challenges to develop their abilities.

Composition studies, then, is in search of productive methods that focus on the needs of writers in the act of composing rather than on writers' mastery of technical decorum or their avoidance of error in finished products. What distinguishes some teachers from others is their sense of role in meeting those needs. Those who believe that teachers can give writers skills and strategies—I will call them "transmission" teachers—offer a variety of tactics, plans, and models to guide the process of composing. Theorists and teachers who currently emphasize invention in their work may be included in this group. Richard Young, for instance, along with his colleagues Alton Becker and Kenneth Pike, designed an invention schema based on Pike's tagmemic grammar, which is intended to assist a writer in finding ways to approach a subject. Similarly, Frank D'Angelo has returned to classical rhetoric to offer the topoi as a means of assisting writers in discovering ideas to write about and in organizing complex material (*Process*). He argues that the topoi are cognitive processes, suggesting that when writers engage in such exercises they are extending their abilities as thinkers and writers (*Conceptual Theory*). Other composition specialists emphasize different sorts of tactics and schemes to help writers develop. Linda Flower, for instance, bases her teaching recommendations on her observations of professional writers at work (*Problem Solving Strategies*). She has developed problem-solving strategies and planning diagrams for writers by reasoning that if professional writers plan their texts in particular ways then students should explicitly learn to plan their texts in those ways as well. Some teachers even attempt directly to affect such subtle aspects of development as syntactic maturity; hence the popularity of sentence combining. Because students who practiced sentence combining for fifteen weeks gained in syntactic complexity over students who were taught in traditional ways (Daiker, Kerek, and Morenberg, *Sentence Combining*) researchers concluded that sentence-combining practice might generally assist students' writing performance. Thus sentence-combining exercises (Daiker et al., *Writer's Options*, and O'Hare) have been used in composition teaching to develop technical competence and stylistic diversity. Finally, some theorists and teachers have looked to the depiction of cases, a long-popular method of instruction in business and law schools, to provide students with "simulations" of real-world audiences and purposes for their work, hoping to guide composing with reference to helpful rhetorical constraints. They reason that students will be motivated to learn how to write if they are given instances in which to practice the forms that they are learning and if they are given problems to solve that are similar to those they might encounter in the future.

Meanwhile, the other group of teachers, those who emphasize encouraging writers to use the latent resources they already have—whom I will call "reactive" teachers—are offering their own perspective. Essentially, this group advocates engaging writers in intellectually provocative issues or imaginatively challenging tensions, usually of students' choice, so that the students have an internal need to write, to seek response to ideas, and to revise their pieces so that their intentions can be realized. Teachers in this group describe ways to stimulate committed writing and to bring about communities of writers in the classroom (Martin; Murray, *Learning*; Elbow, *Writing with Power*). Collaborative learning, having peers read and respond to one another's work in cooperative projects, is regarded as an essential aspect of establishing this context (Barnes and Todd; Bruffee, "Collaborative"; Clifford, "Composing"; Beaven). Multiplying the number of readers of the students' work not only gives students a sense of the diversity of readers' reactions but also demonstrates the need to become critical readers of their own texts. Teachers' responses are also crucial, of course, and they have become an important research interest of those who emphasize a "reactive" approach. Traditionally, teachers have read student writing in order to find fault with it and to correct those "errors" that they perceive as distracting from the meaning the writer is attempting to convey. Interesting new research reviewed in this volume by Glynda Hull points out the oversimplified concept of error that leads many teachers to a restrictively evaluative, and therefore largely unhelpful, style of responding to students' work. Some theorists now suggest that teachers can better assist writers by responding as facilitators rather than as evaluators and that the time to respond should be when work is in progress rather than when the student writer and the teacher reader alike view the writing as completed (Sommers, "Responding"; Brannon and Knoblauch; Knoblauch and Brannon, "Teacher Commentary"). They also suggest that the best way to guide writers is by sustaining their intellectual and rhetorical choice making through successive drafts and according to the unique potential and problems of individual texts rather than by offering generalized strategic and planning principles in advance.

Predictably, each group of teachers finds limitations in the other. The "transmission" group finds the "reactive" group limited, because they believe that students in a reactive classroom are left without a structure and so may never figure out for themselves what to do. In other words, students may never understand, or gain control over, procedures for systematic inquiry without being taught specific strategies for writing. Transmission teachers believe that students need ways of exploring a subject and making connections and that reactive teachers leave them to wander and stumble into effective activity. Reactive teachers, however, find the transmission teachers limited; they see the a priori systems of these teachers making thinking and writing very mechanized and arbitrary. Reactive teachers believe that organizing structures are already part of one's mental capacity and point to learning theory and other research favoring their vantage points. To them writers do not act as the transmission teachers suppose, by selecting ways of thinking about a subject from a repertory of thinking strategies. Rather, students have the natural capacity to think systematically: by thinking about subjects that matter to them in dialogue with a trusted adult who can challenge their connection making, students exercise and extend their natural human competence. Transmission teachers, however, have their research findings as well, and the debate continues.

Determining what kind of instruction is preferable, what kind will be most supportive for the development of writing abilities, is finally dependent on our answering those prior questions about the nature of composing and about the growth or "development" of writers. Until that time more personal philosophical commitments regarding learning, composing, and development must continue to shape teaching practice. Even after we understand the nature of composing and the development of writing abilities—assuming we reach that point—the problems of teaching will not be automatically solved. Teaching practice is always dependent on the personalities, beliefs, and attitudes of teachers. There is no such thing as a teacher-proof method. Rather, learning happens or fails to happen in the complex social environment of the classroom, where children of various backgrounds and abilities engage with texts, teachers, and one another. Given so many variables, how can we judge what worked in the classroom? How can we determine if one method is as good as another? What will constitute evidence? Finally, the personal creative energy that sustains teaching and engages students will always matter more than the answers to research questions. The happiest fact about the new research interest in composition, therefore, is not that it has solved our problems but that it has brought about a new professionalism among teachers, an intellectual commitment to the field, and a sense that research in composing is a valid intellectual activity. More people are writing on the subject than ever before. New journals have been started, focusing on different aspects of the field as well as on different theoretical or methodological preferences. The major work in composition still remains before us. But the will to do that work and to apply its findings in support of the best possible teaching already vitalizes our practice, insuring the mix of knowledge and practical experience on which the evolution of our profession depends.[1]

Note

[1] I should like to thank C. H. Knoblauch for his comments and suggestions on all drafts of this text and to thank Cynthia Onore and Nancy Lester for their comments on early drafts.

Modern Rhetorical Theory and Its Future Directions

C. H. Knoblauch

Rhetoric is among the world's oldest liberal arts, one of the earliest disciplines, along with logic and grammar, to concern itself with the nature and properties of verbal expression. For over two thousand years, it was also a central, at times *the* central, course in European academic curricula. Its rich history contrasts oddly with the obscurity into which it has fallen in the past century. Rhetoric survives these days as an academic institution at the university level chiefly through two rather parochial offspring, the department of speech or communication, emphasizing oral discourse, and the department of English literature, emphasizing certain privileged written texts. These concentrations, though certainly worthy, represent only fragments of a once encompassing intellectual tradition. Cicero describes that earlier tradition in his *De oratore*, one of the great documents of classical rhetoric, observing that "the whole of the content of the liberal and humane sciences is comprised within a single bond of union [so that] a marvellous agreement and harmony underlies all branches of knowledge" (3.6.21). The instrument of this harmony, he believes, is language, specifically eloquence—the effective use of language, which "is so potent a force that it embraces the origin and operation and developments of all things, all the virtues and duties, all the natural principles governing the morals and minds and life of mankind, and also determines their customs and laws and rights, and controls the government of the state, and expresses everything that concerns whatever topic in a graceful and flowing style" (3.20.76). The domain of rhetoric, according to Cicero, includes all the roles and purposes of verbal expression in human affairs—implying a far broader intellectual and ethical framework for the study of discourse than what is usually to be found in English or speech programs. It seems therefore a sad commentary on the quality of modern philosophical life that so little attention is given to rhetorical theory as the most embracingly coherent statement of the personal, public, and cultural value of language.

Lately, however, rhetoric does appear to be making something of a comeback, particularly with reference to a study called "composition theory." Ironically, from a rhetorician's viewpoint, what was once a generic discipline is now seen as handmaiden to one of its species—the study of writing. But never mind: its service in any capacity augurs well for a future renaissance. A knowledge of rhetoric can offer those who work in the theory and teaching of writing two perspectives on their work that they currently lack, the first philosophical and the second historical. Rhetorical theory through the ages has been distinguished by its consciousness of philosophical, especially epistemological, questions inevitably surrounding any study of language: the relation between language and mind, the relation between language and the world, the relation between discourse and knowledge, the heuristic and communicative functions of verbal expression, the roles of situation and audience in shaping utterance, the social and ethical aspects of discourse. Rhetorical study has also been sensitive to its own diachronic character, to the historical evolution of thinking about language and discourse. Accordingly, it has always tended to represent its arguments with a view to their intellectual heritage: the Roman rhetoricians cited the Greeks; medieval churchmen cited the ancients; seventeenth- and eighteenth-century rhetoricians, although disagreeing with classical thought, nonetheless referred to it as they developed their own; modern rhetoricians are conscious of their debt to Aristotle and Cicero, to Francis Bacon and Condillac, to Kant, Nietzsche, and Ernst Cassirer, to de Saussure and Heidegger, even as they speculate on the implications of word processors and the age of information abundance.

An awareness of the philosophical issues long associated with rhetorical theory can help composition teacher-researchers locate their statements about *how* people compose within a framework of *why* they compose: what significance the activity has for their lives and for the life of their society and culture. In other words, it can help to place writing in a context of human values—self-expression, learning, reaching out to other people, preserving knowledge, conducting business, making laws, playing, creating works of art—the psychological, ethical, political, and aesthetic dimensions of language use that make it so encompassing a human enterprise. This awareness can also help teacher-researchers avoid the naive positivism that occasionally afflicts their recent efforts to adopt a "scientific" ideology—the belief (which no reflective scientist is likely to hold) that we need only observe "what happens" as people compose, and chronicle the "data," without philosophical perspective, in order to achieve a "knowledge" of composition; the belief that investigative conclusions are unaffected by frames of reference, tacit or acknowledged assumptions, and well- or poorly stated hypotheses; the belief that models of composition are "real" rather than discourses in themselves, artful, speculative, and contingent; the belief that such models so reliably normalize human verbal creativity that they should serve as arbiters of "good" writing or as formulas for writing instruction.

At the same time, the historical consciousness that rhetoric has always sustained can help those who teach and study writing to avoid the feeling that they work in a vacuum, without heritage, without precursors, without guidance from the conceptual achievements and failures of the past. Only the rare study in composition today makes reference to thinking about language and discourse prior to around 1960. When researchers address the concept of "writer's stance," they name Wayne Booth but forget Aristotle; when they speak of writing as a learning process, they cite Janet Emig but forget Descartes, Locke, and Kant; when they advocate writing across the curriculum, they name Elaine Maimon but leave out Plato, who first noted the dangers of teaching forms and strategies of expression separate from knowledge of a subject (*Phaedrus; Gorgias*); when they speak of the organic quality of language, they name Noam Chomsky but not Coleridge; when they speak of revision, they mention Nancy Sommers but not Quintilian, who discusses the matter at length (*Institutio* 10.3.5–7, 10.4.1–2); when they speak of the "process" of composing, they point to research since the mid-1960s but not to research in the mid-eighteenth century, following Locke's theory of the association of ideas, which anticipated modern views in several important respects. No one denies the achievements of contemporary specialists in composition. Indeed, seeing their work from a diachronic perspective lends it still fuller significance—within a tradition of speculation about discourse that allows its appraisal against the standard of long-developing lines of argument and prevents its misconstrual as more or less of an accomplishment than it is.

I have been speaking of what rhetoric has to offer the study of writing, since it is in that context that rhetorical theory chiefly matters these days. But I don't really want to encourage the idea that rhetoric is a handmaiden. I would prefer to insist that it is *generically* the study of discourse or language use, that it includes writing as a subdiscipline and directs inquiry into written composition, and that a generic view is most proper for understanding its future as well as its past and present. To say so is, of course, to offer a definition of "rhetoric," specifying the nature and extent of its intellectual field, not just its relation to composition theory. And I am obliged to make my definition more explicit. Interestingly, however, the philosophical and historical consciousness that preoccupies rhetoricians makes achieving a definition more than usually problematic. As an ancient discipline that has been affected not just by shifting social and political conditions but also by deeper intellectual and epistemological revolutions, rhetoric has never had a fully stable definition or focus of attention. Indeed, its history has been in no small measure a history of controversies about its scope and content—as early a rhetorician as Quintilian feels obliged to review conflicting opinions before offering his own (*Institutio* 2.15). To define the field today is, as it has always been, to take a certain philosophical stance—to fashion an argument that is neither neutral nor absolute nor timeless about the nature and purposes of discourse, the issues and concepts pertinent to a study of discourse, and the means by which that study can be undertaken most effectively. Having betrayed this relativity, I will assert as boldly as I dare that rhetoric is the *process* of using language to organize experience and communicate it to others. It is also the *study* of how people use language to organize and communicate experience. The word denotes, as I use it, both a distinctive human activity and the "science" concerned with understanding that activity. All human beings are "rhetors" because they naturally conceive as well as share their knowledge of the world by means of discourse. Certain individuals are also "rhetoricians" because they study the nature, operations, and purposes of discourse. I suggest further that rhetoric, as a generic discipline, encompasses all forms of written as well as oral expression and includes the efforts of undeveloped speakers and writers as well as the achievements of literary artists. But I must also reassert my qualifier that rhetoric has not always been defined in this manner—and that indeed not even all contemporary rhetoricians would necessarily define it so broadly. Aristotle, for instance, states that rhetoric concerns itself only with suasory discourse and the strategies of persuasion (*Rhetoric* 1354a). Some modern rhetoricians, say Donald Bryant or James Kinneavy ("Restoring"), would agree with Aristotle; others, Douglas Ehninger, for instance ("On Systems"; *Contemporary Rhetoric*), or Tzvetan Todorov, have offered opinions resembling mine. The definition I propose, like anyone else's, is an argument, not a Platonic universal.

The competing arguments derive from more than casual differences of opinion. They sometimes reflect changes of historical circumstance—the fact, for instance, that deliberative oratory has been more influential in societies and times that have valued participatory government and therefore has often been more central to a definition of the scope of rhetoric in such circumstances than at times when participation was discouraged. They also reflect technological realities—such as the fact that oral discourse held priority of place over written discourse in ancient Greece, so that the principles of rhetorical theory in that period tended to assume an oral context. They reflect differing intellectual and educational convictions—as when Boethius argued in the early sixth century for the priority of logic over rhetoric, leaving the discovery and arrangement of arguments to that discipline and little more than a superficial regard for form and style to rhetoric. They reflect different concepts of literacy, different estimates of the range of practical and aesthetic uses of discourse, and alternative views of the variety of "legitimate" media as well as the worthiness of more popular media for academic study. They reflect alternate epistemologies—for instance, disagreements about knowledge (whether stable and bounded or eternally evolving), about the relation between knowledge and discourse (the separateness or indivisibility of "content" and "form"), and about the extent to which language is thought to serve a heuristic rather than merely communicative function. Depending on an individual rhetorician's view of these issues, and perhaps others besides, the definition of rhetoric will be more theoretical or pragmatic in emphasis and more or less encompassing in scope. If, in addition, we accept Michel Foucault's arguments (*The Order of Things*) about periods of radical epistemological disjunction, whole intellectual eras may differentiate themselves according to their ways of regarding the nature and purposes of discourse. The very dimensions of rhetoric as an intellectual construct may change with the displacement of one perspective by another.

I defend my argument about the scope and substance of rhetoric, though other rhetoricians may argue differently, because it seems to me at once congenial with the modern epistemological temper and suited to the social and cultural circumstances of modern life. Inevitably, I also depend on it for estimating the past, present, and future character of the field. That estimate is itself a discourse, one rhetorician's credible fiction about the intellectual space he inhabits. What follows, then, is no more and no less than a "text" about the present and future of rhetoric. My text will begin with the past, naturally, because that is the customary starting point for rhetoricians, and with some continuities and discontinuities that bear importantly on the current shape of the field as I see it. The first point to make about contemporary rhetoric, therefore, is that it essentially shares and preserves the spirit of the ancient tradition, although in many ways it differs in intellectual substance. Modern rhetoric continues to endorse the ideals of classical humanism, its regard for the personal and cultural value of language, its practical, not just theoretical, interest in the applications of discourse, its concern for the public responsibilities of speakers and writers, its commitment to discovering and speaking the truth, its awareness of the power of literacy, and its subsequent advocacy of educating the young to be thoughtful, productive language users. These ideals are nowhere better articulated than in Quintilian's *Institutio oratoria*, a work intended for teachers of his own time and no less relevant in spirit to teachers today. Quintilian speaks of the goals and the ultimate importance of education in the arts of discourse:

> The man who can duly sustain his character as a citizen, who is qualified for the management of public and private affairs, and who can govern communities by his counsels, settle them by means of laws, and improve them by judicial enactments, can certainly be nothing else but an orator. . . . If we constantly have occasion to speak of justice, fortitude, temperance, and other similar topics, so that a cause can scarcely be found in which some such discussion does not occur, and if all such subjects are to be illustrated by invention and elocution, can it be doubted that, wherever power of intellect and copiousness of language are required, the art of the orator is to be there preeminently exerted? . . . We are to form, then, the perfect orator, who cannot exist unless he is above all a good man. We require in him, therefore, not only consummate ability in speaking, but also every excellence of mind [and] the principles of moral and honorable conduct. (*Institutio* 1: 9–13)

The humanistic spirit of these remarks seems well worth preserving both in classrooms devoted to the development of verbal literacy and in society at large, dependent as it is on literacy for the quality of life enjoyed by its citizens.

At the same time, however, the content of modern rhetoric—its epistemological assumptions, its focuses of attention, even in some respects its methods of inquiry—differs substantially from that of the classical tradition. And the difference is important to a consideration of how our ideas about discourse have been formed and the extent to which they are serviceable or insufficient. The essential distinction between classical and contemporary theory concerns the relation between discourse and knowledge, one of the most fundamental disagreements in the history of European intellectual life, dating from the Renaissance and emerging gradually between the seventeenth and the twentieth centuries. Cicero's and Quintilian's remarks about the importance of effective communication notwithstanding, classical arguments about language generally assume the subordinate relation of *verba*, the world of words, to *res*, the prior and substantial world of their references in nature. Accordingly, suspicion about the capacity of language to distort and deceive exists side by side with admiration of its capacity, when properly controlled, to display the truth in pleasing apparel. The suspicion finds powerful voice in ancient rhetoric when Plato attacks the Sophists (fairly or unfairly) for attending to the verbal surface of things rather than to things themselves, in effect depending on mere trickery to move audiences. The separation of *res* and *verba* is further embedded in the philosophical underpinning of classical discourse theory when Aristotle, in *On Interpretation*, distinguishes the substance of thought from the changing forms of its verbal expression: words denote our ideas, he says, but while words differ from language to language, "the mental affections themselves, of which . . . words are primarily signs, are the same for the whole of mankind, as are also the objects of which those affections are representations or likenesses, images, copies" (16a5–10). To the classical mind, language was a mirror held up to reality, its efficacy inversely proportionate to its degree of distortion. In the best circumstances, it was the nearly invisible membrane of thought (as in classical logic, where the interpretive nature of propositions goes largely unexamined in the belief that they refer directly and reliably to "the world"); but at worst— whenever language began to draw unseemly attention to itself (as in poetry or oratory)—its tendency was to cloud the rational sense of things, beguiling human judgment with its ornamental designs. The forms of language characteristic of oratory, according to Aristotle, are concessions to what he calls "the sorry nature of an audience" (1404a), the inability of most listeners to attend to strictly logical argument, their need for a pleasing or memorable shape to ideas. Effective language is something superadded to argument rather than essential to it, important to the communication of ideas but not to their discovery or their fundamental character. Implicit in Aristotle's reasoning, then, is the split between "logic" and "rhetoric," intellectual "content" and communicative "form," that would plague the study of discourse from his time onward. To be sure, rhetoricians such as Cicero (3.19) struggle against the separation of wisdom and eloquence. But once these parts had been distinguished, the whole, like Humpty Dumpty, could never be quite the same.

The concepts and methods of classical theory depend on its epistemological assumptions. According to George Kennedy's very readable survey, the major works of ancient rhetoric, from which the "classical" tradition chiefly derives, include Aristotle's *Rhetoric*, Cicero's *De oratore*, the *Rhetorica ad herennium*, and Quintilian's *Institutio*. Collectively, these texts describe a discipline that is formalistic in its theoretical underpinnings and taxonomic in its method (Ehninger, "On Systems"). It is formalistic in the sense that it conceives the function of discourse to be essentially, if not exclusively, the display of arguments in a formal dress suited to particular communicative occasions (Knoblauch and Brannon). The arguments themselves have, as Aristotle suggests, an independent integrity, a reality apart from discourse, discernible to the disciplined rational mind though inaccessible to weaker intellects, which require verbal representation to remember and appreciate them. Only the forms of persuasive argument are the province of rhetoric, which describes them as an inventory of technical alternatives available to orators for conveying already conceived knowledge to a given audience. Classical rhetoric is also, therefore, taxonomic or, as Ehninger characterizes it, "grammatical" ("On Systems"), in the sense that it analyzes discourse into structures, parts, and strategies, representing these as systems of information and models of correct performance. Hence, ancient rhetoricians, analyzing samples of completed writing, taxonomized the occasions and purposes of discourse (forensic, deliberative, epideictic), the kinds of argument (enthymeme or example), the topoi or "places" of invention, the parts of an oration from exordium to peroration, the varieties of style, the tropes and figures, all into assorted systems and models. The formalist emphasis of classical rhetoric dominated discourse theory until the later Renaissance. Its taxonomic method remains in service even today, albeit qualified by a more relativistic spirit of inquiry. Contemporary systems or models derived from the analysis of samples of discourse (e.g., James Kinneavy's spectra of scientific, persuasive, and poetic modes of writing, in *Theory of Discourse*, or Francis Christensen's categories of sentences and paragraphs, in *Notes toward a New Rhetoric*) have much in common with those of ancient times, though their nomenclatures differ.

The impact of classical rhetoric on writing theory and instruction has been pervasive across the centuries, and it remains so today, notwithstanding the epistemological disjunction that has brought some of its assumptions into question. Such twentieth-century rhetoricians as Kinneavy (*Theory of Discourse*), Edward P. J. Corbett (*Classical Rhetoric*), and Frank D'Angelo argue for the continuing usefulness of ancient rhetorical concepts pertaining to occasions, modes, and strategies of discourse, though they might well also concede that the changed intellectual circumstances of modern times force a reconsideration of how those concepts are to be applied. D'Angelo, for example, suggests the suitability of the topoi of invention ("definition," "comparison," "illustration," etc.) for describing cognitive processes, arguing therefore some degree of congruence between ancient rhetoric and modern cognitive psychology. Richard Young, Alton Becker, and Kenneth Pike have offered a new system of topoi, comprised of "particle," "wave," and "field" views of a subject, which concedes the changed environment of modern thought but not therefore any inappropriateness in the ancient taxonomic view of invention. Alternative systems of discourse modes, such as Britton's "expressive, transactional, poetic" continuum ("Composing Processes"), are proposed today in place of earlier taxonomies such as Aristotle's logical, persuasive, and poetic modes. Modern "stage" theories of production, such as "prewriting, writing, revising," are offered to replace earlier stage theories such as Cicero's "invention, arrangement, style." Whether ancient rhetorical concepts and methods will continue to be applied in the future may partly depend on the amount of attention paid to fundamental issues of philosophical compatibility between ancient and modern perspectives on discourse. Are the perspectives simply different moments in a single, evolving tradition or are they two (or more) discrete traditions, not equally serviceable in the contemporary intellectual climate because of their opposed epistemological assumptions? My own inclination toward the latter view leads me to suggest that classical concepts are not always usefully adapted to modern concerns, since adapting them tends to perpetuate certain errors to which a formalist and taxonomic approach gives rise—in particular the ancient but discredited distinction between form and content as well as a mechanistic view of the process of composing (Knoblauch and Brannon). But the work of Corbett and others is speaking forcefully for the continuing theoretical value of those concepts. Indeed, a recent collection of articles, *Essays on Classical Rhetoric and Modern Discourse*, edited by Robert Connors, Andrea Lunsford, and Lisa Ede, argues the compatibility of classical and modern perspectives as forcefully as I would argue their disjunction.

Classical rhetoric retains at least as much vitality in teaching today, though not always as a matter of teachers' conscious awareness and not always for the better. James J. Murphy's edition of essays, *The Rhetorical Tradition and Modern Writing*, offers explicit arguments for the propriety of looking to the classical tradition for instructional guidance. Composition theorists such as Susan Miller ("Classical Practice") and Erika Lindemann have suggested the value for writing instruction of consciously applied modern equivalents to the ancient *progymnasmata*—systematized short exercises in the techniques of persuasion. Meanwhile, the continued practice of modes of writing—narration, description, exposition, argument—the continued rehearsal of "strategies" such as definition, classification, and comparison; the descriptions of grammatical correctness, proprieties of style, paragraph structures, and the features of such school genres as the term paper (similar in shape to the ancient oration form) all testify to the durability of classical theory as an unconscious influence. Unfortunately, one result of this formalistic emphasis through the centuries has been that instructional concern for the quality of thought in school writing often takes second place behind a concern for technical control of the medium itself—this despite the larger humanistic values and intellectual concerns that underlay ancient theory. The declamatory exercises popular in schools from Roman times through the end of the eighteenth century offered the model for the largely ceremonial composition exercises seen in so many writing classrooms today—where the subjects of discussion are hackneyed, the forms predetermined, and correctness of execution seemingly more valued than quality of thought. This is not to suggest that the only influences of classical rhetoric on recent instruction have been negative: ancient emphases on the purposes for composing, the needs of audiences, and the constraints of situation carry over in the practice of many writing teachers, as does the regard for good and extensive reading, for constant practice at writing, for disciplined powers of reasoning, and for frequent revision of texts in progress. But Plato's misgiving in the *Gorgias*, that a fascination with the "knack" of manipulating words will jeopardize intellectual integrity, points to the inevitable deficiency of a formalist rhetoric, where quality of thought, however highly regarded in principle, tends to become an issue extrinsic to the primary focus of attention. Enough present-day writing courses continue the exaggeration of technical decorum to suggest that Plato's concern was well-founded.

The question that arises, then, both for research and for teaching, is the extent to which the concepts and methods of traditional rhetoric ought to continue to influence contemporary thought and practice—especially if it is true, as I believe it is, that modern rhetoric differs from classical in some crucial respects. The values of ancient rhetoric are not at stake— they remain properly influential today. At stake, rather, is our sense of what will be regarded as functional knowledge about discourse in the twentieth century. Understanding the differences between Aristotle's rhetoric and that of, say, Kenneth Burke (even despite Burke's own professed indebtedness to Aristotle) is part of that knowledge, important to understanding where the discipline is today and where it is likely to go in the future. The intellectual origins of modern theory lie less in Greco-Roman tradition than in the philosophical upheavals of the past four centuries, the seventeenth-century revolution in empirical science, the eighteenth-century revolution in psychology, the post-Kantian elaboration of the theory of symbolic action. Abrams's *Mirror and the Lamp*, Cassirer's *Philosophy of the Enlightenment*, Howell's two studies of British logic and rhetoric from 1500 through the eighteenth century, and Langer's *Philosophy in a New Key* are classic introductions to these intellectual events, while Foucault's *The Order of Things: An Archaeology of the Human Sciences* is a provocative "modernist" rendering. Briefly put, if ancient rhetoric was formalistic in its intellectual presuppositions, modern rhetoric should rather be regarded as "epistemic," proposing a reciprocally dependent relation between knowledge and discourse, a much closer connection than the ancient rhetoricians had estimated between thought and language.

Consider, for example, two "modern" statements, the first by John Locke, the second by Ernst Cassirer, in juxtaposition with Aristotle's conclusion in *On Interpretation* that changeable words constitute merely the dress for permanently unchanging "ideas." Locke argues, by contrast, that "there is so close a connection between ideas and WORDS . . . that it is impossible to speak clearly and distinctly of our knowledge, which all consists in propositions, without considering, first, the nature, use, and signification of Language" (*Essay concerning Human Understanding* 2.32). Cassirer broadens the point dramatically in *Language and Myth*: "myth, art, language, and science [are] symbols; not in the sense of mere figures which refer to some given reality . . . but in the sense of forces each of which produces and posits a world of its own. [They] are not imitations, but *organs* of reality, since it is solely by their agency that anything real becomes an object for intellectual apprehension, and as such is made visible to us" (8). The opposition between Aristotle and Cassirer makes plain the essential difference between a formalist and an epistemic rhetorical perspective. But as early as the seventeenth century, philosophers such as Francis Bacon, Descartes, Antoine Arnauld, John Locke, and Leibnitz begin to point out the interpenetrating relation between thought and language, knowledge and discourse, the process of learning and the process of articulating through signs. The force of this speculation was to shift rhetorical theory away from the classical view of discourse as a mere display of preconceived ideas for communicative purposes and toward a new view of discourse as a means by which intellectual and imaginative conception occurs. Ancient stress on an inventory of formal vehicles gives way before a new preoccupation with the emergence of form through the very processes of composing and therefore a new regard for the heuristic power of discourse—its ability to create coherence as it orders the composer's experience one assertion at a time. From the mid-seventeenth century onward, discourse comes to be regarded as exploratory and open-ended, a process of articulating connections through the signs and syntactic possibilities of language, a mode of inquiry as free and full of potential as the search for knowledge that it enables. It becomes a process of making meaning rather than a ceremonial dress for what is already known.

Eighteenth-century philosophers, language theorists, and rhetoricians, including David Hume, Vico, Condillac, Adam Smith, Joseph Priestley, Henry Home (Lord Kames), John Ogilvie, and George Campbell develop these ideas, though within the limiting assumptions of a mechanically associational theory of mind. Kant and the German idealists broaden and refine the new view of discourse with reference to a richer, organic philosophy of imagination. Following Kant, in particular, modern philosophers of discourse have elaborated the theory of symbolic action, which resolves ancient polarities of mind and matter, form and substance, discourse and knowledge, by depicting what Coleridge referred to as the "coalescence" of subject and object, processes of mind and the "experience" that mind conceives through the mediation of symbols. Knowledge of the world is an imaginative achievement comprised of symbols. All human beings, not just trained orators, mathematicians, or literary artists, are naturally, unavoidably makers and users of symbols. All verbal discourses, whether viewed as "logical," "persuasive," or "poetic," entail symbolic action. Since rhetoric is concerned with language use as a species of symbolic action, all makers of verbal discourse as well as all circumstances and instances of verbal composition belong within its province. Important twentieth-century philosophers delineating the theory of symbolic form include Ernst Cassirer (*Symbolic Form*), Alfred Whitehead, Ferdinand de Saussure, Edward Sapir, Claude Lévi-Strauss, Susanne Langer, and Michael Polanyi. Among the most important modern rhetoricians to apply a theory of symbolic action to the pragmatic circumstances of speakers and writers are Kenneth Burke, I. A. Richards, Wayne Booth (*Rhetoric of Fiction*; *Modern Dogma*), Stephen Toulmin (*Uses of Argument*), and, to a degree, Chaim Perelman. A readable overview of the work of these rhetoricians, among others, in historical context is *The Rhetoric of Western Thought*, edited by Golden, Berquist, and Coleman. (If "composition theory" is taken as a subdiscipline of rhetoric, several more contemporary theorists could be added to this list, including James Britton [*Language and Learning*], Janet Emig [*Web of Meaning*], James Moffett, and Ann Berthoff [*Making of Meaning*].) Perhaps Douglas Ehninger has best defined rhetoric from this modern intellectual vantage point when he refers to it as "that discipline which studies all of the ways in which men may influence each other's thinking and behavior through the strategic use of symbols." Characterizing the opposed epistemologies of ancient and modern perspectives, he concludes: "[T]he notion that rhetoric is something added to discourse is gradually giving way to the quite different assumption that rhetoric not only is inherent in all human communication, but that it also informs and conditions every aspect of thought and behavior: that man himself is inevitably and inescapably a rhetorical animal" (*Contemporary Rhetoric* 8–10).

Modern rhetoric is "epistemic," then, in philosophical predisposition, where ancient rhetoric and the classical tradition were essentially "formalistic." Societies compose and share their knowledge of the world (and of themselves) through acts of language. The major change that this shift has implied for research has been a reorientation from characterizing structural properties of texts to characterizing the personal and social processes that give rise to them, a line of investigation very much in evidence in composition theory today. If verbal form is not regarded as a ready-made dress of thought, then concern for describing that dress as the means of ensuring the propriety of future texts is bound to diminish. If form is seen rather as the achievement of a search for meaning, then not surprisingly students of discourse will find more value in uncovering the processes by which form is achieved than in classifying features of completed texts, which are as infinitely various as the composers that produce them. This change of research emphasis has been occurring gradually over the past three hundred years. Eighteenth- and nineteenth-century rhetoricians tend to speak of "method" when considering the ways in which people make meaning through discourse, while modern theorists refer more often to "composing processes." But the concern for method or process has distinguished research ever since Locke first made apparent the indissoluble connection between thinking and using language in the *Essay concerning Human Understanding*, thereby tying the activities of learning and knowing to the activities of discourse. Rhetoricians such as Joseph Priestley, Lord Kames, and Adam Smith anticipate modern theorists, albeit embryonically, in their efforts to represent composing (that is, thinking in language) as a process of making successive choices about what to say and where and how to say it within the syntactic, structural, generic, and situational constraints acting on a particular writer. Essentially the same kind of work goes on today in the arguments of Britton, Emig, Winterowd, Berthoff, Murray, and a great many others. It will surely remain the dominant focus of rhetorical research for years to come.

Writing instruction has also been affected in some important ways by the change from a formalist to an epistemic view of discourse and by the subsequent shift of concern from the properties of finished texts to the processes of composing them. If symbolic action is species-specific to human beings, representing a deeply human competence rather than an acquired skill, then the teaching of writing, to the extent that writing manifests that competence, entails nurturing young writers' latent capacities to make meaning rather than "giving" them skills they do not possess. To be sure, there are skills associated with writing, and those skills—such as forming letters with an instrument, spelling and punctuating, managing different genres—are taught. But in its essence as a mode of composition, writing is not merely or even mainly a technology. To teach it as though it were is to undervalue the power young writers bring to classrooms while overemphasizing the formal control they lack—thereby offering little motivation to learn that control since it remains so unrelated to everything valuable about composing in the first place, namely, the personal experience of making meaning. Teachers who accept the arguments of modern rhetoric place more emphasis on students' expressive powers than on their formal control, encouraging exploratory discourse, continuous revision on the basis of teacher and peer responses, individualized (rather than systematic) discovery of new strategies, and a democratic regard for the multiple ways in which diverse writers can achieve their purposes. Resulting texts offer primarily an opportunity to do more composing, not an opportunity to "correct" technical and formal errors as though the decorous shape of an artifact mattered more than the developing quality of the mind that composed it. Skills continue to be taught in this style of instruction, but always in the context of the search for meaning, always in relation to what matters most to writers – the realizing of their own intentions – and always as a priority subordinate to nurturing the power of mind.

Interestingly, the shift of theoretical predisposition in the research activities of modern rhetoric entails – at least logically – a shift as well in investigative methodology, although researchers' awareness of that entailment has been slow to evolve. If it is true that knowledge is an achievement of symbolic representation – that is, a discourse derived from the processes of imaginative conception – then it is also true that a knowledge of verbal action itself constitutes a discourse, possessing the fictive nature of all interpretive behavior, subject along with all discourses to inadequacy and change. Knowledge cannot be divorced from knowers (the makers of discourse); it has no status independent of the individuals and communities that conceive and share it. The process of conducting inquiry into language activity is therefore itself a rhetorical act and the conclusions of inquiry an achievement of rhetorical artifice – the application of some perspective, the choice of some range of "pertinent" information, the selection of some strategy for arranging the information and asserting its significance, the presentation of that significance within authoritative patterns of proof. The method of ancient rhetoric had been taxonomic, with an assumption that the generalizations derived from inquiry, the systems of forms, modes, parts, and operations of discourse, were absolute, universal facts. Still today, with the continuing impact of seventeenth-century notions of science, taxonomic inquiry tends to have a positivistic bias, where research data are presumed to exist independent of the researcher so that conclusions about the data are thought to be "found" rather than asserted, affording them the status of objective (and therefore unassailable) truths. Yet modern rhetoric has laid a philosophical foundation that denies an objectivity transcending discourse, thereby rendering a positivistic style of inquiry implicitly naive. In place of positivistic assumptions, modern rhetoric (necessarily) asserts phenomenological assumptions, tending to resist traditional taxonomic method – the construction of abstract schemes and models that simplify experience while implying a false objectivity – in favor of richly concrete depictions of language acts accompanied by highly self-conscious, contingent assertions of a researcher's conclusions from them.

It is important to insist that phenomenological and positivistic styles of inquiry are not merely alternate possibilities equally useful to researchers given different ambitions on different occasions. They are ideologically incompatible because of their differing views of the status of the data of "scientific" observation and also the status of generalizations proposed to organize that data (Mishler). Historically, taxonomic method has tended to assume the "real" character of empirical evidence (often referred to as "hard data") and a similarly "real" (therefore reliable) quality for the statements intended to order that evidence and assert its "meaning." Given this positivist bias, it has tended to assume the possibility of differentiating what is typical from what is less important or merely idiosyncratic in the object of investigation. By contrast, a phenomenological approach implicates researchers in their research, conceding the imaginative, interpretive nature of both the data yielded by analysis and the assertions organizing the data. Where the classical researcher "locates" information by selecting from the stream of available experience those privileged perceptions that will constitute the basis for generalization, the phenomenological researcher, aware that data are conceptions, not perceptions, "makes" information by recording the stream of available experience as richly and fully as possible. Where the classicist "discovers" an ordering principle by evaluating the data, implicitly raising that principle to the status of "objective" truth, the phenomenologist "creates" an organizing idea, at the same time conceding its fictive quality—its necessarily interpretive, contingent, and endlessly evolving character. The phenomenologist does not deny the possibility or value of scientific inquiry (including the value of taxonomizing) but only insists that scientific knowledge depends on the making of discourse, a rhetorical activity, just as poetic knowledge or mythic knowledge depends on a similar making or creative process. The scientific researcher, not unlike a novelist, asserts "themes" that are taken to be significant within the range of experience under investigation, weaving those themes together as the "narrative" of science. That narrative is both "true" and useful, subject to the constraints of scientific verification, but it is also a creative act, a symbolic representation, a product of mind: it is not unassailable or permanent; indeed, it is not even "objective" in the classical sense of a knowledge that is true independent of human beings who possess it, share it, and cause its growth.

David Hume's theory of history is an early instance of the rhetorical self-consciousness that would eventually evolve into a phenomenological view of research. For Hume, the difference between history and poetry is far

less certain than it had been for Aristotle in the *Poetics*. History, as a suc-
cession of statements ordered to create in readers the sense of some coherence in events, is no less a discourse than is epic poetry. Decisions about
what will be included or excluded in a history, how information will be
arranged, what focuses or priorities will be enforced, what conclusions will
be drawn, are no less artful than those of poetry. Eighteenth-century history writers after Hume are sensitive to the literary quality of their work
even as they grow more sophisticated in historiographic method. Furthermore, the boundaries between the genres of history and prose fiction blur
throughout the century, yielding such epistemologically self-conscious works
as Defoe's *Journal of the Plague Year*, where a fictional narrator conveys historically accurate details of the last outbreak of plague in England, weaving
them together by means of themes intended to explore its theological significance. Phenomenological theory is not peculiar, therefore, to the twentieth century. Its roots lie implicit in the shift of epistemology that
occasioned the change from formalist to epistemic rhetoric, above all perhaps in the seminal arguments and disagreements between Kant and Hegel
in the late eighteenth and early nineteenth centuries.

Yet the "inevitability" of a phenomenological perspective governing research in rhetoric is only philosophical at the moment, not for the most
part a fact of contemporary work. One need not look far in composition
studies to find positivistic values influencing investigation. And to the degree that composition researchers study writing with unself-conscious optimism about the dispassionate objectivity of their findings, as though the
sophistication of modern scientific method reached its highest perfection
with John Locke instead of carrying on to Whitehead, Wittgenstein, Thomas
Kuhn, and Polanyi, they risk discrediting themselves in the larger scientific
community, which understands the value of empirical and experimental
research without succumbing to positivistic assumptions. The way of a future methodology dependent on phenomenological assumptions is, however, visible at the present time. The method currently enjoys its most
sophisticated elaboration and use in the so-called human sciences, particularly anthropology, psychology, and sociology. The writings of Clifford
Geertz are a significant contribution to the development of phenomenological research within anthropology; the work of Amadeo Giorgi represents
its impact in psychology; larger speculative views of the method are available from such theorists as Hans-Georg Gadamer, Maurice Roche, Paul
Rabinow, and—at the radical extreme—P. K. Feyerabend; and finally, of
course, the roots of twentieth-century phenomenology lie in the works of
Martin Heidegger and Edmund Husserl, among others. Since these
researchers in diverse sciences have all reflected self-consciously on the in-

terpretive character of their intellectual fields, Geertz very notably in his subtle studies of Balinese culture, they are perhaps all to be called rhetoricians in the largest sense, scholars preoccupied with the relation between knowledge and discourse in their own disciplines. Compared to them, rhetoricians who work in the field of composition theory remain for the most part rather atheoretical about the interpretive quality of their research and in their efforts to apply phenomenological, or "human science," method by representing the writing process within the richness of actual writers at work.

Still, beginning even in the eighteenth century, the tendency toward a phenomenological method can be detected. There is clearly far less absolutist taxonomizing in the rhetorical theory of, say, Adam Smith or Joseph Priestley than there had been previously. Indeed, throughout the eighteenth century there is considerable mistrust of the formulaic distinctions of ancient theory, including parts of orations, "topics" of invention, modes of argument, and the like (Howell, *Logic and Rhetoric*). Genre distinctions that had been sustained for centuries—epic, tragedy, lyric—assume far less significance in eighteenth-century thought, encouraging an atmosphere of experimentation in writing that resulted in the emergence of several modern prose vehicles, including the periodical essay, the argumentative historical narrative, the biographical narrative, and the novel. While rhetorical theory of the age shows no particular sophistication in evaluating these emergent forms, it does suggest a certain restlessness with generalized taxonomies and a preference for examining the practices of writers as those practices illuminate the nature of mind and language. Only in the twentieth century, however, has this concern for writers in the actual process of writing become a dominant feature of research, and even then only very recently. The focus on individual writers' activities without reference to some overriding conception of how they ought to behave is apparent in the work of James Britton with the Institute of Education (University of London) and the work of Janet Emig in the United States. However, neither Britton nor Emig resorts to the "thick description" characteristic of phenomenological research in the purest sense, nor does either reveal quite the sensitivity of, say, Geertz toward the fictiveness of research conclusions—the implication of researchers in their research. However, Shirley Brice Heath's recent investigation of literacy in the southern United States comes closer to that purity of method. And Sondra Perl, albeit nearly alone among contemporary writing researchers, has largely assumed a phenomenological perspective in her study of students and teachers in the Shoreham Wading River school district (Long Island, NY), though the results of her study, including a description of the method, are yet to be

published. At the same time, the growing number of case studies in composition, the continued emphasis on observing writers at work in naturalistic settings, the improving sophistication of descriptive studies, all point
toward phenomenological rather than classical taxonomic method as the
means of future rhetorical inquiry.

The multiple directions of that future inquiry are, of course, impossible
to predict, though the epistemological and methodological frameworks that
I have sketched seem durable as the underpinnings of continuing research.
The tendency of modern rhetorical study has been to extend its scope to
larger and larger contexts of discourse, oral as well as written, domestic
as well as literary, and that expansion appears likely to continue (recent
theoretical considerations of the "rhetoric" of dance or the "rhetoric" of
clothing suggest even a broadening beyond verbal expression to other systems of signs). Rhetorical criticism of the sort that Wayne Booth has so
powerfully undertaken in *The Rhetoric of Fiction* remains one significant
line of investigation, directed at literary discourse in particular. Another
is "reader-response theory," as represented by the work of Rosenblatt (*The
Reader*), Iser, Fish, Bleich, and others (see Tompkins), which is concerned
to show how the reading process is as active and heuristic in nature as
writing—a process of composing the "text" of a response to some other text.
The study of argumentation, particularly under the influence of Toulmin
(*Uses of Argument*), has grown richer with the new focus on "informal logic,"
which takes the process of reasoning in discourse out of the rarefied environment of scholastic logic and places it in the practical world of human
thinkers. Speech and communication theory are currently extending into
electronic media, from cable television to personal computers and beyond.
Work on the evolving nature, characteristics, and importance of literacy,
particularly as Western societies become more dependent on electronic tech-
nologies for the management and sharing of information, also suggests the
concern for placing the processes of discourse within larger social and ethical
perspectives (see, e.g., Bailey and Fosheim). Composition theory is continuing to pursue the description of writers at work, skilled as well as unskilled, in the richness of the social settings that contribute so much to
their concrete, text-specific, personalized choices. And the teaching of writing is, for the first time in centuries, beginning to examine its assumptions
and goals with reference to a substantial, growing body of theoretical and
research conclusions—becoming, in other words, a self-evaluative, purposeful, indeed, let us say, professional activity. Meanwhile, the historical and
philosophical work that has always distinguished rhetorical investigation
continues to advance. Recent studies by Connors, Lunsford, Berlin, Hal-
loran, Stewart, Horner, and numerous others on the background of mod-

ern composition theory and teaching are typical of that sustained preoccupation. The new Horner bibliographies (*Present State of Scholarship*) represent the best popular catalog of historical research currently available. All these dimensions of inquiry regarding the contexts and processes of discourse will surely continue to flourish into the twenty-first century, and others as well, too numerous to mention (James Kinneavy's contribution to the Horner bibliographies, "Contemporary Rhetoric," details some of them). There may even be reason to hope, at last, that rhetoric will recover the status and stature of an academic discipline that it held for so many centuries, so that modern researchers will no longer be rhetoricians by accident, unaware of the tradition in which they work even as they make their own contributions to it. Perhaps English departments, too, having recognized of late that studying the processes of composition can have as much intellectual integrity as studying Jane Austen, will allow themselves a further concession that rhetoric is the generic liberal art that gives public and cultural significance to what they do. Perhaps.

Composition Theory and Literary Theory

John Clifford and John Schilb

Although courses combining literature and composition are no strangers to the English curriculum, the last few years have witnessed several inspiring attempts to fuse the teaching of writing with the teaching of literature under new theoretical frameworks. In some cases, the word *new* might prove misleading, since the theorists involved actually seek to revive concepts that have fallen into disuse. But these and other efforts to synthesize the two pedagogies seem refreshing, not only because they promise to unify a curriculum that has suffered too long from fragmentation but also because they proceed from sophisticated understandings of what writing and literary interpretation can involve. Despite the range of recent proposals for yoking composition and literature, most of them tend to emphasize certain basic notions. Writing emerges as a process of discovery, enabling students to construct knowledge rather than simply to regurgitate familiar truths or structural formulas. Literary study, too, emerges as a dynamic event, one in which students can be encouraged to draw on subjective insights as well as objective perceptions as they gradually refine their sense of a text. The act of writing and the act of reading literature can therefore become for students mutually enhancing activities, each bolstering the other's capacity to help students build and revise their visions of meaning. Teaching writing and teaching literature become indistinguishable undertakings, with courses actually coming to center on the action of "composing"—whether of the students' own prose, or of their literary analyses, or of their general viewpoints on life.

In analyzing the recent theoretical work on connections between composition and literature, we begin with the influence of reader-response theory on efforts to establish a unified classroom praxis, for this influence has indeed been considerable and could lead to significant change in the way literature in particular is taught. We then discuss what certain theorists take to be the implications of poststructuralism for the teaching of writing as well as for the teaching of literature. Next, we focus on those theorists who look to rhetoric or a similar overarching conception of discourse as the best means of linking composition and literature in the English curriculum. Finally, we turn to the question of what kind of literature might prove most valuable in the simultaneous fostering of students' reading and writing abilities.

Reader-response theory

Reader-response theory has probably been the strongest shaping force in the development of models for bringing the teaching of writing and the teaching of literature together. Names such as Louise Rosenblatt, David Bleich, Stanley Fish, Wolfgang Iser, and Norman Holland have been cited by advocates of course designs that mesh the two pedagogies. It should be noted that these particular figures do not all share the same assumptions, nor have they had all that much to say about how their insights concerning the study of literature might apply to the teaching of composition. Still, resemblances do appear in their accounts of reading, and the resemblances dovetail with results of contemporary research into the process of writing. It is not surprising, then, that certain instructors trying to integrate composition and literature have invoked them as a set of references. More precisely, their collective emphasis on reading as a dynamic interaction of reader and text corresponds with the emphasis of composition researchers on writing as a recursive process that helps the writer make and remake meaning. And such a correspondence points toward courses that intertwine the processes of reading and writing for students' productive engagement in both.

The title alone of Louise Rosenblatt's 1938 book, *Literature as Exploration*, suggests her concern with reading as a self-ordering, self-corrective process in which text and reader come together, each being shaped by the other. Influenced herself by John Dewey and William James, Rosenblatt was saddened by the impact that objectivists were having on criticism and the teaching of literature. She deplored their neglect of the personal elements in the reader's unfolding relationship with the text, along with their focus on a determinate meaning that could supposedly be extracted from it through a method of "close reading." Her book calls for a pedagogy that affirms the role of the reader's feelings, thoughts, and prior experiences in interpretation—not to dismiss the reality of the text but to recognize the variety of forces at play in the making of meaning. While Rosenblatt was not exactly exiled to Elba for her endorsement of the "affective fallacy," the decades-long hegemony of New Criticism eclipsed her ideas. The recent burst of esteem for *Literature as Exploration* and the acclaim that greeted her 1978 book *The Reader, the Text, the Poem* suggest that a full-scale Rosenblatt revival is under way. Several reasons for it can be enumerated, but clearly one of them is the appeal of her focus on the transactional nature of literary response for instructors who hold comparable views of writing—instructors, in other words, who see writing as an active reflection on and continuous reformulation of one's feelings and thoughts.

In *Readings and Feelings: An Introduction to Subjective Criticism*, David Bleich proposes a pedagogy for using subjective criticism in the classroom that involves students writing their responses to a literary text. These writers first "'say what the poem says' in their own prose" (21) and then describe the emotions and associations they experienced while reading. Bleich asserts that such writings demonstrate perceptual differences and provide data for a deeper awareness of individual identity. He elaborates the epistemological basis for his approach in *Subjective Criticism* when he argues that knowledge depends on language as it symbolizes experience. Students, in order to "know" literary works, must examine both the works and their written responses to them. Ultimately, Bleich's students engage in a process of "intersubjective negotiation" whereby they collectively analyze their responses to determine what it is they would like to know and what it is they consider knowable. The primacy that Bleich assigns to written self-reflection in the act of literary response and his emphasis on a group inquiry akin to the give-and-take of peer groups in composition classes make his theory especially congenial to teachers of writing concerned with enhancing the richness of the composing process.

Stanley Fish's collection of essays *Is There a Text in This Class?* shows that he, too, is interested in the structure of a reader's experience. More specifically, the earlier essays demonstrate his concern with the responses that readers make as words succeed one another in a literary text. The essay "Literature and the Reader," for example, proposes a teaching strategy that encourages students to analyze the effects that words of a text have on them during their reading. Such analysis can involve considering the verbal choices that the author makes and the frequency with which the author satisfies or subverts students' predictions as they read. Writing can, of course, be a useful tool for the class as they seek to record and understand the impact of particular words on them, along with the predictions they find themselves forming or abandoning. It should be pointed out that later essays in Fish's anthology reveal an important shift in his thinking. Fish now seems less interested in reader-centered explications of texts and more interested in how "interpretive communities" lead readers to construct, rather than to passively recognize, what they consider the evidence in the text for their claims about it. Rather than conceding the reality of certain textual givens, Fish depicts the facts of a text as the product of assumptions held by the interpretive community of which the reader is a member.

Aware of Fish's recent belief that interpretation cannot be grounded in properties of a text that are objectively there, teachers can still feel justified in taking students through the kind of exegesis that Fish once recommended, especially if they fuse his dynamic inquiry with composing strategies that help readers articulate their perceptions more fully. Janet Emig reminds us that writing provides a record of one's evolving thought, an insight that is particularly germane to the process of making sense of texts ("Writing"). In fact, when readers are confronted all at once with the complexity of reading literary texts, writing seems the only way to fix their responses for analysis and understanding. Fish himself contends that his earlier teaching strategy is indeed still viable, and certainly many instructors concur. Perhaps both the early and the later Fish can be useful in different ways, with the Fish who focuses on interpretive communities relevant to instructors who want to better understand the rationales for establishing peer groups in the classroom, as Kenneth Bruffee has recently suggested ("Collaborative Learning"). Edward M. White points out that this Fish might also help instructors clarify what they are doing when they form group standards in holistic grading sessions.

Wolfgang Iser is another theorist who posits a dynamically complex, unfolding process of reading. He stresses how the act of reading literature entails a construction of the text, with the reader operating within certain schemata or codes. As the title of his book *The Implied Reader* suggests, Iser also believes, unlike Bleich and Fish, that the text provides a number of objectively verifiable cues for the reader's activity. At the other end of what might be thought of as a spectrum of attitudes toward this question of textual reality, Norman Holland, in books like *5 Readers Reading*, tends to depict interpretation as an expression of the "identity theme" that distinguishes the reader's own psychological makeup. Whatever their views on this particular issue, however, all the theorists we have mentioned jointly champion an emphasis on reading as process, an emphasis that guides or at least complements the philosophy of several theorists who would merge literature and composition.

Of the latter group, perhaps Anthony Petrosky provides the most fully articulated attempt to use writing productively in literature classes ("From Story"). He bases his approach on the notion that reading and writing are both composing acts, that understanding itself is a process of composing. Combining literary theory and composition theory, then, helps students understand themselves as readers and writers because these theories yield compatible explanations of human understanding as a process rooted in the individual's knowledge and feelings and characterized by the fundamental act of making meaning, whether it be through reading, responding, or writing (26). This emphasis on an interactive process clearly indicates Petrosky's choice of a response philosophy in the spirit of Rosenblatt. Working with a number of other humanistic and empirical theories, Petrosky maintains there is "compelling evidence to support the claim that comprehension is heavily subjective, a function of the reader's prior knowledge, the text, and the context" (21). Using traditional composition criteria, he argues that written responses to literature can best be evaluated according to the degree of elaboration, coherence, and clarity in them. His further suggestion to use quantity as a criterion might seem superficial, but it is appropriate given the benefits of persistent attention to the recursive rhythms generated between text and writer.

Since, according to Petrosky, readers and writers both create meaning out of "the cultural and contextual frames we happen to find ourselves in" (26), writing about literature can help students unravel the social and psychological complexity of their transactions with texts. Attentive instructors will listen carefully to these responses and will then be better able to see the range of understanding in a class. With such information it is easier for instructors to intervene, helping students "learn to elaborate, clarify and illustrate their responses by references to the associations and prior knowledge that inform them" (24). Petrosky relies on Bleich's response heuristic to structure the writing: students are first asked to write what they perceive in the text, then what they feel about what they see, and lastly what associations "inform and follow from their perceptions" (25). In a literature class, then, readers might write about "A Rose for Emily" with spontaneous responses that are interrogated for clues that enable further explanation. In this way composing becomes a way to represent understanding of text and self. In a larger sense, the pedagogy that follows from these strategies suggests a dialectic between individual response and community reaction that can lead to a thoroughgoing examination of personal and cultural assumptions, the ultimate goal being more mature and informed critical judgments.

Also highlighting critical reading, Rosenblatt's former student John Clifford suggests a composing strategy that might guide students along a "continuum of increasing responsiveness" ("Beyond Subjectivity" 95), beginning with personal statements before moving on to more analytic writing. He has his students write before, during, and after reading a piece of literature in order to "create a more explicit, ordered context for their encounters with literature" (96). Using John Updike's short story "A & P," for example, he had students speculate about their response to the situation the protagonist of the story finds himself in. After reading a third of the story, students were asked to write again, this time focusing on specific feelings about characters in the story. Writing is woven into the process of reading in these ways because it can suggest "unrealized possibilities." Adapting Purves and Rippere's classic research study on response to literature, Clifford sequences writing assignments to move the class through three stages: perception, interpretation, and evaluation. Clifford emphasizes the need to guide inexperienced readers through the process of critical inquiry using a transactional dialectic between reader and text. This kind of composing as a deliberate structuring of the web of meaning (Vygotsky) encourages a continuous, spontaneous stream of thoughts, opinions, ideas, and reactions that help students become active, conscious makers of meaning. This and similar approaches have also been influenced by James Britton's (*Development of Writing Abilities*) and James Moffett's insights into the benefits of rooting language development and knowledge in personal experience and expressive writing.

In a related essay ("Using Intuition"), Clifford creates a composing sequence of nine stages to teach Loren Eiseley's "Dance of the Frogs." Although he realizes that writing is a continuous and recursive process, he also believes it needs to be divided into discrete stages for teaching purposes. In this way instructors can introduce "timely rhetorical information at the appropriate stage" (7). To develop a context for classroom interaction, focused free-writing questions were used as heuristics. Students broke into small groups to read responses, sharing their speculations, beliefs, and doubts about the plausibility of Eiseley's fictional universe. Clifford claims that the free-writing heuristic helped his students discover and clarify their ideas. And because the initial response was written quickly from various perspectives, students "often ended up in unplanned positions that surprised and intrigued them" (8). Citing Kinneavy's belief that expressive writing is psychologically prior to other, more analytic aims, Clifford reports how students were eventually encouraged to turn personal responses into transactional prose. A composing sequence that "values and encourages incubation and growth" (9) can, among other things, allow students the freedom to say something worth the effort.

In a similar vein, Elizabeth Flynn makes good use of exploratory writing in teaching "A & P" herself. She is careful, however, to disassociate herself from an exclusive reliance on response statements, which she sees as only the initial stage in a complex process—as means, not ends. Citing the work of James Britton and Linda Flower on expressive and "writer-based" prose, Flynn believes writers "initially write to and for themselves" (342). Hence, these student papers usually lack explicit causal relationships and score low on the usual criteria: evidence, development, illustration. Her pedagogy encourages movement from "writer-oriented to reader-oriented writing" (343); she notes that in initial statements students frequently identify with characters and display "difficulty stepping back from them to make judgments or find a coherent pattern of meaning" (343). Flynn illustrates these evolutions from "participation to observation, from identification to critical distance" with a journal entry, a draft, and a final paper that a particular student wrote in response to "A & P." Although the student's progress is clear, the motivation or classroom technique that produces the final breakthrough is less so. Flynn does indicate, though, that peer-group discussions are an important factor in promoting her students' cognitive growth. And her overall position is quite lucid: she wants to transform personal responses into "negotiable interpretations." Ultimately she wants to "evaluate and analyze, to decenter, to transcend the limitations of their initial, private responses" (347). She relies on extended and trusting interactions in the class to enhance those rereading and rewriting phases that connect literature with students' experiences. Beneath her strategies is the conviction that writing can enrich the reading of those texts that have the power to transform and enlarge previous visions of the self.

Also echoing Rosenblatt's insight that there is a significant difference between knowing *about* literature and knowing *through* literature, Mariolina Salvatori bases her composition and literature pedagogy on developing appropriate writing and reading skills in tandem. Salvatori's research leads her to believe that the maturity of writers is "the result, rather than the cause, of their increased ability to engage in, and to be reflexive about, the reading of highly complex texts" (659). The key pedagogical move is to allow students to "tolerate and confront ambiguities and uncertainties in the reading process" (662), a strategy she hopes will help them avoid premature closure in the composing of their own texts. Building in particular on Iser's theory, Salvatori tries to move her students from the assumption that reading is an extraction to the more dynamic view that "reading is construction, the composing of oneself and the text through interaction with it" (664). Her tactic is to intervene in the reading process, hoping that students will learn to synthesize various perspectives and therefore better realize that reading and writing are interconnected. Explaining the case of a student trying to analyze Maya Angelou's autobiography, *I Know Why the Caged Bird Sings*, Salvatori depicts the student as moving from "a writer who merely reproduces the texts she reads and writes about, to a writer who more actively interacts with the text she composes as that text composes her" (666).

Many instructors believe that by intervening they can increase their students' awareness of and control over the processes of reading and writing.

Assuming that a reader-response approach can best give instructors access to what happens between text and reader, Russell A. Hunt agrees with Fish's call for a method that will make "observable, or at least accessible, what goes on below the level of self-conscious response" (Fish 32; qtd. in Hunt 348–49). One way to do this, Hunt suggests, is to slow down the reading experience by having students stop at various points in the text to discuss expectations. What Hunt terms "an impromptu exploratory writing assignment" (354) can neatly fit in with this pedagogical technique.

Hunt's preference for such writing and his uneasiness with more orthodox, thesis-oriented, conventionally structured papers as an approach to literary criticism echo Keith Fort's argument against the "formal tyranny" of the traditional written response to literature, its "self-deceptive need for an authority whom we don't consciously believe can exist" (636). More recently Thomas Newkirk, following David Bartholomae ("Writing"), has expressed similar sentiments. Newkirk declares his belief "that the traditional critical analysis paper may discourage students from dealing with reactions that are not easily resolved into a thesis, that they may discourage the student from dealing with the more puzzling (and very likely more complex) issues of meaning and language, that, in sum, they encourage the student to play it safe" ("Looking" 757). As an alternative, Newkirk would allow students to keep reexamining their interpretations of a text through a series of exploratory writings. He also thinks it important for the instructor to share his or her own written reflections on the text with the class, a technique most fully propounded by Frank Smith.

Another proponent of the discovery draft is Bruce T. Petersen, who believes such prewriting techniques can later be reworked into a variety of forms, including narration or description. Citing studies by Walter Kintsch, Charles Bazerman, Robert de Beaugrande, and others that imply "that reading and writing are connected thinking processes which derive from similar, if not identical, mental structures" (460), Petersen presents a theoretical basis and a pedagogical model for a course combining composition and literature. The key to this integration can be found, he believes, in recent composition research from James Britton and Linda Flower and in theoretical statements from reader-response critics like Rosenblatt and Bleich (Petersen's dissertation adviser). He argues that all four theorists hold that "our first approach to knowing is founded on a personal and often affective base" (463). We respond to literature affectively through personal associations, prior cognitive schemes, and private images and memories. Our first responses in writing are expressive and writer-based and filled with egocentric concerns. The similarities between Britton's and Flower's view of writing on the one hand and Rosenblatt's and Bleich's description of readers on the other suggest to Petersen that "both processes are grounded in a psychological process which underlies both learning and thought" (463).

In the classroom, then, students would be encouraged to respond naturally by allowing them to bring their personal experiences to the text. Hence, writing in a wide variety of forms becomes the center of the course. And, as with other similar response-oriented pedagogies, small-group work and peer response to writing are championed as ways to overcome the limitations of "ego-centered or self-confirming thought" (464). Petersen's course unfolds in phases similar to the audience-directed movement from the self to the world in James Moffett's discourse continuum. Students are encouraged to respond, then to generalize from their own experiences and thoughts, and later to move toward critical papers. Throughout, the recursive nature of the reading and writing process is highlighted as meaning emerges from active transactions with texts. W. Ross Winterowd ("Comment") argues that Petersen's theory of reading-writing connections does not necessarily apply to the relation between writing and the reading of literature; Winterowd also suggests that certain special qualities of literature risk being devalued when literature is integrated with the teaching of composition. Yet it seems as if the kind of exploratory writing that Petersen discusses could indeed enhance a student's understanding and appreciation of literature, as well as the act of *reading* literature or anything else.

Although Ann Berthoff has not specifically allied herself with response theorists, her work has been influential in helping the profession see useful connections between literature and writing. In her three texts on imagination and the making of meaning, she has, in fact, gone further than most theorists in blending reading and writing theory into a strong classroom praxis. She does emphasize, however, that her critical orientation differs from the extreme subjectivity of Bleich and others. Although she is not interested in "gut" reactions, she sees little value in objective and intentionalist concerns. Rather, she believes, "the essential significance of criticism in the classroom is that it enables us to teach reading for meaning and writing as a way of making meaning." Since, for Berthoff, meaning resides not in objects but in relationships, it is "unstable, shifting, dynamic" (*Making of Meaning* 42). For both reading and writing, context and perspective are everything. To enhance the critical reading and insight into process that Berthoff wants, she suggests that students "write continuously in a double-entry notebook" (45). To encourage the strong critical attitude that comes from reflective questioning, students should keep reading notes, responses, direct quotations, and such on one side of their notebooks, while the other side is used for notes about those notes, revisions, and insights. This desire for self-inquiry and critical consciousness is indicative of Berthoff's dialectic pedagogy, a strategy where I. A. Richards's "continuing audit of meaning" is central to learning how to read and write critically.

Recently Frank Devlin has proposed a wide range of writing assignments that can help instructors mesh composition and literary study. Devlin contends that such integration has been thwarted because of traditional textbooks, both in literature and in composition. For him, standard literature textbooks wrongly endorse formalistic strategies at the expense of the reader's personal experience with the literary work: "The impersonal, the removed, the objective is clearly the desired stance" (10). In parallel fashion, traditional composition textbooks wrongly emphasize strictly conventional structures and pseudoscientific methods of inquiry. (Here Devlin consciously echoes the important essay of Keith Fort.) An alternative account of literary study for Devlin would be that provided by reader-response theory, particularly as voiced by Holland and Rosenblatt. An alternative composition theory would be the "new rhetoric," which "posits a variable reality, interpreted and shaped by individual response" (11). Devlin submits that these two alternative theories complement each other well, and therefore could provide the foundation for a pedagogy that unites the teaching of writing with the teaching of literature.

The assignments that Devlin explains build on this conceptual unity in various ways. For a first assignment, he has students write about R. H. Munro's short story "The Open Window" by reading through the story section by section and responding in a particular manner at the end of each one. When they finish reading the first section, they are to analyze Mr. Nuttel and the young girl by describing, comparing, and associating each character; then, they are to talk on paper about how they think the story will develop and why they have this expectation. At the end of the second section, they are to analyze Mr. Nuttel and Mrs. Sappleton by again describing, comparing, and associating; then, they are to review their responses to Mr. Nuttel. Finally, they are to explain their reactions to the last two paragraphs in the context of their whole reading experience (12). Devlin's later assignments have the class writing down memories or their own methods of storytelling before reading a work, a process that enables them to understand after reading the work how the context they brought to it matched or failed to match the author's themes and techniques. Charles Moran makes a similar case for having students try out various approaches to rhetorical situations before reading how a particular novelist handles them. In noting how the interplay of writing and reading in his own course leads to reciprocal benefits in both areas, Devlin points out how this combination of reader-response theory and the new rhetoric produces writing that has an impressively personal voice: "Though students often write about identical selections, their papers are strikingly different, in tone, emphasis, and approach" (15).

Devlin's article prods his reader to envision other writing assignments based on his apparently fruitful premises. The new examples he is able to cite within the confines of a short essay stir the imagination to conceive of numerous possibilities. The generativity of Devlin's piece suggests at least two important things about current work on the role of reader-response criticism in a truly unified literature and composition course. First, even though many theorists draw on the insights of figures like Rosenblatt and Iser, they are not mere synthesizers of other people's thought. Instead, they have used it as a resource in the evolution of their own fertile pedagogies. Second, the relation between reader-response strategies and the teaching of writing is still being formulated. If all these theorists emphasize the idea of process in discussing reading and writing, their own philosophical inquiries can be said to be still in process. In other words, even more stimulating insights might yet come forth.

Poststructuralist theory

Of course, reader-response theory is not the only kind in force on the critical scene. Indeed, most people working in the field of literature would first point to the surging influence of poststructuralism, especially deconstruction. Composition theorists have, admittedly, proven more hospitable to reader-response pedagogies, but some are now turning to poststructuralist concepts as guides to the teaching of writing as well as the teaching of literature.

W. Ross Winterowd, for example, has often tried to imagine the effects of poststructuralism on composition praxis. In "Post-Structuralism and Composition," Winterowd ponders the implications of the radical indeterminacy that Jacques Derrida (*Of Grammatology*) attributes to linguistic operations. He notes that if composition teachers can never hope to know what a student's paper really means, they might feel compelled to ignore ideas, development, and structure, concentrating instead just on the teaching of style. But Winterowd himself greets the advent of deconstruction more optimistically. He apparently anticipates with pleasure one possible consequence of it: a composition pedagogy of "endless dialogue and dialectic" rather than of "conclusiveness" (86). Traditional lecturing, where instructors pass out knowledge, will be given up in favor of a "problematized," ongoing process with no ultimate goal (81). Other implications of Derrida's

skepticism, self-reflection, and irony might include a privileging of complexity for its own sake and the debunking of composition as an empirical
science. There might also be an increased reaction against the authority
of handbooks and rhetorics. That exploratory writing "will gain stature"
(90) in this poststructuralist vision Winterowd sees as double-edged, however, since traditional expository prose with a clearly stated thesis will be
devalued to coincide with the epistemological assumptions of deconstruction.

Again, in "Black Holes, Indeterminacy and Paolo Freire," Winterowd
speculates that poststructuralism could alter "the way we perceive and teach
the universe of discourse" (29). The essay relates poststructuralism to several
of Freire's pedagogical concerns, especially the need for critical awareness
and the need for students to be "critical co-investigators in dialogue with
the teacher" (33). Interestingly, Winterowd here seems quite willing to dismiss the pedagogical consequences of Derrida's work in favor of Freire's
and Kenneth Burke's concern with literature as equipment for living and
literacy as revolutionary, "where rhetoric is the best hope for peace and
understanding" (35).

More pedagogically concrete is William Covino's analysis of Burke and
Derrida. Central to Covino's thinking is the idea that invention is "the
unifying term for the whole process of composition" (1). And invention
should encourage a free play of the mind, an attempt to invent something
new, "something that creates new categories which complement and advance the old ones" (3). Covino notes that Derrida questions the given,
"the self-assured certitude of consciousness" (2), using "differance" to indicate the slippage of language, its inability to capture essences, to locate meaning in one place, one word, one text, so that we are left with traces of
meaning that recede before our inquiry. "Differance" involves a playful attitude that encourages constant questioning and rearranging. Covino observes that this idea is consistent with Burke's "perspective by incongruity":
a method of invention that would encourage in students playful exploration and discovery and the rejection of formulaic approaches to writing.
Rigidity, sameness, and certainty are renounced in favor of free play, multiple perspectives, and tentativeness, even skepticism. In this sense, then,
Burke's and Derrida's ideas on invention can be seen as "epistemological
heuristics," helping writers to discover how they know the world.

After surveying recurring themes in the poststructuralist critical milieu,
Tilly Warnock nominates Kenneth Burke's rhetorical theory of language
as symbolic action as a catalyst for department "coherence and even, perhaps, that longed-for sense of Kairos, of harmony and wholeness" (176).
Hoping for a new way for composition and literary theorists to talk to one

another, Warnock is essentially optimistic that these two supposedly disparate endeavors can find a common ground. She unpacks the usual themes
of deconstruction—centerlessness, imprecision, indeterminacy, free play, slippage, and instability—as an indication that the old ways no longer hold,
that the time is ripe for dialogue. She wants composition theory to be more
than technique. To upgrade the humanistic caste of rhetoric, Warnock suggests we juxtapose what writing theorists know and do with what "for example, a specialist in Renaissance drama knows and does with language"
(176). More interesting but no less operationally opaque is her reference
to Burke's metaphorical anecdote in *The Philosophy of Literary Form* about
life as an ongoing cocktail-party conversation. It is, she proposes, an image of language learning that may be possible for English departments to
enact in a poststructuralist climate.

Recently one of the major theorists of deconstruction, J. Hillis Miller,
has explored its implications for the teaching of writing. In doing so, he
affirms the inseparability of reading and writing, maintaining "that no skillful composition is possible without that prior act of decomposition practiced through reading models of composition by others" (42). Reflecting
on deconstruction's concern with the essentially figurative character of all
discourse, Miller additionally contends that composition handbooks should
not treat metaphor as mere ornamentation that the student writer can do
without. A deconstructive stance leads to a more realistic and profitable
composition course, in part, he suggests, because it encourages writers and
readers to think about how tropes pervade what they write and what they
read. Interestingly, this important theorist of deconstruction does not call
for or exemplify Winterowd's vision of poststructuralist discourse; indeed,
Miller's argument is expressed in a most accessible, traditional fashion, as
probably befits an address at the Modern Language Association convention and as certainly befits the academic writing in which Miller has articulated his views before. Miller's orthodoxy of form here might indicate that
poststructuralism will not necessarily have the transformational influence
that Winterowd associates with it; then again, perhaps Winterowd is, in
a sense, more poststructuralist in temperament than Miller is. Or perhaps
Miller's emphasis on the basic figural quality of discourse is the most radical conceptual move of all, considering how the received wisdom of composition handbooks is obviously subverted by it and how students would
indeed be engaging in intense self-reflection if they concentrated on un-
packing all the assumptions latent in the metaphors they were using
throughout their writing.

Undoubtedly there will be further efforts to synthesize the insights generated by poststructuralist perspectives with the principles of an identifiably

sound composition pedagogy. Many composition instructors, however, will find poststructuralist theory uncongenial, given its emphasis on indeterminacy. John Gage, for example, holds to the traditional notion that composition teaching should get students to implement their self-acknowledged intentions, and in adhering to this idea, Gage worries that literature courses nowadays confuse students if they present the contradictory notion that readers can never really know what an author meant. Far from proclaiming the virtues of indeterminacy in composition classes and literature classes, he wants the principle of intentionality to be inculcated in both. Of course, not only advocates of deconstruction might object in turn to Gage's proposal. James Britton's notion of shaping at the point of utterance ("Shaping") and Janet Emig's notion of writing as a mode of learning ("Writing") both suggest that writers do not, in fact, clearly "know" their intentions when they write but instead discover them during the process of writing. Still, many instructors currently maintain a praxis that reflects sympathy with the position represented by Gage.

Therefore, it remains the task of poststructuralist theorists to show how their philosophical premises might indeed have beneficial consequences for the teaching of writing as well as the teaching of literature. The possibility of a convincing demonstration is suggested by the intriguing speculations already voiced by the theorists we have mentioned. It should be noted at the same time, however, that even more speculations about poststructuralist composition and literature pedagogy might appear. For example, how might the writing of literary criticism be taught if the instructor assents to the claim of a Geoffrey Hartman, in a book like *Criticism in the Wilderness*, that criticism should not be deemed parasitic on literature and therefore considered a mere adjunct to it but rather that criticism and literature are equally creative, equally worthy modes of discourse, with their separateness not as real as the discipline of English has made it seem? Hartman's deconstruction of the classic distinction between criticism and literature is merely one of the areas in poststructuralist thought that could yet be tapped for a new approach to the teaching of composition as well as of literature.

Unified theories of reading and writing

There are, however, even more ambitious possibilities for connections between the literature and composition components of the English curriculum. A number of theorists are formulating broad paradigms that would enable instructors in English departments to feel that they are carrying out a common enterprise rather than toiling in different fields and subfields of a painfully heterogenous discipline. Susan Miller's attempt at an intellectually flexible synthesis is promising, as is Richard A. Lanham's attempt to show how literature and composition can occupy places on the same theoretical spectrum. Rhetoric has also been put forth as an inclusive and systematic theory to unite English faculty.

In an exploratory essay, Miller offers a satisfying and intellectually rigorous attempt to specify ways that composition and literary study might be combined. Miller believes a description of "writing" that can "comprehend both research interests is urgently needed" ("What Does It Mean" 220). She cogently points out apparently irreconcilable differences between the two fields, such as the privileged status of the literary text in contrast to the usual evaluative reception of student writing. She also notes that the "perceived purposes" (223) of the two fields vary, each having roots in rhetoric and poetic theory that posit literature as the transforming humanistic study and composition as the utilitarian and vocational tool of public humanity.

There are other differences: methods of research vary, with literature focusing on the texts of individual writers while much empirical work in composition stresses the composing processes of groups of writers, usually without reference to resulting writing. With these differing perspectives on writing, how is more than a cosmetic rapprochement possible? Relying on the multivariate and highly contextually oriented work of the sociolinguist Dell Hymes, the rhetorical ideas of Kenneth Burke, and the tagmemic linguistics of Kenneth Pike, Miller constructs several multidimensional figures of the writing event, the development of writing ability, and written discourse that she hopes will enable theorists to study, for example, texts in literature and composition in a cultural, historical, and situational context. In her comprehensive matrices there would be no absolutes, no automatic responses either to Shakespeare or to a student writer. Approaching either with limiting preconceptions about aesthetics or research paradigms instead of a dedication to "evocative problematics" would "reduce our scope" (234). Miller's piece encourages a synthesis of composition and literature, but only if the resulting view of writing embraces a wide range of intellectual perspectives, in the manner of Pike's wave, particle, and field heuristic.

Richard A. Lanham argues that if the study of literature is to be seen as bearing a definite relation to the teaching of composition, the long-prevailing paradigm underlying English studies has to change. More precisely, Lanham claims that with the traditional framework of the discipline, "Composition becomes the study of communication in a world posited to be 'real,' admittedly 'out there,' in contradistinction to literature's imag-

inative reality" (18); therefore, the two areas of the curriculum really do
not seem to have much to do with each other. Lanham articulates an alternative epistemology that does hold greater promise of authentic recon-
ciliation. Assuming that "literature does not constitute a separate reality,"
that "Life . . . is full of 'literary' elements," he envisions a spectrum where
at one end lies "neutral 'real life', detached from man and his recreative
imagination," and at the other end lies "a world of fantasy"—"with all kinds
of mixed states in the middle." He then conceives of another spectrum
"for the perceiver rather than the perceived" (18). At the left of this one
lies what he calls "*Through* Vision," a state of affairs when someone is reading
purely for information. At the other end lies "*At* Vision," when the reader
is paying attention to the aesthetic qualities of a work. Again, a perceiver
or reader is usually somewhere in the middle of this spectrum during the
act of perceiving or reading. Lanham declares that if English studies accepted the conceptual validity of these two spectra, then as far as literature
and composition are concerned, "*the problematic relationship between the
two simply disappears*," because "They represent different points on the same
series of spectra." Basically, then, "Teaching literature and teaching composition form different parts of the same activity" (19).

One of the especially appealing features of Lanham's conception of English studies is its conscious analogies with recent theoretical developments
in other disciplines. He feels that literary critics who hold to the old paradigm are at odds "with the sociologist who examines role theory; with the
cultural anthropologist who finds 'ordinary' communication astoundingly
full of literary ingredients; with the perception psychologist who stresses
the active, participating, integrative role of perception . . . and above all
those who study the social behavior of animals" (21). We should note, too,
that Lanham criticizes traditional composition teaching for its emphasis
on what he denigrates as the CBS style: in other words, a style that emphasizes clarity, brevity, and sincerity in the mistaken belief that an objectively distinct reality exists and that it can best be rendered by a prose
that aims to be utterly transparent. For Lanham's paradigm to be implemented, therefore, both literary critics and composition teachers would
have to surrender their traditional epistemologies.

Other theorists have called for a revival of rhetoric to unify the English
curriculum. James Murphy, for example, bemoans the separation of reading and writing that developed along with the waning of rhetoric as a cen-
tralizing force in the study of literature and composition. Of course, when
theorists nowadays look to rhetoric as an important new conceptual bridge,
they do not have in mind reductive popular notions of the term. They
do not see rhetoric as simply ritualistic patterns of argumentation or the

study of metaphors as mere ornamentation. Instead, they believe an attention to rhetoric in its fullest, most wide-ranging sense can promote the making and remaking of meaning as a constant, dynamic activity in the classroom, involving both composition and the reading of literature.

Wayne C. Booth envisions courses that in effect challenge "the assumed dichotomy between rhetoric and reality" by featuring reading and writing sequences pivoting around "the question; 'What kinds of reality can be made only – or made best – with planned, artful speech?'" ("LITCOMP" 64). He states that underlying such courses would be "one fundamental assumption about all of us, teachers and students alike: that we have an unlimited need, even when we don't know it, to improve our capacity *to shape reality with words*" (64). In Booth's ideal classroom, therefore, teacher and students would concern themselves with "four kinds of making that are achieved, or botched, with discourse":

> They are implicit in every serious treatise on rhetoric: With our discourse we can (1) make or remake our characters and commitments in the *present*; (2) we make and remake (as "revisionists") our *past*; (3) we help to make our *future*; and (4) we sometimes hope to share accurate reports on what is "neither past nor passing nor to come," since all of us "at one time or another" – note the phrase – attempt a "rhetoric of the timeless." (65)

Frequent writing assignments, proceeding from study of various texts, would characterize this kind of learning. As with Lanham's plan, one of the attractive aspects of Booth's thinking is that it would enable English departments to draw on similar ideas from other disciplines; Booth finds, for example, that "perhaps the richest current literature about reality making in rhetoric is that of anthropologists who study how people constitute each other in symbolic exchange" (77). Another attractive aspect is Booth's emphasis on the potential ability of his model to engage the various members of an English faculty in a common, intellectually invigorating pursuit, one that might counteract the hierarchal patterns that have otherwise marred the relationship between teachers of literature and teachers of composition.

Although Nancy R. Comley and Robert Scholes do not explicitly invoke the word *rhetoric* to summarize their proposed conception of an English curriculum, it seems fair to assign that label to what they have in mind. Comley and Scholes see the current English curriculum as threatened by a number of false polarities. To them, English faculty privilege literature over nonliterature, consumption of texts over production of texts, and the academic world over the outside world (96–97). Focusing on how freshman English in particular might be changed, they believe that "the first step in arriving at a new approach to freshman English is to locate the qualities of good writing that are shared by 'literary' and 'nonliterary' texts." Then the staff "can devise an arrangement of readings and writings that will point toward them" (102). For the purpose of demonstration, Comley and Scholes show their own rhetorical leanings by concentrating on the quality of voice, pointing out that "it suggests a person behind the words, whose personality is one focus of organization," that it "also suggests the presence of the receiver of the text, a reader or 'listener' also conceived in human terms," and that "finally, voice suggests a consistent attitude toward the subject under discussion" (102). Comley and Scholes observe that study of genres like lyric poetry can help students develop appropriate voices in their writing. Using as a model Gwendolyn Brooks's poem "We Real Cool," for example, student writers can present lively accounts of their personal classroom experience.

W. Ross Winterowd, believing that English departments need a "unifying theoretical basis for activities" ("Getting It" 30), also sees a cure for departmental fragmentation in rhetorical thought, especially the ideas of Kenneth Burke. Moreover, Winterowd finds in the classical rhetorical categories of logos, pathos, and ethos, including structure and style, enough depth and breadth for rhetoric to be a framework for both writing theory and literary criticism. He goes further, however, claiming that rhetoric is vital to literature, "for the field has a robustness that can be a healthy corrective for the effeteness of some — perhaps most — literary studies" ("The Three R's" 63).

Winterowd is especially fond of representing the links between rhetoric and poetics with schematic charts and diagrams. In a typical arrangement, Burkean ratios are drawn among M. H. Abrams's four critical viewpoints (mimetic, expressive, pragmatic, and objective) and the three main divisions of classical rhetoric (logos, ethos, and pathos). For example, he derives a poem-reality ratio from Abrams's mimetic and Aristotle's logic. This blending of rhetoric and literature is typical of Winterowd's confidence in Kenneth Burke's dramatistic perspective, one that creates knowledge by analogy, metaphor, comparison, and opposition. For Burke, perspective is everything and knowledge comes "by extralogical processes," with conclusions preceding arguments: "From what we want to arrive at, we deduce our ways of getting there." Winterowd highlights this Burkean quest for appositional thinking instead of propositional or logical activity in an open letter to Peter Elbow. Winterowd develops from gestaltist, imagistic thought a prose style that he argues would be consistent with an appositional rhetoric. The "representative anecdote as conceptual pivot" is favored over the enthymeme, organizational flexibility over rigidity, specific examples over general examples, a foregrounded style over a background style, and great presence over little presence ("Dear Peter Elbow" 99). Typical of the propositional style is, of course, the conventional academic essay that supports arguments with appropriate examples. In the appositional style, however, Winterowd says writers would follow examples "to their limits" (99). Apparently, writers would reach for the generalization only after giving rein to the concrete, the representative anecdote. By making these comparisons and observations, Winterowd also hopes to show the sweeping, holistic nature of rhetoric and the eclectic and fragmented state of literary criticism.

Winterowd's resistance to the separation of rhetoric and literary criticism in "The Realms of Meaning: Text Centered Criticism," for example, has influenced others to search for useful parallels. Steven Mailloux, for example, attempts to indicate concrete similarities between rhetoric and poetics. Like Winterowd, Mailloux tries to use the traditional rhetorical categories of invention, arrangement, and style to make connections between composition and literary theory. Fish's simple question—What does this word or sentence do?—is cited as an invention resource for composition teachers, along with Burke's pentad. Moving on to a discussion of form, Mailloux relies again on the theories of Burke and Fish, noting that Fish's "structure of the reader's experience" is similar to Burke's theory of form, especially his insight in *Counter-Statement* that form is "an arousing and fulfillment of desires" (124). Style is also seen as a source of connections between literary and composition theory. Mailloux mentions sentence combining as a promising exercise, demonstrating to student writers the wide-ranging stylistic choices available. Enhancing syntactic fluency, improving structure, and discovering topics are the pragmatic teaching goals in Mailloux's attempt at synthesizing rhetoric and poetics.

Although Terry Eagleton's call for a revival of rhetoric at the end of his controversial book *Literary Theory: An Introduction* does not bear explicitly on the role of composition in the English curriculum, his remarks certainly have implications for the teaching of writing, the teaching of literature, and the ways that the two pedagogies might be related. Before his invocation of rhetoric, Eagleton reminds his reader of two main assumptions he has made throughout the book: that "literature" does not really exist as a distinctive mode of discourse, since no sound, consistent definition of the term has ever been put forth, and that most schools of "literary theory" have sadly ignored the problems of society at large, promoting principles that insulate the study of "literature" from the concerns of the wider public realm. For an alternative to the traditional English curriculum, Eagleton therefore seeks a form of study that would entail a greater range of discourse and that would focus on the influences that discourse has in the world. Rhetoric seems to be this form of study for Eagleton, at least given his conception of rhetoric:

> Rhetoric, which was the received form of critical analysis all the way from ancient society to the eighteenth century, examined the way discourses are constructed in order to achieve certain effects. It was not worried about whether its objects of enquiry were speaking or writing, poetry or philosophy, fiction or historiography: its horizon was nothing less than the field of discursive practices in society as a whole, and its particular interest lay in grasping such practices as forms of power and performance. (204)

Eagleton does not think the vocabulary of ancient rhetoric needs to be revived as well, because the resurrection he has in mind could no doubt work with aspects of the various critical theories he details in his book. But clearly his curricular framework would go beyond these theories because of its emphasis on discursive practices other than those traditionally identified as "literature" and because of its determined attempt to concentrate on their social effects. Eagleton also develops this concern with effects in his discussion of the ultimate aims that English education should have. More precisely, he believes that teachers should consider their choice of particular materials and methods as "strategic": "It all depends on what you are trying to do, in what situation" (210, 211).

In explicitly embracing a pragmatic conception of curriculum, Eagleton considers himself to be endorsing again the original nature of rhetoric. It is important to point out, however, that although Eagleton seems to be suggesting that a variety of pedagogical choices is fine with him, he also seems committed to "any method or theory which will contribute to the strategic goal of human emancipation, the production of 'better people' through the socialist transformation of society" (211). Overall, then, the Eagletonian curriculum studies all kinds of discourse, emphasizing their social effects and ultimately concerning itself with the enlargement of human freedom instead of with the disinterested pursuit of knowledge because of its supposedly intrinsic worth.

Perhaps Eagleton's most radical move in his championing of rhetoric is his conviction that if his vision of learning were to be implemented, "departments of literature as we presently know them in higher education would cease to exist." They would be replaced by some other kind of organizational structure that would concern itself with "education in the various theories and methods of cultural analysis" (213).

Given Eagleton's ideal scenario, student writers would probably be encouraged to consider the social effects of their own discourse and to write about the signifying practices in their society—both kinds of learning having the ultimate aim of human emancipation. While he really does not have anything to say about student writing directly, Eagleton does make a passing observation that could have highly intriguing implications for the subject: "On other occasions what might prove useful will not be the criticism or enjoyment of other people's discourse but the production of one's own. Here, as with the rhetorical tradition, studying what other people have done may help. You may want to stage your own signifying practices to enrich, combat, modify or transform the effect which others' practices produce" (212). Working with such an assumption, students in a composition class would feel that their writing could indeed have an important purpose. They would be motivated to write from a sense that they were intervening in the established network of communications so as to alter it for the greater public good. Furthermore, students in an Eagletonian composition class would probably not just be *writing* but instead producing a whole range of discourse. The current dichotomies lamented by Comley and Scholes—literature versus nonliterature, consumption versus production, the academy versus society—would therefore totally break down, with a dedication to a theory of rhetoric presiding over the newly unified curriculum that would result.

What kind of literature?

Terry Eagleton would acknowledge that there would probably be a great deal of resistance to such curricular transformation, from many different quarters. But his daring questions and ideas are still worth debate in the present, even if they are ultimately embedded in what might be thought of as a utopian scheme. We wish to conclude our own discussion of the relation between composition theory and literary theory by focusing on one particular issue he raises, albeit somewhat indirectly: what kind of literature would most help students become better writers? As we have already suggested, a number of contemporary theorists have indicated their unwillingness to restrict textual study in composition pedagogy to works traditionally classified as "literary." Besides Eagleton, Comley, and Scholes, for example, Wayne C. Booth would also include more than just "literary" texts. While not everyone might endorse Eagleton's claim that "it may seem best to look at Proust and *King Lear*, or at children's television programs or popular romances or avant-garde films" (211), clearly several instructors would endorse the principle of letting composition pedagogy bring in a wider field of discourse than traditional courses have encouraged.

Does that mean any teacher of writing ought to feel free to bring in any

texts that he or she wants, as long as the texts promote the students' capacities for meaning making? This question has received new prominence
as a result of recent theoretical work by E. D. Hirsch. In contrast to his
previous work in composition theory, Hirsch now focuses on the content
of composition students' reading. In attributing so much importance to
their reading instead of focusing on the development of their writing techniques, Hirsch renounces his prior allegiance to what he terms "pedagogical formalism," "the idea that we could teach people how to write in a short
time by teaching them the underlying principles common to all writing
tasks" ("Reading" 143). Now he believes that:

> Teaching that emphasizes the linguistic and rhetorical features of writ-
> ing is . . . inherently incomplete. The manipulation of technical
> features—including rhetorical, audience-oriented features, carries so
> much hidden, unspoken information that the linguistic and rhetori-
> cal features themselves are the smaller part of the transaction. (144–45)

Composition courses must, for Hirsch, therefore inculcate "cultural literacy," in other words, "that knowledge that enables a writer or reader to
know what other writers and readers know within the literate culture" (146).

To a certain extent, it is hard to quarrel with Hirsch. For one thing, even
the most idealistic composition teacher would probably admit that students cannot be taught how to write in a short time. Moreover, students
certainly have more resources for writing if they have more information
about their culture. And all the theorists we have mentioned so far would
shrink from endorsing as the main activity in a composition course "the
manipulation of technical features"—insisting instead that, in one way or
another, they wish composition pedagogy to concentrate on the process
of how people come to know what they know, how people come to mean
what they mean.

Since Hirsch's argument does not have much to say about the epistemic
character of a composition course, many of these theorists might quarrel
with him for that reason alone. But a larger source of contention between
Hirsch and others trying to unite composition and literature might be the
method of selection he proposes as he discusses the cultural knowledge
that he feels student readers and writers must have. He seems to endorse
what might be called a "top-down" scheme for choosing the texts that would
be read in freshman English and other classes, suggesting that they can
be decided through negotiations among "the Modern Language Association, National Council of Teachers of English, state councils on education, and the various national academies" ("Reading" 146). Probably a great
many people would feel that, despite the virtues of the organizations he

mentions, it would not be good for education to be so much a matter of centralized decree.

Furthermore, many might object to the definition of culture that Hirsch supports in his proposal. He seems to promote "culture" in the sense of the academy's traditionally valued texts—basically, the tradition of the Great Books. By contrast, Terry Eagleton calls for attention to "culture" in a more anthropological sense of the term—one that would embrace "mass culture" as well as "high culture" because it encompasses the whole range of a society's signifying practices, including those in forms other than writing. Of course, as we have indicated, many people interested in bringing texts into writing classes might not wish to go along with Eagleton's catholicity.

Is there a middle ground? Hirsch suggests that his ideal syllabus would not restrict itself simply to literature but would include works from other disciplines ("English"). Still, he does not seem disposed to include a significant number of what might be considered "noncanonical" texts; he appears much closer to Matthew Arnold than to Terry Eagleton. It is probably safe to say that the whole question of whose vision of texts to promote—Hirsch's or Eagleton's—will be one of the central issues for the discipline of English during the coming years, especially as the discipline concerns itself more and more with the relation between the teaching of writing and the teaching of literature.

In reviewing what various theorists have had to say about that relation, we have not included all the commentators on it. Rather, we have chosen to focus on those whose theoretical frameworks seem especially cogent and provocative. Which framework might eventually be implemented on a wide scale will not, of course, be decided without intense discussions in individual English departments as they contemplate their future. And for better or worse, such discussions will be influenced by the political arrangements existing in those departments. Yet whatever the effects of their institutional structures on their faculty's thinking, the adventurousness of much current theory on the possible connections of composition and literature might just make such theory the center of many departments' plans. It deserves to be.

Linguistics and Writing

William Strong

Twenty years ago, when teachers of writing asked about the contribution of linguistics to composition instruction, the answers were often evasive, usually centering on a rationale for "humanizing" writers-to-be. Although the work of Noam Chomsky offered a far more coherent explanation of English syntax than did the traditional and structural grammars of earlier days, the problem was one of *application*—and for many practitioners in schools and colleges, the transformational-generative model gathered dust on the professional bookshelf. What was intellectually provocative was nevertheless remote from everyday realities.

It was during this period of heightened interest in language study that certain teacher-linguists attempted to relate emerging insights in the field to writing pedagogy. Among the most notable of these efforts were those of Paul Roberts, Enola Borgh, Hans Guth, Owen Thomas, and Jean Malmstrom and Janice Lee, all "translators" of theory into practice. Regrettably, however, much of their advice was either ignored by those distrustful of analysis or swept away in the later wave of enthusiasm for "naturalistic" approaches to writing—ideas popularized by Ken Macrorie (*Writing to Be Read*), Donald Murray (*A Writer Teaches Writing*), and Peter Elbow (*Writing without Teachers*) and theoretically formulated by James Moffett. Attempts to infuse new linguistic content into federally sponsored Project English curricula for the schools proved almost uniformly disastrous; the gap between "knowing about" and "knowing how" was simply too wide for most teachers of writing—or their students—to bridge. Even the best of linguistically based efforts—for example, Freeman Anderson's pioneering work on *New Directions in English*, which deemphasized formal grammar in favor of structured thinking-writing tasks—enjoyed only brief popularity.

Paralleling the work of "popular" linguists were the research efforts of Kellogg Hunt (*Grammatical Structures*), Roy O'Donnell, and Walter Loban, whose conception of the T-unit established not only a research tool but also a way of connecting linguistics and writing. Hunt defined the T-unit as a single independent clause plus any grammatically attached subordinate elements. This definition—like the concept of "morpheme" in relation to "word"—provided much more precision than the general notion of "sentence." By coupling the T-unit with insights gleaned from transformational theory, Hunt documented what had only been intuitively sensed by many observers: that as human beings grow older, their written language naturally becomes more structurally complex and elaborated. Hunt provided individuals of varying ages with rewriting tasks that consisted of semantically related "kernel" sentences. Analysis of task results established developmental norms for written syntax that have since been widely used in experimental studies to judge the effectiveness of instructional treatments in writing. From one point of view, Hunt's work provided a vital link between linguistics and writing by operationalizing descriptive (and qualitative) studies; but from other perspectives, Hunt was engaged in what Michael Holzman has labeled mere "scientism"—"the practice of the forms of science for their own sake, or for the sake of wearing those gorgeous cloaks over a poor reality" (74).

In more recent years, text analysis (or text linguistics) has been an area for concerted research thrusts and for model building related to composing processes. Probably the best overview of linguistic approaches to text analysis is provided by Charles Cooper in "Procedures for Describing Written Texts." Cooper explains the background and relevant research for a range of approaches—cohesion analysis, the management of "old" and "new" information, sentence roles, abstraction levels in discourse, and thematic analysis (an approach based on propositional analysis and case grammar). Reading Cooper's treatment of these topics in tandem with his application of the approaches—"Studying the Writing Abilities of a University Freshman Class: Strategies from a Case Study"—provides an excellent introduction to current research. Another superb discussion of linguistics in relation to writing is provided by Miles Myers in *A Model for the Composing Process.* Myers relates insights from linguistics to three functions of writing—"Writing for discovery (*processing*), writing for establishing social relations (*distancing*), and writing for making texts and sending messages (*modelling*)" (7). The treatment is intellectually challenging yet very readable. Not to be overlooked in this work is the appendix, which makes connections among models for composing research in linguistics and writing, suggesting implications for classroom practice.

Because Cooper and Myers each provide such fine overviews, I limit my discussion to two current connections between linguistics and writing—one pedagogical, the other analytic. The first of these connections is an instructional approach based on various forms of rewriting tasks alluded to above—an approach called sentence combining (SC). While Hunt initially made no claims for the SC approach, an implicit message of his studies—that increased syntactic maturity was a necessary condition for "better" writing—was not lost on those who followed. Today, SC pedagogy seems not only an application of ideas underlying transformational theory but also, ironically, a kind of heuristic for promoting dialogue about certain aspects of the writing process. The second connection pertains to cohesion analysis. In recent years there have been important developments in advancing a grammar of discourse. The most widely known of these taxonomies, M. A. K. Halliday and Ruqaiya Hasan's *Cohesion in English*, has illuminated our understanding of textual cohesion in powerful ways and led to other theoretical refinements, specifically related to writing. The ultimate contribution of this perspective will no doubt prove as revolutionary as that provided by Chomsky—and probably more so.

Sentence combining and writing

To say that sentence combining is a "contribution" of modern linguistics to writing instruction is not quite accurate. As Edward P. J. Corbett notes in "The Theory and Practice of Imitation in Classical Rhetoric," the fourteenth-century rhetorician Erasmus showed how a single sentence could be expressed in 150 ways by altering syntax or diction (310); and as Shirley Rose demonstrates, SC work was a part of turn-of-the-century composition textbooks—among them Hitchcock's *Composition and Rhetoric*, Scott and Denney's *Elementary English Composition*, and Genung's *Outline of Rhetoric*. In summarizing the rationales behind including SC exercises in classroom work of the period, Rose observes that the exercises were regarded as offering "training to develop analytic-synthetic skills in construction of both thought and expression" (489). Moreover, they were considered "a logical and integral step in teaching composition, built as they were on a foundation of grammar study and foundational themselves to later work in paragraphs and essays" (489).

Thus, it is the "rediscovery" of sentence combining that is a fairly recent development. This rediscovery was triggered in part by key Chomskian concepts—distinctions between competence and performance and between deep structure and surface structure—and in part by the widely read research of John Mellon and Frank O'Hare, both of whom reported dramatic "syntactic fluency" gains (syntactic "maturity" in the parlance to others) as a result of SC treatments. O'Hare's research essentially replicated Mellon's, with two important differences: while Mellon cued students with grammatical terms derived from earlier study, O'Hare explicitly provided connecting words and other "signals" for achieving target sentences; and while Mellon's instructional emphasis was "a-rhetorical," O'Hare explicitly related SC exercises to work in composition. The outcomes of these studies, based as they were on the developmental norms established earlier by Hunt, suggested empirical validation for a commonsense notion: that explicit and systematic attention to putting-together processes in language might well enhance linguistic performance, at least in the area of syntax. O'Hare's conclusion—that SC instruction had not only accelerated the acquisition of more complex, syntactically mature structures but also promoted gains in writing quality—sparked a flurry of follow-up research that continues unabated. (As of October 1984, there were 69 studies on sentence combining listed in *Dissertation Abstracts* and 292 citations in ERIC.)

Of course, research and theory are one thing, classroom practice another—and without materials or training to change what goes on behind closed doors, one might reasonably expect "business as usual." The first textbook devoted exclusively—some would say exhaustingly—to SC practice was William Strong's *Sentence Combining: A Composing Book*, a series of "whole discourse" SC problems without explicit cues for combining. Developed in almost blissful ignorance of SC research, these exercises contrasted with those that Mellon and O'Hare had investigated. They not only invited a range of grammatical "right answers" (stylistic options) but also assumed that instruction would focus on decision making—choosing the "best sentence" within a context of previous sentence choices. Among their theoretical strengths, such exercises contextualized SC practice; but an accompanying weakness was that systematic sequencing of grammatical transformations—as in the discrete SC problems researched by Mellon and O'Hare—could not be assured. The reaction to such work was predictably diverse. For some writing instructors, "open" exercises, like the "models" approach of classical rhetoric, seemed a reasonable adjunct to the writing program—a way of building student self-confidence, not to mention syntactic maturity and awareness of stylistic options; but for others, SC work was perplexing in its assumptions, problematic in its application, and of dubious value for teaching processes of composing.

Francis Christensen was among the first to warn that SC practice might ultimately reinforce "bad writing"—more specifically, the highly embedded, nominalized style characteristic of government documents and certain professions. Christensen also argued against the use of the T-unit as a measure of syntactic maturity, contending that such analysis did not describe interconnecting levels of free modifiers, a key structural feature of "cumulative sentences" ("Problem of Defining"). James Moffett voiced similar misgivings—"syntactic complexity is no virtue in itself, surely" (72)—as part of his view that SC practice was a poor substitute for experiences that engaged students in real discourse. Moffett's basic point was that the ends of language education were better served by "interaction" than by "imitation," however skillfully orchestrated. And, finally, in "On Defining Complexity," Joseph Williams pointedly summarized the implicit concerns of many writing instructors, particularly those who were less than enthusiastic about the latest laetrile for English education:

> Most [sentence-combining researchers] have simply assumed that bigger is better. . . . [But] every program that attempts to teach adults how to write . . . concentrates on the ways that those adults can write less complex, simpler clauses; not longer, but shorter sentences. Every such program attempts specifically to undo what sentence combiners specifically want to do. (597, 598)

In responding to such criticism, many SC defenders have taken a developmental line, citing Moffett's premise that "sentences must grow rank before they can be trimmed" (172). Related to this assumption, the research of Elaine Maimon and Barbara Nodine showed increases in the frequency of error as the result of practice with more sophisticated embedding, but studies by Macey McKee and Rebecca Argall point in the opposite direction. The key seems to lie not in the materials themselves but in the use to which they are put. Strong contends that "the intent of SC is to make good sentences, not to make long ones" (4), arguing further that SC exercises are "self-teaching" tools that provide a means to an end—increased "automaticity" in syntax so that attention can be focused on larger problems of composing, one of which is style. Donald Daiker, Andrew Kerek, and Max Morenberg take a similar stance in *The Writer's Options*, pressing for conscious control of structures that may not be within the student's repertoire. The emphasis, always, is on shaping language to match intention. And, finally, on the issue of syntactic complexity, Strong discusses the relation between sentence length and writing quality as follows:

> Some people, seeing the correlation between growth in syntax and qualitative gains have mistakenly concluded that quality writing is necessarily comprised of complex sentences and that making longer sentences *causes* one to write better. Obviously, this contradicts what we usually admonish regarding lean, direct writing; but even more to the point, it mistakes correlation for causation—a dangerous kind of logical fallacy. . . . What matters, developmentally speaking, are gains in intuition and judgement about prose effectiveness, not in some mindless ability to pack as many details as possible into individual sentences. (4–5)

For further discussion of syntactic fluency and writing quality, see

Crowhurst's "On the Misinterpretation of Syntactic Complexity Data" and Lester Faigley's "Names in Search of a Concept: Maturity, Fluency, Complexity, and Growth in Written Syntax."

The diversity of claims made by SC zealots and the absence of a coherent framework to support its classroom use have created confusion over the role – if any – that SC instruction should play in writing instruction. Indeed, an implicit expectation of some school programs has been that increased clause length is itself the end of instruction and that SC practice is a means to that end. To SC moderates, such thinking is wrongheaded in the extreme. The power of the SC approach, so the argument goes, lies not so much in the fact that it promotes increased depth of modification, though for many students this is a key learning; for most, the power of SC work centers on the heightened sense of control over syntax that seems to accompany thoughtful, disciplined practice. Basic to this control are a sense of linguistic play and attention to syntactic detail. Thus, the instructional issue is not how to help students write longer sentences; the issue is how to inform a variety of decisions, syntactic and otherwise, that impinge on writing performance. More specifically, say the proponents, it is the relation between propositions – and the effectiveness of sentences in an emerging context – that should be the focus of SC instruction.

A second critical thrust, far more penetrating on theoretical grounds, has recently been articulated by William Michael Kleine in an important dissertation. In addition to subjecting SC research to close scrutiny and pointing out contradictions, dubious conclusions, and theoretical "leaks," Kleine examines alternative explanations for reported gains in syntactic fluency and/or writing quality. Part of his case is that exercises themselves represent a covert cue – an implicit message to "write complex sentences" – and that other kinds of treatments – for example, focused work on paragraph revision – can produce statistical gains like those in SC experiments (30–38). Kleine notes also the problems of SC research methodology – its reliance on T-units and clause length as maturity measures even though these fluctuate in differing discourse modes (51–52). And he is especially critical of the neglect of discourse theory in SC research, particularly as regards considerations of audience in relation to syntactic maturity. His contention, clearly, is that so-called gains are neither real nor durable: "Though the transformational cuing becomes internalized and leads to short-term gains in T-unit and clause length, it does not supplant – or even reflect – the kind of growth that can come from a deepening of mind and the kind of decentering that enables a writer to take control of syntax, distance it from herself, and assess not only its complexity but also its effectiveness" (39).

Kleine summarizes five reasons why sentence combining is an inadequate technology for developing real skill in student writers:

1. Discourse production involves a dynamic interaction between pragmatic, semantic, and syntactic process components. The whole-text exercise advocated by sentence-combining researchers makes no effort to specify pragmatic context, discourse situation, audience characteristics. Thus, the student combiner is forced to invent a fictional context for a fictional discourse: because she is not negotiating a real communicative transaction, her effort to assess syntactic effectiveness differs from the kind of self-assessment characteristic of genuine and successful human production.

2. Because the sentence-combining exercise provides and orders propositional content, there can be very little interaction between the semantic and syntactic components. Moreover, the design of the exercise makes it impossible for syntactic process to influence or change semantic and pragmatic process. Although Kerek, Daiker, and Morenberg encourage students to delete propositional content, the general design of the exercise provides little motivation for rearranging and inventing content—and no motivation for rethinking pragmatic implications.

3. Self-assessment of syntactic choice is for the student combiner, a text-bound experience. Because the only means of evaluating a syntactic choice is to consider its relationship to surrounding textual artifacts (S's), the student combiner is not challenged to see the relationship between a given transformation—many times cued—and real discourse production.

4. Because sentence-combining does not tap the stored propositional hierarchies of the individual combiner, it cannot seriously affect cognitive growth. As Mellon claims, the embedding characteristic of sentence-combining is, at heart, non-restrictive embedding.

5. When it is cued by specific transformation, sentence-combining necessarily works against genuine production behavior. Since syntax is responsive to pragmatics and semantics, an effort to achieve a specified transformation in a discourse environment makes "effective choice" impossible. (101–02)

Kleine's alternative to conventional SC—what he calls an "integrated cuing system" based on the student's own writing—is persuasively detailed in the remainder of his dissertation.

To address the issues raised by Kleine is a major task for those who see SC as something more than a busywork curriculum—and a task well beyond the scope of this essay. The point here is to lay out the challenge and give it wider visibility so that theory can catch up with classroom practice. So far, no one has articulated a real rationale for SC—a rationale related to language learning, writing process, and "naturalistic" classroom pedagogy. Given the present situation—in which SC is "defined" by an incredible variety of materials, some beyond belief in their banality—perhaps such a rationale cannot be developed. The problem is compounded by a wide range of objectives for SC practice and an even wider range of teaching practices. Indeed, as James Kinneavy pointed out in his analysis of SC materials, what may really be at issue is context—how such materials are used. Although it is possible to use SC as a prewriting stimulus or as an approach to promote lean, direct writing, the popular emphasis has been on "combining" narrowly defined. "Sentence relating" or "sentence revising" would actually be a more generic description.

But if it remains for others to deal fully with the substance of Kleine's critique—Sandra Stotsky seems the most promising hitter in the SC lineup—perhaps a few thoughts can be ventured in brief response. First, while most SC exercises force the student "to invent a fictional context for a fictional discourse," this is hardly to say that contexts cannot be specified or that the student's own writing might not serve as source material for an exercise; many teachers already use SC exercises in precisely this latter way. Second, while most SC exercises are static in their propositional content, this is hardly to say that exercises cannot be designed in which content is rearranged or elaborated—or for that matter invented; "heuristic" exercises—ones with built-in (or follow-up) questions—seem entirely possible, especially given the advances now being made in computer software. Third, while most current SC exercises do not focus attention on syntactic choices in relation to considerations beyond the text, this is hardly to say that diction-centered SC work cannot be imagined; variations of closure-style reading exercises suggest interesting formats for experimentation. Fourth, while SC exercises in their present form do not tap propositional hierarchies of the student, this is hardly to say that exercises related to course content cannot generate thought; indeed, SC work might provide entry into a topic and encourage the student to find a personal way out, using ideas generated in a class discussion. Fifth, while the cuing of specific transformation has little, if anything, to do with general discourse behavior, this is hardly to say that most students have all the discourse skills—syntactic or otherwise—for realizing their aims; work with certain "moves"—say, concession in argument—may build up the student's repertoire of available structures so that progress can be made with real writing.

An issue not raised by Kleine—but one of concern to persons interested in the scope and sequence of language-development curricula for school-age children, ESL learners, and basic writers—centers on the transformational framework for a coherent program. If one accepts implicit hypotheses advanced by Hunt in "Early Blooming and Late Blooming Syntactic

Structures," such curricula should be based not on the logical structure of grammar (as defined by grammarians and textbooks) but rather on the psychological and developmental facts of language acquisition. In Hunt's view, there is no question but that such a foundation of information is now taking shape. He states the implications of this view explicitly: "Surely it is possible to test whether a transformation can be taught at a certain age by a certain amount of repetition, or cannot be taught at all until later" (102). Hunt is arguing, of course, for an empirically tested curriculum, one based on a verified sequence of syntax acquisition. His assumption—one not necessarily shared by those who stress the pragmatic basis of language acquisition—is that development of syntax can (and should) be promoted through direct classroom instruction. Almost needless to say, Hunt is not "against" naturalistic approaches; rather, he is laying the philosophical groundwork for approaches that might systematically complement a naturalistic framework for discourse instruction.

The work that seems most likely to help realize Hunt's aims is that of Joseph Lawlor, especially as articulated in "Sentence Combining: A Sequence for Instruction." From his review of developmental research on written syntax, Lawlor notes two broad trends regarding elaboration—the first relating to position, the second to structure: elaborations "occur first in the predicate phrase," he notes, and "there is a general tendency to elaborate with full clauses first, followed by phrases and words that are derived from full clauses" (56). Lawlor uses these principles to construct a developmental sequence for five structures—coordination, adverbial modifiers, restrictive noun modifiers, noun substitutes, and free modifiers—each based on research in written syntax, each divided into "levels" of increasing difficulty. While space does not permit a reprinting of Lawlor's taxonomic framework, its value should be strongly emphasized. Not only does it provide still another link between linguistics and writing, but it also establishes a point of departure for curriculum developers, researchers, and teachers who are interested in syntax development. Revisions in the framework will undoubtedly be made as it is tested in varying contexts, ranging from elementary school to adult ESL instruction. What is important for now is that such a framework engage the imaginations of persons interested in a more rational basis for SC work. Indeed, research with SC instruction will probably be a primary vehicle for validating such a framework in years to come.

In summary, SC is a "linguistic" approach to writing that has received considerable attention because of its impressive track record in empirical research—but one that has not passed muster with many skeptics. As Marion Crowhurst notes, "increases in syntactic fluency have been reported for virtually every sentence-combining study" ("Sentence Combining" 69).

Not all studies, however, have reported improvements in writing quality as a consequence of SC treatments. Her thoughtful conclusions follow:

> Since composing is a complex act involving many skills, it is not to be expected that a few months' sentence combining will automatically produce a general improvement in writing quality. Sometimes, however, an improvement in overall writing quality may be noted. This may be due, partially, to increased practice in writing sentences during sentence combining, partially to greater facility in constructing sentences, and partially to the fact that increased skill in constructing sentences releases energy for other aspects of composing. Quality improvements are most likely to result if substantial time is spent on open, rather than cued, exercises, on whole-discourse problems, and on discussing the rhetorical effect of the various versions produced. (69–70)

What proportion of time, if any, should SC play in a coherent writing program? What types of exercises complement or enhance the discourse development of writers? What SC methods produce the best results? These are questions that must be addressed if SC is to come of age as an educational technology.

Cohesion and writing

If any linguistic topic has captured the imagination of writing instructors in the past few years, it has surely been the study of "cohesion"—a focus on relations between and among sentences (or T-units). Interest in intersentence connections, however, is hardly "new." In the 1866 edition of *English Composition and Rhetoric*, Alexander Bain instructed that "the bearing of each sentence upon what precedes shall be explicit and unmistakable." Moreover, as Connors has shown in "The Rise and Fall of the Modes of Discourse," the principle of coherence was regarded as one of the three foundational "elements" of writing in composition textbooks from the nineteenth century forward.

What is different about the current interest in cohesion is its explicitly linguistic basis, the formulation of descriptive "rules" for textual relations. The key work to set forth a taxonomy for such relations is Halliday and Hasan's *Cohesion in English*. While certainly not the first attempt to formulate a grammar of intersentence connections, the Halliday and Hasan effort is the fullest; and like Noam Chomsky's *Syntactic Structures*, it seems to have strongly influenced the way the profession now looks at language. Indeed, the influence of *Cohesion in English* is evidenced in part by the fact that writers such as Jean Fahnestock, Sandra Stotsky, and Robin Markels have each developed major statements using the work of Halliday and Hasan as a point of departure. Significantly, each writer has pointed to *Cohesion in English* in text analysis, suggesting modification in the taxonomy or revision of its assumptions.

But why study cohesion? On a personal level for writing instructors, cohesion seems worth knowing about because of the relentless frequency of prose that simply does not "hang together." Such writing typically surfaces during a special kind of Sunday evening despair—twenty papers yet to go and a feeling that random numbers were used to arrange sentences into paragraphs. Besides being the prose that sends one to the liquor cabinet before (and sometimes after) retiring, this is the writing on which one scrawls, "Read aloud and *listen* to what you're saying!" The focus in this frustrated, but reasonable, advice is not so much correctness on the one hand, content on the other; rather, the focus is the near absence of inter-sentence connections.

The pedagogical point is a basic but tricky one: quality writing is always encoded by, or realized through, good sentences; but good sentences, even on the same topic, do not in themselves ensure quality writing. The reason for this is metaphysically simple: meaning inheres not only in but also between sentences. And the between-sentence connections—what we often call "flow," "continuity," "development," "logic," or "connectedness"—are always central to judgments about prose quality.

The following illustration may demonstrate in a primitive way how cohering text is a web of meaning, with each clause like a thread in the overall structure:

1. The pedagogical point is a basic but tricky one:
2. quality writing is always encoded by, or realized through, good sentences;
3. but good sentences, even on the same topic, do not in themselves ensure quality writing.
4. The reason for this is metaphysically simple:
5. meaning inheres not only in but also between sentences.
6. And the between-sentence connections—what we often call "flow," "continuity," "development," "logic," or "connectedness"—are always central to our judgments about prose quality.

What should be noted from the above example is that cohesion occurs as certain words require the reader to refer elsewhere in the text to recover meanings. Clearly, certain words "point" to one another, sometimes with the help of punctuation cues such as colons.

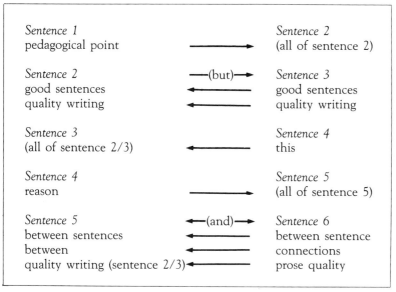

Fig. 1. *Textual Cohesion: Web of Meaning*

Cohesion, as defined by Halliday and Hasan, is a semantic (not syntactic) system of ties that extends across sentence boundaries and binds a text together. For cohesion to occur, one textual item is interpreted by reference to another. It is this feature of presupposition—the fact that linguistic items "point" to one another—that Halliday and Hasan explore in great detail. The pointing can be back to previous linguistic items (anaphora) or ahead to new information (cataphora); cohesion can be "immediate" (a tie between two linguistic items), "chained" (a sequence of immediate ties), or "remote" (a separation of one or more sentences between linguistic elements). Some ties are realized through syntax; others, through vocabulary. This distinction, it turns out, is really one of degree, but it does serve to organize the elaborate taxonomy that Halliday and Hasan construct. Grammatical cohesion—linkage via structural items—is composed of three separate but related categories: reference, substitution, and ellipsis. Lexical cohesion—linkage via vocabulary items—constitutes a single category. And between these two extremes—mainly grammatical but also lexical—is the category called conjunction. These five types of cohesion, with all their subtypes, are the universe of semantic resources for creating ties across sentences (or T-units).

As a practical matter for writing instructors, the categories of substitution and ellipsis pertain far more to spoken discourse than to writing; hence, it is the other three categories—reference, lexical cohesion, and conjunction—that should probably receive most classroom attention. Halliday and Hasan exclude from consideration, incidentally, the information of text—the interweaving of "old" and "new" ideas—as well as devices such as parallelism, rhythm, and rhyme, even though these often reinforce meaning-based ties between sentences.

The idea that cohesion is a necessary (but not sufficient) condition for coherence needs to be emphasized here. In other words, a text may be cohesive in terms of its explicit linking mechanisms—the ties between and among linguistic items—and still not be coherent. The following text illustrates this point:

> I particularly like classical music in the evenings. Evenings are the best time to run. Running is a little like writing a poem. A poem has rhythms that . . . .

For a text to be perceived as coherent, it must first of all be congruent with the reader's expectations for a particular mode of discourse. As discourse expectations change, however, the reader's perceptions of coherence may also change—as the following illustration should make clear:

> In the evenings
> classical music,
> the best time to run:
> like writing a poem,
> rhythms that . . . .

In addition, of course, texts are viewed as coherent only if they mesh with a reader's existing knowledge structure. A text that violates a reader's expectations about a known topic—or addresses a topic about which a reader has no fund of knowledge or reference points—cannot be perceived as coherent.

Cohesion, then, is a subconstruct of coherence—and coherence, in turn, is a subconstruct of writing quality. Or to put the matter another way: Judgements about writing quality must necessarily take into account the reader's perceptions of coherence, a major factor of which is textual cohesion. While such distinctions may seem like scholasticism of an arcane kind, they are also basic to a more informed conception of product-process relations in writing—a necessary (but, again, not sufficient) condition for better instruction. Two current questions related to cohesion, coherence, and writing quality are these: how do the texts of able and less able writers differ with respect to number of ties, types of cohesion used, and "distance" between ties? to what extent do measures of cohesion correlate with measures of coherence at one level, writing quality at another? Empirical answers to such basic questions could well inform the content of future writing instruction.

On the question of cohesion differences between "high rated" and "low rated" essays, Witte and Faigley found certain "gross differences" (195–96) — among them the fact that in high-rated expository essays about 32% of all words contributed to cohesive ties, whereas in low-rated essays the figure was about 20%. Also of interest was that in high-rated essays, there were substantially higher percentages of immediate and mediated ties, with low-rated essays using more remote ties. As for types of cohesion, Witte and Faigley report that high-rated essays used about twice as much referential cohesion and over three times as much conjunctive cohesion as low-rated essays (196). Striking as these differences are, the data for lexical cohesion are even more dramatic. Not only were lexical ties by far the most frequent type of cohesion, but writers of high-rated essays managed a lexical tie every 4.8 words — as compared with 7.4 words for less able writers. Moreover, for skilled writers, the frequency of lexical collocation was 94 times per 100 T-units, easily three times more than for their counterparts (197). In short, whereas good writing was characterized by both more frequent and more immediate ties — a denser, "elaborated" texture — poor writing was marked by just the reverse. Significantly, less able writers "excelled" only in simple repetitions of lexical items as a cohesive strategy.

Cooper, Cherry, et al. report similar findings in their study of persuasive writing of freshman students at the State University of New York at Buffalo. As part of a detailed examination of several textual and rhetorical features, Cooper and his colleagues learned that the best writers used 4.9 cohesive ties per T-unit, whereas the less competent writers composed texts of noticeably "thinner" texture — 2.8 cohesive ties per T-unit (37). Closer analysis revealed other facts: the best writers used not only twice as many referential ties (as in the Witte and Faigley study) but also twice as many types of reference as weak writers, including comparatives such as *the same as*, *similar to*, and *different from* — all explicit signals of relations between ideas (36). With regard to conjunctive ties, the analysis showed that better writers used about ten times as many additive conjunctions — evidence, again, of a tendency to elaborate assertions or evidence (37). And, finally, with regard to lexical cohesion — the most powerful linking device in terms of frequency — there were striking differences: the best writers used over eleven synonyms per 100 T-units, whereas the least competent writers used none; equally important, the best writers used two and a half times as many general items (and twice as many collocational ties per 100 t-units) as their less able counterparts (37).

All this evidence, of course, provides empirical validation for the intuition of writing instructors, but what more can be made of it? Witte and Faigley make these observations:

> The better writers . . . elaborate and extend the concepts they introduce. The poorer writers, by contrast, appear deficient in these skills. Their essays display a much higher percentage of lexical and conceptual redundancy. (197)

Following a content analysis of the essays in their study, Witte and Faigley draw a conclusion that is rich with instructional implications:

> Besides lacking adequate vocabularies, writers of the low-rated essays seem to lack in part the ability to perceive and articulate abstract concepts with reference to particular instances, to perceive relationships among ideas, and to reach beyond the worlds of their immediate experiences. (199)

To deal strictly with cohesion, one might infer from the above, would be to treat merely the symptoms of a deeper problem—a problem of thinking generally and thinking on paper specifically. At the same time, one might also infer that work with cohesion could well provide more functional instruction than that afforded by models, exhortations, grammar drills, and error analysis. An emphasis on cohesion would at least center the attention of students on how their texts are being read.

On the question of relations between measures of cohesion, coherence, and writing quality, one of the first attempts to validate such constructs empirically is a doctoral dissertation by George McCulley titled "Writing Quality, Coherence, and Cohesion." McCulley examined the extent to which cohesion frequencies correlate with coherence ratings and quality scores in the persuasive mode of discourse. He found that coherence scores explained 41% of the variance in writing quality when manuscript length was held constant—and that textual cohesion explained 53% of the variance in coherence scores under the same conditions.

These findings suggest validation for Bain's notion of coherence as a fundamental—even central—aspect of writing quality; more to the point for current research, however, they help to describe relations between cohesion and coherence. When manuscript length was held constant, McCulley found that both the total number of cohesive ties (with a partial correlation coefficient of .41) and the lexical cohesion category of "near synonyms" (with a partial correlation coefficient of .54) were highly significant correlates of coherence (p < .001); however, only two other cohesive strategies—reference through personal pronouns and lexical repetition—were significant correlates of coherence (p < .05). Besides confirming the importance of lexical cohesion in persuasive discourse, McCulley's findings suggest that cohesion and coherence are hardly synonymous terms and that other factors within text—either syntactic or rhetorical—influence coherence. But the results of McCulley's multiple regression analysis also produced a very high multiple correlation coefficient (.82), perhaps indicating that cohesion contributes more to coherence than most people realize.

A key question addressed by McCulley's study is the extent to which cohesion frequencies correlate with scores of writing quality. Only one Halliday and Hasan index—that related to cohesion through synonyms, with a partial correlation coefficient of .39—was found to have construct validity with quality scores (p < .001). This finding presents a strong argument not only for enlarging student vocabularies but also for making in-class revision exercises focused on lexical cohesion a regular part of instruction. When T-units were held constant, other cohesion frequencies—including the total number of ties—did not meet the correlation range (.30 to .65) for construct validity. When T-units were not held constant, however, the correlation between quality scores and the total number of cohesive ties was .68, statistically significant at the .001 level, with $r^2 = .38$. This finding implies that in-class instruction should probably address the relative density of cohesive ties to help students make qualitative improvements in text.

But aside from research implications, what commonsense cautions might be offered about an explicitly "linguistic" approach to revision through cohesion analysis? The first point to be made, surely, is that unless students have real commitment to their writing—meanings they want to communicate—attention to cohesion will be as pointless, arcane, and intimidating as transformational diagrams. In other words, a writing instructor's first task in many classrooms is working with motivation; for until students can genuinely attend to instruction, not much learning will occur. The second point is that attention to larger issues of revision—subject, audience, and purpose—must necessarily precede cohesion analysis for the same reasons that talk about a poem's meanings inevitably precedes discussion of prosody. Put another way, cohesion analysis is always explicitly or implicitly governed by rhetorical aims; it is one's sense of a text "unfolding" during reading that provides a monitor for checking the cohesive links between and among sentences—and for making changes in text.

Related to the preceding points, a promising area of recent research has been to fuse a close study of revising behavior with insights from text linguistics. In "Measuring the Effects of Revisions on Text Structure," Faigley and Witte build on the research in cohesion, coherence, and text hierarchy to construct a taxonomy for analyzing "surface changes" and "meaning changes" as writers revise. Their aim is to synthesize work in text analysis with work in psycholinguistics. In other words, the taxonomy attends to an area not directly addressed by cohesion research—namely, how readers process meaning in text and construct its gist in memory. Moreover, this research focuses specifically on revising, one of the most crucial aspects of the writing process. In short, Faigley and Witte are using the analytic and conceptual tools of linguistics, particularly psycholinguistics, to help us understand different "levels" of revision.

Surface changes are predictable matters of conventional form as well as several types of changes that preserve meaning in context. These latter changes are basically acts of paraphrase, not acts of revised conception. The consolidation of two clauses into one, for example, would be categorized as a surface change. By contrast, meaning changes are those that alter the gist of how the text is to be constructed by a reader. Faigley and Witte classify meaning changes into two broad subgroups—those affecting meaning but not altering a summary of the text and those affecting both meaning and summary. With their taxonomy, they analyze six different lengths of revision: graphic changes, lexical changes, phrasal changes, clausal changes, sentence changes, and multi-sentence changes. Significantly, they not only count textual features but also interpret them.

As in so much research connecting linguistics and writing, Faigley and Witte empirically corroborate what others have studied in different ways: that revision is highly recursive, with attention to "internal" features of text (such as diction) at one stage, to "external" considerations (such as audience needs) at another level. Of course, for many student writers, text is not revised in the light of intentions, because intentions are unclear. Faigley and Witte caution that when this is the case, aimless revision may actually weaken the final text. What counts, they say, is the ability to hold the text at arm's length and *think* about it: "The important thing is for students to discover what, exactly, they have to say and to think about how potential readers might react to their text" (107). The implicit promise of such research is a fuller understanding of how texts "emerge" with gains in cohesion, coherence, and overall quality.

In summary, the basic assumption of cohesion analysis is that certain words presuppose others and that whenever one word is interpreted by reference to another, a semantic link (or "tie") occurs. A second assumption is that cohesion is directional; each tie always involves one item "pointing" to another. Most of the time an item points back to some previous item in another sentence, but occasionally the presupposition is reversed. This "pointing" is essential for coherence.

Cohesion analysis emphasizes relations of meaning—a topic that writing instructors generally regard as central to their work. The assumption is that certain objective features distinguish cohering texts from random collections of sentences and that these features operate in highly systematic and patterned ways—not within a structural system (as sounds cohere to form syllables or as words, phrases, and clauses cohere to form sentences) but rather within the semantic, meaning-based system of the language. Research has shown that certain aspects of cohesion distinguish high-rated and low-rated essays; other research has suggested relations that may exist between cohesion frequencies and perceptions of coherence and writing quality. From this research, two implications regarding explicit attention to cohesion can be drawn: lexical cohesion and frequency of ties are both likely targets for productive classroom work.

Recent research has gone beyond the limits of cohesion analysis, narrowly defined, to approach writing from the angle of psycholinguistics, a field concerned with the act of reading. In effect, this new research creates a bridge between explicitly textual features and their representation in human memory. Attention so far has focused on analyzing different revising behaviors as reflections of different acts of mind, acts related to a writer's presumed intention. In the final analysis, then, it is meaning that matters—whether one is reading text, composing it, or researching its processes and pedagogy.

Connecting linguistics and writing

In an educational climate where *process* is the buzzword, it may seem heretical to suggest that linguistics—with its emphasis on product—may hold some promise for teachers of writers. But attention to sentence basics and text relations would still seem essential if we presume to teach, and not merely assign, writing. In fact, the idea of not working with sentences in some disciplined way seems ludicrous—a little like "studying" mathematics without learning number operations or "studying" pottery without putting one's fingers in the clay. Writing, after all, *is* sentences.

When skill building is viewed as an adjunct to instruction about writing process, both sentence-combining work and some form of cohesion analysis may help students with text revision. Of course, both approaches are tools for teaching—and limited ones at best. To expect a tool to do all things—or to confuse a means of instruction with desired ends—is to subvert any connection between linguistics and writing. Some instructors are disappointed, for example, when SC practice does not automatically transfer to the invention skills of students; others have taught their students the simpleminded notion that "more transitions make for better writing"—an admonition almost guaranteed to produce dreadful prose. While the research on SC practice confirms its usefulness for developing syntactic fluency and perhaps for improving writing quality—particularly when exercises demand rhetorical decision making—exercises as presently conceived and generally used have little to do with the development of genuine discourse production; and while the research on cohesion analysis suggests its value as a powerful research tool and, more practically, as an index of coherence, a foolproof technology for classroom application has yet to be developed.

So, twenty years after the first broad wave of enthusiasm for linguistics, new gifts of knowledge have washed up on the beach. The question is: What do writing instructors do with their find? One option would be to take the curriculum approach of the middle sixties and teach linguistic insights as an intellectual system, a program that is somehow "humanizing" in and of itself. A second option would be to take the dominant approach of subsequent years—what might be called "educational nihilism"—and simply ignore the gifts, trusting in "practice" to solve writing problems. The third option is by far the most exciting. It is to translate new linguistic insights into activities that reveal, by induction and indirection, what we want students to internalize and transfer to their prose. The challenge, in short, is to use analytic approaches to extend understandings of writing process.

Collaborative Learning and Teaching Writing

John Trimbur

Collaborative learning is a relatively new term in composition studies. It begins to appear in the late sixties and early seventies, in journal articles, textbooks, conference papers, and professional conversation about teaching writing. Collaborative learning is a generic term, covering a range of techniques that have become increasingly visible in the past ten years, practices such as reader response, peer critiques, small writing groups, joint writing projects, and peer tutoring in writing centers and classrooms. The term refers to a method of conducting the business at hand—whether a freshman composition course or a workshop for writing teachers. By shifting initiative and responsibility from the group leader to the members of the group, collaborative learning offers a style of leadership that actively involves the participants in their own learning. Collaborative learning, as Kenneth A. Bruffee says, is "a form of indirect teaching in which the teacher sets the problem and organizes the students to work it out collaboratively" ("Collaborative Learning" 638).

Collaborative learning practices were developed initially from experimental insights. Following an intuition that collaboration could help students learn to write, teachers proceeded by trial and error to organize students in groups—so that students could pool their knowledge and experience by working together. From such improvised beginnings, experiments in collaborative learning have grown into a sizable body of theory and practice. The work of Bruffee, Peter Elbow, Nan Elsasser, Elaine P. Maimon, and others has not only produced important models of collaboration for the classroom. The influence of this work has also produced a heightened awareness among composition teachers of the importance of social interaction to learning how to write. Through accumulated experience and a widening theoretical discussion, experiments in collaborative learning now constitute, as it were, a method for composition teachers and a problem for theorists: how to organize and interpret the activity of learning to write through the group interaction of the learners.

As we will see, these theoretical and practical issues are by no means resolved at present. If anything, distinct trends of collaborative learning have started to emerge. There is nonetheless a shared assumption in the various forms of collaborative learning, an assumption that operates from the original experimental insight that students can learn together and from one another in new and potentially significant ways. Such an assumption, of course, is new only to teachers. It has been operating all along in the folkways of student culture, in the rap sessions and informal study groups outside the official academic structures. Students have always banded together to interpret and cope with their undergraduate experience. The shared social status of being undergraduates seems to unionize students, to organize them in self-help circles to deal with the intellectual demands of their course work.

Educators have recognized since at least the early sixties that peer relationships are an important potential source of learning. In 1962, Theodore M. Newcomb presented his findings that peer-group influence is the single most powerful force in shaping college students' attitudes toward their learning. What is new about collaborative learning is that it attempts to tap the educational potential of peer-group influence and to mobilize that influence in formal academic contexts. Collaborative learning attempts to channel the informal learning that occurs in student culture into the academic structures of the classroom and the writing center, to formalize (and often to require) what had existed before only informally—the networks of mutual aid students have always developed on their own.

Based on the spontaneous mutual aid rooted in student culture and the growing professional consciousness of the importance of social interaction to learning, collaborative learning brings to composition studies a recognition of the social context of the writing class and its effects on student writers. In a sense, collaborative learning is an experiment in context—in organizing new ways of being with the text during the process of composing. The models of collaboration Bruffee, Elbow, Elsasser, Maimon, and others have developed involve a reorganization of the relations between students and teachers and among the students themselves in their roles as writers and readers. Such a reorganization not only augments the existing body of pedagogical techniques in composition. As Andrea Lunsford and Lisa Ede point out, it also approximates more closely than the traditional classroom the actual conditions of writing in business, government, and those academic disciplines where collaboration is the norm rather than the exception ("Why Write").

This reorganization, moreover, raises important theoretical issues for composition studies concerning the relation between writers and readers and the social and cultural dimensions of composing. Drawing from recent trends in anthropology, literary criticism, philosophy, and the sociology of knowledge, theorists interested in the implications of collaborative learning have extended the discourse of composition studies by developing conceptual frameworks that treat writing as a social process and the authority of the text as the product of the social interaction between writers and readers.

So far, however, the influence of collaborative learning and the practical and theoretical issues it raises have not been systematically organized and assessed. The purpose of this essay is to provide an overview of collaborative learning as a trend in composition studies. I go about this by treating (1) the historical and conceptual background of collaborative learning as a current of educational reform, (2) the theory and practice of collaborative learning as applied to teaching writing, and (3) the larger issues implied by collaborative learning and possible directions for research and theoretical development in composition studies.

Historical and conceptual background

Implicit in the experimental origins of collaborative learning in the 1960s and 1970s is a critique of the traditional structures of teaching and learning. According to the traditional conventions that regulate the social life of the classroom, education operates on a hierarchical model. Authority is centralized in the figure of the teacher, and knowledge is passed from the top down. In the traditional teacher-centered classroom, the students are atomized; they are an aggregate of individuals organized to learn from and perform for the teacher as individuals. In contrast to this model, collaborative learning attempts to decentralize the authority traditionally held by the teacher and to shift the locus of knowledge from the sovereign domain of the teacher to the social interaction of the learners. Collaborative learning replaces what John Dewey calls the "nonsocial character of traditional education" with participatory communities, where learning takes place not through the one-to-one relation between teacher and student but instead through the social relations among students.

Collaborative learning, and its implied critique of traditional education, emerged in the late sixties and early seventies from a set of social and cultural pressures. On college campuses across the country, students challenged the prevailing doctrine of in loco parentis in higher education and demanded a greater role in determining the scope and content of their education. Suspicious of authority, students rejected the traditional hierarchy of the academy, calling instead for a "community of scholars"—for the public space of a decentralized, participatory, democratic culture. The "free universities," the teach-ins and study groups of the antiwar movement, the consciousness-raising groups of the women's movement, the communes of the counterculture—all reveal a deeply felt desire for community, self-organization, mutual aid, and nonauthoritarian styles of leadership and decision making. If much of what appeared to be subversive in the sixties degenerated during the Me Decade of the seventies into narcissistic self-realization fads, the antiauthoritarian values and communal ethos of the sixties nonetheless initiated critical thinking about social relations in higher education.

The arrival of nontraditional students through the open-admissions programs of the early seventies prompted a further reevaluation of the prevailing social relations in the traditional classroom. Open admissions seemed to offer the institutional framework for Mina Shaughnessy's vision of a literate democracy, where those who had been excluded from higher education could take their place as participants in public life and discourse. The faculty at open-admissions colleges, however, were largely unprepared and unequipped (and sometimes unwilling) to deal with the learning problems of nontraditional students. Traditional classroom practices proved rather quickly to be unsuited to nontraditional students who had not yet learned the behaviors expected of students in traditional educational systems. Most traditional college-bound students learn these behaviors in grade school, when they learn to keep their social and academic lives apart by internalizing the radical separation of work and play that traditional forms of education demand. Nontraditional students, by contrast, often are not fully socialized to the discipline of the classroom and the rules and values of the academic game. So though traditional modes of education could impart information, these traditional modes lacked any way to connect learning to the enormously stressful social transition nontraditional students were attempting to make by entering college.

Collaborative learning, however, seemed to offer a method to overcome the separation of learning and social experience in traditional education. Learning in groups, Kurt Lewin and Paul Grabbe point out, is often more effective than learning individually because learning involves more than simply acquiring new information. It also involves the acceptance of new habits, values, beliefs, and ways of talking about things. To learn is to change: learning implies a shift in social standing—a transition from one status and identity to another and a reorientation of social allegiances. As many teachers in open-admissions programs found, the mutual aid and participatory style of collaborative learning helped ease the social transition their students were undergoing by reducing or making more manageable the anxiety and resistance to change learners often experience.

Collaborative learning connects learning and the social experience of students by organizing students in transitional communities, to bridge the gap between their indigenous communities and the community of college-educated men and women.

The practical insight that collaborative learning can help students make the transition into the academic community is by no means limited to open-admissions programs or nontraditional learners. Recent educational innovations at leading colleges and universities—such as the writing fellow and the science mentor programs at Brown, the peer tutoring programs at Harvard and Yale, and the learning communities at Rollins and the State University of New York, Stony Brook—indicate that collaborative learning moves students from a passive to an active role in their learning and revitalizes faculty interest in the social dynamics of teaching and learning.

Theories of collaborative learning

Collaborative learning is not a theoretically unified position but a set of pedagogical principles and practices worked out experimentally. In an effort to raise these experiments to a theoretical level—to codify them and to provide a conceptual rationale for collaborative learning—a number of teachers involved with collaborative learning have drawn on the work of educational reformers such as John Dewey, M. L. J. Abercombie, Edwin Mason, and Paolo Freire.

A good introduction to John Dewey's theory of education can be found in *Experience and Education*. Published in 1938, over twenty years after Dewey first articulated the premises of "new education" in *Democracy and Education* (1916), *Experience and Education* offers Dewey's retrospective assessment of the progressive schools as a reform movement in education. Dewey challenged the rigid rules of conduct, authoritarian patterns of school organization, and static subject matter in traditional education. He called instead for a new education based on the "organic connection" between education and experience. For Dewey, learning should be experiential and should occur through the interaction of the learners and the wider social environment, not through the teacher's imposition of subject matter from above and outside the experience of the learners.

As Dewey's analysis of the progressive education movement indicates, the conditions for experiential learning cannot be created simply by rejecting traditional forms of social control in the classroom. "When external control is rejected," Dewey writes, "the problem becomes that of finding the factors of control that are inherent within experience" (21). The abolition of authoritarian structures, for Dewey, cannot be an end in itself. Dewey thought it perhaps inevitable that reform movements in education, such as the progressive schools, must pass through a "negative phase, one of protest, of deviation, and innovation," a reaction against all forms of authority and social control. Dewey's point, however, is that this reaction against traditional authority only creates the need for a "more effective source of authority" (21–22). In the traditional classroom, the teacher keeps order because, as Dewey says, "order was in the teacher's keeping, instead of in the shared work being done." Dewey wanted to replace the traditional hierarchy of teaching and learning with the "moving spirit of the whole group" when the group is "held together by participation in common activities" (54–55). Dewey wanted to constitute the social interaction of the learners as the "normal source of order" (63).

At the end of World War II, the reform spirit of Dewey's new education had largely faded in the United States. What began with Dewey's call to reform the social relations of schooling had lapsed into "life adjustment education" (Ravitch 43–80). By the early sixties, however, signs of a revival of experimental education began to appear in England. A. S. Neill's *Summerhill*, for example, initiated a new wave of interest in free schools and libertarian education. Others, such as M. L. J. Abercombie at University College, London, and Edwin Mason and his associates at Goldsmith College, based their innovative teaching practices on the connection between social interaction and learning.

Abercombie's experience teaching diagnostic skills to medical students led her to conclude that while her students learned information quite readily, they had considerable difficulty when confronted with a situation, such as clinical diagnosis, that required evaluative judgment and the practical application of information. In *The Anatomy of Judgement*, originally published in 1960, Abercombie argues that small-group interaction can foster development of the evaluative judgment her students lacked. What students learn best from small-group work, Abercombie says, is not so much new information as how to use the information they have already acquired but have not yet assimilated to the point of applying it to solve problems. According to Abercombie, group interaction helps students learn judgment by "canceling biases." As she notes, students often begin group discussions by trying to impose their own preconceptions on one another. When, in the process of discussion, contradictory inferences emerge that the group cannot leave unreconciled, students begin to uncover first the biases in others' judgment and then, more important, the biases in their own thinking. For Abercombie, the social pressure of reaching consensual solutions helps students see and modify their limited perceptual schemes.

In the book that coined the term collaborative learning, Edwin Mason makes explicit what Abercombie implies: namely, that the emphasis on individual learning and performance in traditional education teaches students to "compete for esteem" and encourages an "anti-social use of aggression." For Mason, the participatory style of collaborative learning offers an alternative to bureaucratized educational institutions and a model of noncompetitive social relations that promise to "transcend both personal egocentricity and the displaced egocentricity of nationalism" (52). Mason, moreover, anticipates one of the central themes in subsequent discussions of collaborative learning when he suggests that collaborative learning not only represents a more humane way to organize teaching and learning. According to Mason, knowledge itself is a social construct, produced by collaborative activity. Human beings, Mason says, "realize their world and life with language which is not only common social property but a living product of human collaboration. Realities are made, not found, and authenticity of knowledge depends on authenticity of relationship" (21).

The Brazilian educator Paolo Freire argues that the social construction of knowledge occurs within, and reproduces, structures of power and cultural domination. Traditional education, Freire says, is based on a "banking" metaphor: the bank clerk–educator makes deposits to fill up the student's account. Since students "receive" the world as "passive entities," traditional education is a force for domestication – not freedom. According to Freire, the purpose of traditional education is to teach students how to live passively within oppressive and alienating structures, to adapt to the world as it is, instead of developing their subjectivity as historical actors.

In contrast to the banking concept of education, Freire and the teachers he has influenced, such as Nan Elsasser and Vera John-Steiner, propose "conscientization," the process of cultural action in which the everyday experiences of the oppressed and powerless – experiences devalued by the dominant culture – can be reclaimed and reinterpreted. Conscientization is a method of resistance where learners are no longer passive recipients of knowledge but rather knowing subjects whose learning leads them to a deepening awareness of the social forces and relations of power that shape their immediate experience. The role of the teacher is not to make "deposits" but to join with students as "critical co-investigators" in a "dialogical" relation. Freire's goal is to recover historical agency through the dialogue of teachers and students as subjects "who meet to name the world in order to transform it" (97).

Dewey, Abercombie, Mason, and Freire all underscore the importance of the social and cultural contexts of teaching and learning. How we teach, they argue from various perspectives, is what we teach. Teaching conventions, in this view, constitute what educational theorists call the "hidden curriculum." According to Henry A. Giroux, theorists have defined the "hidden curriculum as those unstated norms, values, and beliefs embedded in and transmitted to students through the underlying rules that structure the routines and social relationships in school and classroom life" (47). In the traditional classrooom, these norms, values, and beliefs remain unexamined and taken for granted; the social structures and relations they rest on appear as "natural" or "normal." For educators concerned with the connection between learning and social experience, however, the social forms of teaching and learning cannot be neutral means of transmitting knowledge. Instead, as Bruffee argues, the form of learning is as much the content of a course as the subject matter is. Bruffee says, "While students often forget much of the subject matter shortly after the class is over, they do not easily forget the experience of learning it and the values implicit in the conventions by which it was taught" ("The Way Out" 468).

Collaborative learning is potentially important not only as a reform of teaching methods but also as a kind of critical practice. To reorganize the classroom is to probe the traditional hierarchy of teaching and learning and, as Bruffee points out, traditional beliefs about the authority of knowledge. Recent intellectual trends, Bruffee notes, have fostered critical thinking about the social production and authorization of knowledge. The theorists Bruffee cites—Thomas Kuhn in the history of science, Stanley Fish in literary criticism, Richard Rorty in philosophy, and Clifford Geertz in anthropology—all present the view that knowledge is a social artifact, generated and authorized by the assent of members of knowledge communities. The challenge this view presents to the traditional canonical concept of knowledge as permanent and determinate truth passed from generation to generation is only just beginning to influence thinking about pedagogy and undergraduate education. Bruffee, Maimon, Elbow, and others have started to explore the connection between collaborative learning and the social construction of knowledge. If their work so far has been tentative, it suggests at the same time that the reinterpretation of knowledge going on in current critical theory contains important implications for classroom practice, curricular reform, and the study of discourse. We return to some of these issues in a later section. First we should turn to applications of collaborative learning to teaching writing.

Collaborative learning and teaching writing

If collaborative learning emerges in higher education as a critique of the traditional structures of authority in the teacher-centered classroom, the application of collaborative learning to teaching writing grows more specifically out of a critique of what Richard Young calls "current traditional rhetoric." According to Young, the paradigm that underlies current traditional rhetoric emphasizes the written product, formal modes, correctness, and style. The pedagogy associated with current traditional rhetoric is not only teacher-centered, where the teacher instructs students in the principles of good writing. It is also text-centered, grounded in the objectivity and autonomy of the text. Part of the appeal of current traditional rhetoric is its fit with the New Critical practices most English faculty learned in graduate school, the formalism that institutionalized literary studies in the postwar period by constituting the text apart from authorial intention or reader response. This formalism pervades the current traditional paradigm, making the text an autonomous object that can be analyzed in isolation from the conditions under which it was produced.

The pedagogical practices that flow most often from this paradigm assume that students learn to write by studying and imitating the rhetorical principles found in good writing, in the authoritative texts passed to them from the teacher, from the top down. Over the past two decades, however, a shift in composition theory and practice has taken place, one that parallels in certain respects the rejection of New Criticism by poststructuralist currents in literary theory. The process-oriented approach to teaching writing has challenged the centrality of the written product in the writing classroom and, by implication, the objective authority of the text. By replacing the prose models of the traditional text-centered classroom with workshop practices based on the processes of composing and responding to prose, composition teachers and theorists have participated in the wider redefinition of the status of the text—as an event produced by the interaction of reader and writer and not as an autonomous object.

Feedback

This challenge to the objective authority and determinate meaning of the text has also called into question the authority of the teacher as the reader of student texts. Influenced by James Moffett, Donald Murray, Ken Macrorie, and others, advocates of the workshop approach to teaching writing tend to be skeptical about the role of the teacher as the primary audience for student writing. As James Britton's seminal study of writing assignments and their implied audiences concludes, students write most often for the teacher as an evaluator. Recent studies by Nancy Sommers and by C. H. Knoblauch and Lil Brannon have extended Britton's work, suggesting that teacher evaluation of student writing tends toward narrowly prescriptive justifications of an "ideal text" in the teacher's mind and thus interferes with the development of writing ability by turning composing into an attempt on the student's part to second-guess the teacher and conform to the "ideal text."

The social context of the classroom would seem to guarantee a problematic role for the teacher as an audience for student texts. As James Moffett writes, "For the teacher to act as audience is a very intricate matter fraught with hazards that need special attention. . . . The teacher is at once parental substitute, civic authority, and wielder of grades. Any one of these roles would be enough to distort the writer-audience relationship; all together, they cause the student to misuse the feedback in ways that severely limit his ability to write" (193). Peter Elbow points out, moreover, that the relationship between student writers and teacher readers doesn't affect just students. It affects teachers too. The conventional performance of a pupil for an evaluator circumscribes the teacher's response to student writing. In fact, it can make the teacher's response downright unreliable because the origins of that response are often obscured, filtered through the teacher's norms of evaluation and need to justify grades. As Elbow says, grading papers made him look for something the matter.

Elbow's "teacherless class" suspends the rigors of grading to allow for a different kind of rigor, the investigation of the reader's response to writing. For Elbow, "writing without teachers" changes the ambience of a classroom by replacing the traditional teacher-centered "doubting game" with the "believing game." According to Elbow, the "doubting game" refers to the standard operating procedures of academia—skepticism, the rules of evidence, the logic of argumentation, and so on. The "believing game," in contrast, isn't interested in proving or disproving statements. Instead, it asks the players to try to see statements from others' point of view. In the "doubting game," the teacher has the authority of the final arbiter, the last word that closes student writing. The "believing game" keeps writing open. It fights the urge to argue and settle things, so that fuller and more amplified responses to student writing can emerge. The "believing game" lets student writers begin to see what effects their words have on readers (*Writing without Teachers*).

Elbow's approach grows out of his sense that what blocks student writing is the fear of error and messiness, the tyranny of wanting to get it right the first time. This editorial impulse operates as a kind of superego, a wrathful father sitting in judgment, the internalized stereotype of the English teacher as faultfinder. Since students think of teachers as paper markers, the relationship between student writers and teacher readers is a difficult one at best. As Elbow points out, students write not *to* but *for* teachers, and thus the authority of past and present teachers always hovers over the act of student writing.

One of the rationales for a workshop approach to teaching writing, then, is that it replaces the teacher as the primary audience for student texts, with peer readers organized to give oral or written feedback. Feedback is a term drawn from cybernetics, information science, and systems theory. According to Walter J. Lamberg, feedback "is information on performance which affects subsequent performance by influencing students' attention to particular matters so that those matters undergo a change in the subsequent performance" (66). Experienced writers have already developed a sense of how readers are likely to respond to their writing; they are capable in effect of providing their own feedback as they write. This is the function of what Donald Murray calls the writer's "other self," the reading writer doing the kind of recursive scanning Sommers and Sondra Perl have documented as central to revision ("Teaching"). Inexperienced writers, by contrast, need feedback from others in order to internalize reader response as part of their composing process. Peer feedback provides what John Clifford calls the "necessary experience of witnessing the reader's need for precise syntactic relations and coherent organization" ("Composing" 50).

This experience of the "reader's need" can enhance audience awareness and promote habits of revision with readers in mind. E. D. Hirsch argues that "the difficulty of writing good prose arises very largely from the linguistic abnormality of addressing a monologue to an unseen and unknown audience" (*Philosophy* 58). Peer feedback can help students cope with the monological quality of written language by materializing an audience for them. The dialogue of a writing workshop employs the ongoing exchange of verbal and nonverbal feedback inherent in oral situations in order to help student writers initiate and sustain the kind of monologue that the writing situation imposes on them. The concrete presence and face-to-face interaction of peer readers and writers in a workshop setting help novice writers infer information about their audience.

From the cognitive developmental perspective of Kroll and of Kantor and Rubin, social interaction can lead to a heightened awareness of others' points of view and thereby promote a "decentering" of the writer's frame of reference essential to audience awareness. For Mina Shaughnessy, the cognitive egocentrism that makes it difficult for inexperienced writers to imagine an audience for their writing also leads to "premature closure" in their writing, where meaning seems to short-circuit. "One of the most notable differences between experienced and inexperienced writers," Shaughnessy says, "is the rate at which they reach closure upon a point. The experienced writer characteristically reveals a much greater tolerance for what Dewey called 'an attitude of suspended conclusion' than the inexperienced writer whose thought seems to halt at the boundary of each sentence rather than move on, by gradations of subsequent comment, to an elaboration of the sentence" (*Errors* 227). The function of peer feedback, as Elbow puts it, is to "fight the urge for closure" and to keep student writing alive and open longer so that writers can discover and elaborate the meanings in their writing. Peer feedback helps student writers understand the potentialities in a piece of writing as it passes through loops of feedback created by a community of readers and writers.

A practical advantage of peer feedback, Mary H. Beaven and others point out, is to reduce the teacher's paper load, the endless hours of grading student essays. Teachers can assign more writing, serial drafts, and revision, while at the same time making sure the writing receives immediate feedback. Not only is the response immediate, it is also multiple. As Moffett says, "multiple responses to a piece of writing make feedback more impersonal and thus easier to heed" (193). Suspending the authority of the teacher as the primary reader of student writing creates a new kind of authority in the classroom, the authority student writers and readers invest in one another.

Writing as a social activity

Peer feedback is no doubt the most common form of collaborative learning used in teaching writing. A number of composition teachers and theorists, however, have argued that collaborative learning does more than promote audience awareness and the need for revision. By socializing the process of learning to write, collaborative learning also promotes important kinds of affective, social, and cultural change.

Richard Gebhardt, for example, extends the notion of feedback to aspects of the writing process that are often ignored by teachers who use peer feedback ("Teamwork"). Gebhardt argues that collaborative learning can help overcome the isolation and loneliness that often plague student and experienced writers alike. For Gebhardt, it is not simply the information but the "tone" that make peer feedback useful to student writers. Collaborative learning offers emotional as well as intellectual support, helping students who experience writing as a solitary act to see that they are not alone, that others, too, feel isolated and trapped in the private world of their own words.

Recent research helps explain why students experience writing as a private activity, displaced from its social and cultural context. Studies of the origins and consequences of literacy have shown that the technology of writing itself tends to decontextualize language use by divorcing the author from both audience and the text. Jack Goody and Ian Watt, David Olson, Eric Havelock, Walter Ong, and others have noted how the emergence of writing separates knowledge and learning from the social context of everyday life. According to Goody and Watt, in the transition from oral to literate culture, with the advent of written signs, concepts no longer are "tied to occasions" but rather are isolated from the traditional social setting of speakers and hearers. The graphic isolation of words from the flow of speech creates the cultural space of writing. This graphic isolation, Goody and Watt argue, objectifies words and, "by making their meanings available for much more prolonged and intensive scrutiny than is possible orally, encourages private thought" (27). But if the decontextualized quality of the written word promotes formal thought and systematic logic in literate cultures, it can also make the contexts of knowing and writing invisible to writers, a situation that is especially disorienting to inexperienced writers.

The displacement of the writer from the context of writing, Lunsford and Ede point out, is further underwritten by the romantic image of the artist in the garret, suffering the personal agon of writing in isolation ("Why Write"). This image of the author, so deeply impressed in the consciousness of English teachers, makes collaboration seem suspect because writing is pictured as an inherently private, intensely individualistic activity. Poststructuralist critics such as Roland Barthes and Michel Foucault, however, have challenged this image of the author. Foucault argues that the author is not so much the creative center of a work as a "privileged moment of individualization in the history of ideas" ("What Is an Author?" 141). The author is accorded status outside of and antecedent to the text. According to Barthes and Foucault, the authority and autonomy traditionally ascribed to the author conceals the historicity of the notion, the emergence in the eighteenth and nineteenth century of the idea of the author—a legal fiction by which society allocates ownership of writing to the writer and the text becomes private property. Instead of picturing the author as the sovereign creator and owner of the text, they have reduced the author to a function of the text, a social construct created by the activity of writing.

In composition studies, Bruffee, Patricia Bizzell, and others have questioned traditional notions about the autonomy of the author and traditional assumptions that writing and reading, in Bruffee's words, are "intrinsically individual, asocial activities." They use the idea that writing takes place in social contexts to argue that the production of meaning in written language itself is a social or collaborative process. What goes through a writer's mind during composing—what the Soviet psycholinguist Lev Vygotsky calls "inner speech"—is not the preparation of private and individual thought for public presentation. Rather, Bruffee argues, the writer's consciousness is constituted by public and social talk internalized, by conversation taking place within. In this view, the author is no longer the nineteenth-century individualist but rather a social function in a larger system of dependencies. Writing is not so much the personal expression (and property) of the individual author. Instead, Bruffee says, if "thought is internalized conversation, then writing is internalized conversation re-externalized" ("Collaborative Learning" 641).

One implication of this view of writing as "conversation re-externalized," Bruffee suggests, is that writing teachers need to pay more attention to the forms and workings of "community life that generate and maintain conversation." Bruffee's point is not simply to add social context to a definition of the writing situation but rather to see composing as an activity embedded in what Stanley Fish calls "interpretive communities." Interpretive communities are formed by readers who share interpretive strategies and construct meanings according to conventional norms of acceptability. Fish argues that "understanding is always possible, but not from the outside." Communicating, learning, and knowing take place within community structures, "within a set of interests and concerns" (303). In this view, the genres and formal features of writing—whether a case study, a belletristic essay, a business report, or a scholarly article—are neither expressions of underlying rhetorical principles nor manifestations of deeper cognitive structures. Instead, they are discursive practices, historically derived through a process of group ratification, that bind interpretive communities together.

Collaborative learning, then, involves students in the conversation of readers and writers in interpretive communities. If, as Bruffee argues, writing "is not an inherently private act but is a displaced social act we perform in private for the sake of convenience," the function of collaborative learning is to recontextualize composing and to externalize the process by which writing acceptable to an interpretive community is generated and authorized. In this regard, Bruffee says collaborative learning "is not merely a helpful pedagogical technique incidental to writing. It is essential to writing" ("Writing and Reading" 165).

This emphasis on the social production of texts, moreover, carries beyond pedagogy to suggest new approaches to the study of discourse and to curricular development. For one thing, the social perspective on writing redefines the rhetorical situation. As Bruffee says, it no longer assumes that "people write to persuade or to distinguish themselves and their points of view and to gain the acquiescence of other individuals." Instead, it assumes the opposite: "that people write in order to be accepted, to join, to be regarded as another member of the culture or community that constitutes the writer's audience" ("Collaborative Learning" 641). The forms and genres of writing are not tactical moves in the adversarial enterprise of winning over the reader. Instead the conventions of writing are community-constituting forms of recognition, acceptance, and exclusion.

For Elaine P. Maimon, writing as a community-constituting activity converges with her interest in writing across the curriculum. To learn to write, Maimon says, "introduces students to the concept of thinking in context" ("Knowledge"). To learn to write is to learn to join in the conversation of the various subcommunities—the disciplines within academia. Students, Maimon points out, often experience such conversation as alien, a foreign language. For this reason, the role of the writing teacher cannot be simply to organize students to give and receive feedback. The teacher serves rather, in Maimon's words, as a "native informant," a translator between communities.

If the use of peer feedback is most often associated with a pedagogical stance that asks students to write for their peers as a "natural audience," Bruffee, Maimon, and others treat peer readers and writers as a transitional community. As Thomas Newkirk points out, the criteria students use to evaluate their peers' writing differ from the norms of the teacher's interpretive community. To identify peers as the writer's intended audience, therefore, can be misleading because, as Newkirk says, it may "claim to take one position (assessing writing on its probable affect with any intended audience)" but at the same time "actually take another (assessing on the basis of the norms of the academic community)" ("Direction" 309). By emphasizing the social activity of writing, collaborative learning can play a significant role in helping students make the transition from one community to another, from one discourse to another, from one identity to another. Collaborative learning can help students generate a transitional language to bridge the cultural gap and acquire fluency in academic conversation.

Issues in practice

Although most students have had significant experiences collaborating with their peers outside of school in the course of growing up, they may well not have had any experience working collaboratively in the classroom. Collaboration, after all, verges on plagiarism in the minds of many teachers. Since traditional education evaluates students on the basis of individual performance, collaboration seems to undercut the prevailing reward structure in education. Traditional educational practices rarely provide the opportunity for students to assume the kind of responsibility for one another that collaborative learning demands. For these reasons, teachers who use collaborative learning have recognized that expecting students to give effective feedback or to work collaboratively without careful training is unrealistic.

In the writing classroom, collaborative learning not only asks students to enter into what may be new and unaccustomed relationships, but also asks them to read and respond to one another's work in ways they have generally not been trained to do. As Mary K. Healy points out, students often have had little opportunity to articulate their responses to what they read and therefore need practice and encouragement to become conscious of how they react to written language. But if teachers agree that students need training, the growing discussion about what kind of feedback students should be trained to give has only opened the issue.

Peter Elbow draws a useful distinction between "reader-based" feedback and "criterion-based" feedback (*Writing with Power*). Reader-based feedback presents the reader's experience of a piece of writing, the "raw data" of perceptions and reactions. Criterion-based feedback translates the reader's experience of the text into a judgment by measuring it according to recognized standards such as unity, coherence, style, correctness, and so on. Reader-based feedback strives for richness in describing the effects a writer's words produce in the reader. Criterion-based feedback strives for critical awareness and the development of discriminatory judgment.

Some teachers, such as Brannon and Knoblauch, emphasize reader-based feedback but employ a different terminology. They distinguish "facilitative" from "directive" response on the part of teachers and peer readers. In their view, facilitative response focuses on the relation between the writer's intentions and the effect of a text on a reader. Such feedback will tend to take the form of questions "aimed at making the writer more reflective about the sufficiency of choices" in a piece of writing. Directive feedback will tend to impose the reader's own agenda by specifying changes that need to be made in a text. Since facilitative response is concerned with the clarity or uncertainty in a reader's mind about the writer's intentions, it will tend to treat the content of a text. Directive feedback, Brannon and Knoblauch argue, will tend to mimic teacher feedback and to stifle the development of the writer's meaning by leapfrogging ahead to matters of form and correctness.

In contrast, Bruffee argues that students should learn to do formal analysis before commenting on the content of a text or attempting to make evaluative judgments of one another's work. According to Bruffee, discussions of content are premature and may in fact be counterproductive until students have learned to read carefully and to trust one another's responses (*Short Course* 116–18). The latter point is important because peer feedback inevitably pulls students between two audiences and two sets of feelings — the authority of the teacher and loyalty to peers. For this reason, feedback should begin with description and proceed only gradually to evaluation. What Bruffee calls "descriptive outlines" teach students to do rhetorical analysis that explicitly separates form and content. Students are generally used to doing what we might call "semantic readings," paraphrases of what a text says, but structural or rhetorical reading, statement of what a text does and how it does it, is likely to be new to them.

Beside the question of the kind of feedback students should be trained to give are questions concerning when and how peer feedback is best given. Gebhardt argues that the "restriction of group feedback to relatively late points in the writing process" can undercut the power of collaborative learning by reducing feedback to "collaborative editing" ("Teamwork" 71). Gebhardt's sense that students can profit from collaborative discussions throughout the writing process is supported by the important connection Britton, Douglas Barnes, and others have drawn between talking and writing. In this view, students need to talk through a piece of writing at every stage in its development.

The connection between talking and writing is raised too by the issue of whether peer feedback should be oral or written. Anne Ruggles Gere notes some of the advantages of oral response ("Language"). The immediacy, economy, and contextuality of oral response, she argues, account for its conveying greater specificity than written response does. Bruffee, however, argues that since peer feedback demands that peer critics be "tactful and circumspect, pointed but constructive, sympathetic and firm all at once" (*Short Course* 115), it is the most difficult and the most real writing students must do. For this reason, he says, peer critics learn more from written than from oral response.

The issues surrounding peer feedback are far from resolved. At present, we have different emphases — one approach emphasizes the function of reader-based feedback in revealing to the writer the interaction between reader and text; the other emphasizes the function of criterion-based feedback in developing critical and rhetorical reading skills. There does seem to be growing agreement, however, about the importance of students developing their own language to talk about writing. In fact, as Donnalee Rubin notes, student ability "to make discriminating judgments about their own work and the work of their peers" may well run ahead of their ability to incorporate these judgments in improved written products. Rubin suggests that peer feedback and peer critiques may teach students more than we measure when we evaluate student writing, that students acquire skills in giving feedback that their papers may not reflect. To understand why this is true and how students can transfer their enhanced reading abilities to their composing processes is a topic that awaits systematic investigation.

Another set of issues raised by collaborative learning concerns group dynamics and the role of the teacher in a collaborative classroom. Thom Hawkins's *Group Inquiry Techniques for Teaching Writing* and the collection *Learning in Groups*, edited by Clark Bouton and Russell Y. Garth, offer practical advice on designing group tasks and structuring collaborative work. Diana George identifies types of groups and typical problems in group dynamics that occur in collaborative settings. Gebhardt argues that teachers need to pay more attention to group dynamics, to "explore more candidly the emotional flow in collaborative writing groups, perhaps by finding ways to blend group process instruction into writing classes or by finding ways to use values-clarification and sensitivity-building exercises in writing classes" ("Teamwork" 70). Bruffee notes the importance of work on small-group dynamics, especially Bennis and Shepard's analysis of the interplay of authority and intimacy in the stages of group development.

Teachers such as Abercombie, Mason, and Bruffee have noted that the changes in social relations among students also imply changes in the role of the teacher. Developing new teaching practices, Mason argues, is more difficult than developing new teaching materials because teachers are tied into a self-perpetuating system and set of expectations that are resistant to innovation. Most teachers, Abercombie notes in *Talking to Learn*, "have usually had little or no experience of having been taught in small groups themselves. . . . They consequently have no model of the teacher's behavior to follow and no basis for empathy with students in the small group situation" (1). Trained by the conventions of the lecture and the seminar, teachers seldom have an opportunity to examine their attitudes about teaching and learning. For this reason, Bruffee asserts, "the first change we must make is not in our students but in ourselves." The "latent authoritarianism" in higher education makes it hard to shift power and responsibility from teacher to students. To run collaborative classes, Bruffee says, teachers must "be able to bear the acknowledgement that learning can go on without their immediate presence" and to see their role not as a purveyor of information but as a *"metteur en scene* whose responsibility and privilege it is to arrange optimum conditions for others to learn" ("The Way Out" 470).

Most teachers who use collaborative learning would agree with this formulation, but they differ about how to go about making such arrangements. Some teachers, for example, see their role as collaborators who facilitate small-group interaction. Others, however, argue that the teacher's active participation in group work will only reestablish traditional authority surreptitiously and thus inhibit the power of collaboration between students. Implied here are larger issues about the institutional context in which teaching and learning occur. For Bruffee, John Trimbur, and others, teachers cannot be simply facilitators, because such a role ignores the institutional context and the authority it ascribes to the teacher. They argue that we should recognize the teacher's role as a representative of the academic community in order to help students understand and demystify the workings and structures of power in that community. In this view, teaching in a collaborative setting involves negotiating the teacher's authority and social standing as well as facilitating group processes.

Finally, there is a set of issues concerned with the use of peer tutors in writing centers. Peer tutoring is perhaps the most extensive attempt to apply collaborative learning to teaching writing, in this case outside the classroom. Bruffee's article "The Brooklyn Plan: Attaining Intellectual Growth through Peer Group Tutoring" is a seminal statement of the connections among collaborative learning, peer group influence, and peer tutoring. Much has been written about the selection, training, and use of peer tutors. Stephen North's "The Idea of the Writing Center" offers an overview of the basic issues. While a good deal of the discussion about peer tutoring has been program description, Nathaniel Hawkins's "An Introduction to the History and Theory of Peer Tutoring in Writing" identifies a "dilemma" in the literature—"of whether to emphasize the tutor's role [as a peer and collaborative learner] or his knowledge of theory and grammar." The training and use of peer tutors involves what Marvin Garrett calls a "delicate balance." If tutors are not trained in the theory and methods of tutoring writing, they cannot effectively help their peers. "Yet if they're too well-trained," Bruffee notes, "tutees don't perceive them as peers but as little teachers, and the collaborative effort of working together is lost" ("Training and Using" 446). Trimbur argues that peer tutoring in writing centers contributes to the formation of student culture that takes writing and intellectual activity seriously. To treat peer tutors as instructional staff or adjuncts to the classroom, Trimbur says, not only threatens to exploit the tutors but, by identifying the tutor with the authority of the teacher, can also undercut the peer relations collaborative learning is grounded on ("Students or Staff"). Harvey Kail puts peer tutoring in a wider context by showing how it involves students, faculty, peer tutors, and writing-center administrators in a complex web of influences and relations.

Research and theoretical development

Researchers thus far have focused largely on the question of whether collaborative learning demonstrably helps students improve their writing. Beaven summarizes the research completed by the early seventies: "Research studies dealing with peer groups and evaluation of writing . . . indicate that improvement in theme-writing ability and grammar usage, when students engage in peer evaluation, may equal or even exceed the improvement that occurs under evaluation procedures carried out by the teacher" (151). In a more recent study, John Clifford reports comparable results ("Composing in Stages"). However, the general consensus that experimental groups using collaborative practices improve as much or more than control groups using conventional instruction raises as many questions as it answers. As in any research study employing experimental design, the central question is, what are the questions? What, in fact, have these researchers measured? Ostensibly it is some perceptible gain in writing ability. But how can we know that such improvement was determined by peer evaluation and not by some other variable? The experimental-control model, after all, employs a "context-free" methodology, when in these cases the research is supposed to measure the influence of elements that constitute part of the writer's context. Instead of trying to show whether collaborative learning works, we need to know first of all how it works. We need to frame questions that treat collaborative learning not as a pedagogical technique to be compared to other techniques but as a "naturalistic setting" that allows researchers to examine language development through social interaction.

Lunsford and Ede take an important step in this direction. In "Why Write . . . Together?" they argue that the process of collaborative writing and coauthorship has been ignored by writing teachers even though it is a common form of composing in business, government, the professions, and certain academic disciplines. The questions they pose ask "what specific features distinguish the processes of co- or group-authoring from single authorship," how collaborative writing affects the traditional reader-writer relationship, "what epistemological implications does co-authorship hold for traditional notions of creativity and originality," and what ethical concerns are raised by joint authorship. The results of the research they have projected should enhance considerably our understanding of how writers function collaboratively in a variety of contexts and what the implications are for composition teaching.

Anne Ruggles Gere has initiated another promising research project. Gere's study of the "naturally occurring language" of writing groups contributes to our understanding of the dynamics of peer response and feedback. Gere describes the language of peer response first in quantitative terms, by applying a "three part coding system which identified the language function, the general focus of attention, and the topic of utterance." Then, in order to understand the language in qualitative terms, Gere compares peer response to what we know about teacher responses. Her findings confirm the work of Sommers and of Brannon and Knoblauch:

> By trying to form an ideal text, one which conforms to certain features which can be abstracted from an indefinite number of exemplary texts, all with different meanings, the teacher assumes that the purpose of writing is pedagogical. . . . Concerned with an actual text, writing group response might be predicted to show the features we've described here as genuine response: questions about meaning, information about effective and ineffective passages. . . . ("Language")

Recent research by Carol Berkenkotter and Thomas Newkirk considers some of the problems raised by peer response and evaluation in the writing classroom. Berkenkotter studied the way three student writers responded to peer feedback. What she found is that student writers "respond to their readers in significantly different ways depending on the writer's personality, level of maturity, and ability to handle writing problems" ("Student Writers" 318). Though her findings are based on only three case studies, her work suggests we need to know more about how student writers make use of peer feedback and how they can maintain control over their writing when the feedback includes unwarranted criticism or misleading advice. Newkirk's "Direction and Misdirection in Peer Response" found that student response differs in important respects from teacher response, suggesting that the identification of peer readers with the student writer's audience may be misleading.

What is especially interesting about this recent research is that it extends an examination of reader-text interaction beyond literary studies, where it has already been well developed by Louise Rosenblatt, David Bleich, Stanley Fish, and others, to study reader response to student texts. Not only does work such as Gere's suggest that collaborative learning is a useful pedagogy, it also establishes a common ground for the integration of composition studies and literary theory. What this may lead to is a much fuller sense of how readers respond to texts and how this information can be incorporated into composing processes. For example, if texts, as Gere's work suggests, invariably produce a plurality of readings (or "misreadings," as reader response critics might put it), then we must revise the conventional view of audience as a concrete entity and of the writer as the controller and possessor of meaning. The sense of ownership that writing teachers such as Berkenkotter want to encourage in student writers may well dissolve in the reader-text interaction because the text becomes, as it were, communal property, the result not of a straightforward exchange between reader and writer but of the wider social activity of text construction that constitutes both readers and writers as functions of the discourse.

Further theoretical development on how readers and writers construct themselves in a textual field will have to balance (or, as a critic such as Stanley Fish might say, dismantle the distinction) between objective and subjective readings, between the implicit authoritarianism of criterion-based feedback and the anarchy of reader-based feedback. This can be done, Fish says, only by situating meaning and text in the context of interpretive communities:

> The claims of objectivity and subjectivity can no longer be debated because the authorizing agency, the center of interpretive authority, is at once both and neither. An interpretive community is not objective because as a bundle of interests, of particular purposes and goals, its perspective is interested rather than neutral; but by the same reasoning, the meanings and texts produced by an interpretive community are not subjective because they do not proceed from an isolated individual but from a public and conventional point of view (14).

Once we think that readers and writers operate within interpretive communities, we raise a number of questions: what interpretive communities do we mean by teaching writing and what discursive practices characterize such communities? how do such communities produce and authorize knowledge that's acceptable to the community? what are the structures of power and authority that govern the production and circulation of texts within such communities? These questions assume that we can't teach literacy in any pure or unmediated sense but that reading and writing always take place within social and cultural contexts. How then in teaching writing can we externalize contexts that usually remain implicit and unexamined? Answers to such questions can enrich composition studies by developing a much fuller sense of the social and cultural contexts of composing—of what context, being with the text, means for students and for writing teachers.

Empirical Research in Composition

Anne Ruggles Gere

For many of us in English studies, the word *empirical* evokes, initially at least, images of white-coated scientists following procedures that have no relation to our wrestle with words. More thoughtful consideration, however, reminds us of a broader view of empiricism, one not limited to experimental design or statistical procedures. It is a view consonant with the old saw that there are two ways to find out how many teeth a horse has. One way is to speculate about the nature of horses and teeth, and the other is to open the horse's mouth and count the teeth. Empiricism begins with the opening and counting and includes many forms of observation and experimentation.

The word *empiricism* derives from the Greek *empeira*, meaning experience, and in philosophical terms encompasses two doctrines—one concerned with concepts and the other with propositions. The first, a theory of meaning, holds that concepts can be understood only if their users can connect them with things they have experienced or could experience. In other words, the word *writing* can be understood only by individuals who have experience with writing. The second, a theory of knowledge, assumes that at least some propositions depend on experience for justification. That is, a proposition such as "Jane is a writer" would require having seen Jane actually writing. As these doctrines suggest, empiricism rejects claims of authority, intuition, conjecture, and reasoning. Although composition research does not always adhere to both doctrines completely or remain entirely within the boundaries of empiricism, it does give primacy to experience. To the extent that we embrace composition studies as part of English studies, we encompass empiricism because composition studies has, nearly from its inception, involved empirical research.

During its first century of existence, English studies has shifted its theoretical center several times, moving, for example, from historical-biographical work to New Criticism to deconstruction. These shifts have reflected changes in the larger intellectual community as well as in scholarship within English studies itself. Historical-biographical approaches to literature resulted, in part at least, from the emergence of Charles Darwin's theory of evolution. This idea of growth and development led to a historical approach in both literature and language study (comparative philology, study of Anglo-Saxon and related courses in the history of the English language entered the curriculum during the latter part of the nineteenth century at the same time that historical approaches to literature emerged). So too, the theoretical center of empirical research in composition has changed during its nearly one hundred years of existence. Shifting theories of science have influenced research in composition just as changing interpretative approaches have shaped literary interpretations. In this chapter I trace the changes in empirical research in composition.

College-level composition instruction appeared almost simultaneously with English studies. In 1874 Harvard instituted a prescribed composition course for sophomores and two years later institutionalized English studies by appointing Francis James Child the first professor of English literature. These two events and the 1885 introduction of a required freshman composition course, English A, at Harvard resulted from the influence of Charles Eliot, who became the university's president in 1869. In his inaugural address Eliot lamented "the prevailing neglect of the systematic study of the English language" (2), and he retained this concern throughout his administration. In 1884, for example, he asserted that:

> less than half as much instruction, of proper university grade is offered in English as in Greek or in Latin. The experience of all other colleges and universities resembles in this respect that of Harvard. . . . The first subject which, as I conceive, is entitled to recognition as of equal academic value or rank with any subject now most honored is the English language and literature. . . . English should be studied from the beginning of school life to the end of college life (100).

His commitment to English studies led Eliot to keep written composition as a required course even though the rest of the university curriculum was shifting toward the German system of electives. Predictably, this requirement directed a high proportion of Harvard's resources toward composition instruction, and, just as predictably, this allocation of resources disgruntled faculty and, therefore, administrators. Accordingly, in 1891 Harvard's Board of Overseers appointed a committee to investigate English A. This committee was charged with conducting what can be called empirical research in composition. The work of Harvard's Committee on Composition can be described as empirical research because it adhered to a theory of meaning that connected words such as *English A* and *composition instruction* with experience. Rather than rely on conjecture or intuition, the committee looked at several kinds of evidence before making a recommendation about English A at Harvard. It collected and examined writing samples from English A and from Harvard's 1892 entrance examination (which included a written composition section); it solicited and scrutinized information about the curriculum from instructors in English A; and it surveyed students to gather data about their high school composition courses. The committee's work culminated in a report published in 1892, the first of three "Harvard Reports." This report not only placed composition studies in the empirical tradition but also shaped the direction of composition research for future decades because of the kinds of questions it asked and answered.

These questions, generated by Harvard's growing dissatisfaction with allocating a high proportion of its resources to composition instruction, were primarily administrative rather than theoretical or instructional. That is, the committee was not as interested in learning about writing or how to teach it effectively as it was in reallocating resources. Although administrative questions remained implicit, they influenced the committee's interpretation of data generated by empirical investigation. The committee's implicit questions included: (1) How can we make composition instruction more cost effective? (2) How can writing instruction keep pace with expanding enrollments? (Between 1889 and 1899 enrollment by men increased 62.4% and among women it increased 153.3% [Kitzhaber, "Rhetoric" 72].) (3) How can we relieve college instructors of the burden of composition instruction?

The history behind these questions included the earlier (1874) establishment of a Harvard entrance requirement in composition, a requirement designed to "relegate to the lower schools the responsibility for the more mechanical details of writing so that the university could devote itself to higher instruction on the pattern of European institutions" (Kitzhaber 71). This relegation was not so easily accomplished, however, because many students were either failing entrance examinations or passing them with low scores that indicated they lacked control of these mechanical details. In effect, the members of the committee were charged with finding a way to make these "mechanical details" the concern of someone other than Harvard faculty. Not surprisingly, the committee's report reiterated the position that schools, not colleges, should teach composition:

> It is obviously absurd that the College—the institution of higher education—should be called upon to turn aside from its proper functions and devote its means and the time of its instructors to the task of imparting elementary instruction which should be given even in

ordinary grammar schools, much more in those higher academic institutions intended to prepare select youth for a university course (*Reports* 119).

The committee went on to recommend that admission requirements be raised to eliminate students underprepared in composition and to suggest that if schools did not devote more time to teaching writing they could not expect their students to be accepted at Harvard. Others (notably Albert Kitzhaber and Donald Stewart) have detailed the widespread and largely negative effect of this and the two subsequent Harvard Reports (issued in 1895 and 1897) on writing instruction, not just at Harvard but, because of Harvard's enormous prestige, at colleges across the country. Under the influence of Harvard many colleges adopted entrance examinations, required courses in composition, and even the text used at Harvard (Adams Sherman Hill's *The Principles of Rhetoric and Their Application*). I argue that the Harvard Reports had an equally powerful and deleterious effect on composition research. Powerful because administrative questions like those underlying the reports dominated composition research for decades thereafter, and deleterious because the Harvard Reports excluded the theoretical and instructional concerns that could have enriched the early decades of composition research.

Not only did the Committee on Composition focus on administrative issues, but it operated out of a very narrow definition of writing, one characterized by statements such as "[It is] little less than absurd to suggest that any human being who can be taught to talk cannot likewise be taught to compose. Writing is merely the habit of talking with the pen instead of with the tongue" (*Reports* 155). This reductionist view of writing was accompanied by emphasis on the mechanical details of writing, specifically surface features of correctness. The authors of the 1892 report evinced no concern with development of an argument, with attention to audience, with sustained discourse. Instead, they made comments about grammatical errors, neatness, and handwriting. The questions asked and the answers provided by the Committee on Composition shaped future research by suggesting these priorities: (1) written products, not processes of writing, deserve scrutiny, (2) formal aspects of writing are more important than rhetorical ones, (3) composition instruction (and therefore composition research) should be the province of elementary and secondary schools, not colleges and universities, (4) the problems of writing instructors, not the problems of student writers, deserve attention. While general principles of empiricism (at least the central idea of connecting belief with experience) guided the committee, the empiricism was not particularly conscious or

rigorous. The psychological methods that later influenced composition research had not been adopted in 1892, and the lay status of the committee
mitigated against theoretical questions. The priorities for research, then,
emerged not from careful consideration of either methodology or theory.
Rather, they evolved from institutional constraints and concerns.

An alternative set of priorities, one that illustrates the limitations of that
established by the committee, appears in the work of Fred Newton Scott,
professor of rhetoric at the University of Michigan from 1889 to 1927. Scott
examined the materials collected by the Harvard committee and wrote this:

> I have recently been reading over again the reports of the Harvard
> Committee on English Composition in which a number of exami-
> nation papers are produced in facsimile, and the distorted English
> of the writers is almost indecently exposed. Upon this same English
> there is much sarcastic comment in the committee's report, and the
> exhibits seem to justify it; but for my part I could not view these
> reelings and writhings of the adolescent mind without a feeling of
> pity. It was all so unreal. Back of this mess and confusion were genu-
> ine individuals with likes and dislikes, with budding ambitions, with
> tingling senses, with impulses toward right and wrong. Where did
> these individuals come in when judgment was passed upon their faulty
> English? What were they trying to do? What motives lay behind these
> queer antics of the pen? If one could only tear away the swathings,
> set the imprisoned spirits free, and interrogate them, a strange new
> light might be thrown upon the causes of bad English (18–19).

Not only does Scott approach the student writing with sympathy (sensitive to the "indecently exposed" language), but he raises completely different questions. Instead of sharing the Harvard committee's interest in
administrative issues of cost effectiveness, rising enrollments, allocation of
instructors' time, and formal aspects of written products, Scott concerns
himself with the student writers ("genuine individuals") and the processes
they engaged in ("What were they trying to do? What motives lay behind?
. . . "). In other words, the empirical methods of the Harvard committee
did not contribute as much to the subsequent shape of composition research as did the questions with which the committee was charged and
the backgrounds of the members of that committee. The exigencies of composition instruction at Harvard and the persons involved in assessing the
situation were at least as important as the view of science under which
those persons operated. Empiricism, like any other approach, serves the
predispositions and priorities of its users.

Rollo Lyman's 1929 summary of investigations in writing reveals that in
the decades after 1892 composition research retained many of the priori-

ties established by Harvard's Committee on Composition, but the methodologies changed as views of empiricism shifted. Composition researchers began to emulate scientific methods, particularly those of psychology. Science had always fit comfortably within the boundaries of empiricism because of its assumptions about the structure of the universe and the singular items of evidence used to confirm its theories. Psychology, like other social sciences, attempted to emulate science in the late nineteenth century. Specifically, experiments in clinical psychology were adopted directly from physics, and psychologists used the classic experimental model, with its emphasis on objectivity and strict controls.

Composition research imported the psychological model and carried out projects emphasizing objectivity and careful controls. There was a convenient consonance between this methodology and the types of questions composition researchers asked. In keeping with the priorities established by the Harvard Reports, composition research gave most of its attention to administrative concerns, specifically, the issue of how to evaluate student writing. The Harvard Reports' emphasis on written products and on the problems of writing instructors (as opposed to student writers), led composition researchers of the early decades of the twentieth century to focus on the development of composition evaluation scales. These scales were intended to rank student writing, thereby making the instructor's evaluation duties less onerous. Designed to make comparisons and minimize the injustices of unequal standards for grading, these scales consisted of a selected set of compositions ranging in quality on a scale of, say, one to ten. Rating according to such scales meant comparing the paper in question to those on the scale and assigning it the number of the sample closest in general quality. At least seventeen composition evaluation scales were developed between 1910 and 1926 (Lyman 134–73). All these scales gave attention to mechanics such as spelling, punctuation, capitalization, and thoroughness in content.

Researchers who developed these scales adhered to the scientific model of empiricism by seeking objectivity. That was the goal both of the scales in general and of particular researchers who developed such scales as the Hillegas Scale for the Measurement of Quality in English Composition, Willing's Scale for Measuring Written Composition, and the Hudelson English Composition Scale. The difficulty of translating scientific standards of objectivity into composition research is evident in researchers' frequent calls for more precise measures within these scales (Lyman 157–61). More important, the very basis of the scales could not be objective because there was no way of comparing a given piece of writing with one on a composition scale without calling the evaluator's opinion into play. It was the evaluator, after all, who decided where an individual paper fit on a given scale, and that decision was inevitably subjective. Developers of composition scales could not maintain scientific objectivity when they attempted to translate qualitative features of writing into quantitative terms.

A related line of research during the early decades of this century concerned itself with teachers' judgments when aided or unaided by standards such as those of composition scales. The findings in this area were almost equally divided. Some researchers found that composition scales reduced disparities among teachers' evaluations, and others found that the scales made no difference (Lyman 196). An important variable in these studies was the amount of training teachers were given in the use of a scale, but even with training, teachers continued to make subjective responses to writing.

During the first thirty years of this century, nearly all composition researchers, even as they attempted to emulate the empirical model of psychology, adhered to the priorities established by the Harvard Reports. They gave their attention to written products (not processes of writing), they gave more attention to formal aspects of writing than to rhetorical ones, they concentrated their attention on the writing of elementary and secondary students, and they focused on the problems of instructors, not of students.

Although most composition researchers accepted the priorities of the Harvard committee, some, like S. Colvin, operated from a different set of assumptions. The central question of Colvin's 1902 study was whether student writers' inventive powers could be directed and improved. Colvin's question was significant in several ways. It focused on writers rather than on their instructors, it looked at a rhetorical issue rather than at form alone, and it suggested an interest in processes of writing. Colvin gave high school students five consecutive assignments; the first two assignments asked students to select their own topics, and the assignments for the remaining three allowed students to choose from among topics that had generated the most imaginative writing in the first two sets. Among these topics were "A Voyage in an Airship in the Year 2000," "A Practical Joke," and "The Adventures of a School Desk." The papers resulting from each of the five assignments were grouped according to excellence in formal correctness and according to excellence in invention to determine whether increased power of invention was accompanied by a decrease in formal correctness.

While the validity of Colvin's criteria for the groupings and the reliability of papers' placements were not completely certain, Colvin recognized the limitations inherent in his work. For example, he found a high correlation between increases in formal correctness and increases in inventive ability, but he recognized that correlation is not causation and posed a number of questions for future research:

> Does an increase in formal correctness cause an increase in inventive ability, and does an increase in inventive ability tend to improve formal correctness, or are the variations in these elements controlled by a cause that lies behind them both? The supposition that an increase in formal correctness directly causes an increase in inventive power seems hardly justifiable, since processes contributing to inventive ability precede its expression. It is difficult to imagine how a mere correctness in the expression of a psychic state could in any way influence the state itself. On the other hand, may it not be reasonably assumed that the character of an affective, intellectual, or conative state determines somewhat the form in which the state shall seek expression, and that, if we succeed in stimulating the elements of inventive ability, we shall likewise succeed in improving the mode in which those elements find expression? (418)

Colvin's findings and the questions he drew from them offered a challenge to future researchers, but it was not, as Rollo Lyman noted, a challenge they accepted:

> Twenty-five years ago Colvin pioneered in attempting to discover whether the inventive abilities of pupils can be improved through composition. With the possible exception of the studies made by Hudelson concerning composition topics, this significant line of inquiry has been neglected (196).

The same general pattern of emulating the psychological model of empiricism and following the priorities of the 1892 Harvard Report persisted into the second half of this century. Braddock, Lloyd-Jones, and Schoer assumed in their 1963 retrospective on composition research that the psychological model was the only viable one, excluding from consideration studies that did not employ "scientific methods like controlled experimentation" (1) and relying on the evaluations of a "specialist in educational research" (21). Of the 504 studies included in this report, only two deal with processes of writing (the remaining 502 focus on various aspects of written products). Rhetorical aspects ("larger than the unit of the sentence – in expository writing, for instance, the main idea and its analysis; the support of subordinate ideas with details, examples, statistics, and reasons; and the organization of the previous elements into an orderly and meaningful whole" [38]) are considered in only three studies (39), and all these suffer from serious limitations. A significant number of the studies examined in this report deal with the writing of elementary and secondary school students, and the existing research is divided into the two categories of "rating compositions" and "frequency counts."

Many of the studies included in the Braddock et al. category of "rating compositions" were legacies of earlier research on composition scales. They concentrated on the instructor's problems with grading and led to the development of alternatives to composition scales. Notable among these were "general impression" (or holistic) systems of evaluation and "analytic" systems designed to identify specific features in writing without requiring evaluators to match compositions to a set on a scale. Braddock and his colleagues faulted researchers in this category for failing to give attention to variables of writers, assignments, rates, and interrater reliability, and they urged frequency counts as an attractive alternative to rating compositions. "Frequency counts" (primarily quantification of error types) have, according to the editors, the advantage of "describing composition in fairly objective terms which *can* mean the same things to most teachers and investigators and which are subject to more statistical analyses than are ratings" (16).

This recommendation of frequency counts underscores the scientific approach dominant in composition research of 1963. The need for objectivity, for quantifiable features in writing, persisted. Implicit in this approach is what Manicas and Secord call a standard view of science. The standard view assumes a closed system (such as that in a laboratory) where all variables can be controlled or at least accounted for. When Braddock et al. urge composition researchers to control outside influences such as "the time of day classes meet, motivation by classroom guests or rewards, size of classes, and demands upon time and initiative" (25), they are urging composition research to conform to a standard view where closure can be assumed. Another aspect of the standard view of science is the assumption that theories are tested against "facts," that it is possible to assume a set of givens against which hypotheses can be measured. For instance, many of the studies discussed in *Research in Written Composition* proceed from the theory that grammar instruction will improve the quality of student writing. Implicit in such studies is another standard-view assumption, that causal relations are regular and contingent, that explanation and prediction are exactly symmetrical.

Although one should not attribute too much significance to the placement of sections in a book, the arrangement of sections in *Research in Written Composition* merits attention. The section on methodology precedes and is considerably longer than the section on questions about composition. This arrangement suggests that the editors accepted the standard view of science and accorded greatest importance to methodology. One explanation is that the power and authority attributed to science led composition researchers to emulate it at all costs. Robert Connors, for example, has argued for this position ("Composition Studies"). An alternative explanation is that the empiricism guiding composition researchers assigned a priori status to a number of central concepts; composition researchers assumed that words such as *writing* or *composition* needed no definition. The priorities established by the Harvard Reports certainly made this assumption and implicitly encouraged researchers to concentrate on methodology rather than to question definitions to which a priori status had been assigned.

Certainly those who conducted the research discussed by Braddock et al. did not raise questions about what words such as *writing* or *composition* might mean. Braddock et al. did, however, in a section titled "Unexplored Territory," suggest that the meaning of such words might not be assumed after all. Among the items in this section are, for instance, questions about motivation toward writing, effects of audience on writing, the relation between maturation and writing, and, even, "what is involved in the act of writing?"

Braddock et al. were not the first to ask such questions. As already noted, in 1909 Scott had wondered about the nature of writing, about what writers "were trying to do," about "what motives lay behind" the "queer antics of the pen," as he read the samples collected by Harvard's Committee on Composition; and in 1902 Colvin had raised questions about invention in writing. These kinds of questions were reiterated by Lyman in his 1929 summary of research in composition. Lyman argued that research should give more attention to invention in writing, claiming:

> National English committees insist that in composition *content* is of first importance; *organization* of ideas, second; and *form* (matters of careful scrutiny), third. Yet research has been confined almost exclusively to form. In general, measurements in the field of composition, quite in line with the customary practices in teaching, have exalted mechanical and rhetorical elements and have neglected originality, freshness and inventiveness (197).

In making this statement Lyman questioned the prevailing definition of "writing" as being primarily concerned with form, and he urged that researchers look in new directions: "Techniques of investigation need to be developed which will reveal the growth of thought processes necessary for effective expression" (196). Lyman, like Scott and Colvin, wrote for an audience unable to respond to his urgings. Not only did Lyman's collection appear on the eve of a great national depression, when all research was curtailed, but he wrote at a time when the standard view of science was in full sway. The new techniques Lyman sought were not developed, because the dominant empirical model could not accommodate complex issues such as the growth of thought processes in writing, issues that meant a shift away from assigning terms such as "writing" to an a priori category and a willingness to reexamine the basic premises on which composition research proceeded.

When Braddock et al. raised similar questions, however, the time was much more opportune. Their book was published during a period of economic growth, increased enrollments, and expansion in educational research. Increased federal funding for research led to a number of investigations in composition, but there was a simultaneous burgeoning of activity not directly connected with federal funding. The 1958 *Directory* of the National Council of Teachers of English mentions a Standing Committee on Research with "functions and additional membership to be named later" (31), and the 1960 *Directory* indicates these functions: (1) to stimulate research, (2) to determine those aspects of Council activities where research is needed, and (3) to provide technical assistance to NCTE committees engaging in research. The 1966 minutes of the Executive Committee of NCTE include this item: "The Executive Secretary then presented plans for the bulletin on *Research in the Teaching of English* which would be edited by Richard Braddock with N. S. Blount as associate editor," and with that a new journal was created, one that provided a forum for researchers interested in issues associated with the teaching of English. Not surprisingly, a significant percentage of the articles in this new journal were on the topic of composition research. This convergence of events created a very favorable environment for composition researchers.

In addition, empiricism in this country underwent a major shift. The 1962 publication of Thomas Kuhn's *The Structure of Scientific Revolutions* popularized a critique of the standard view of science that had been circulating among philosophers for over a decade (see David Bohm; Mario Bunge; and Stephen Toulmin, *Philosophy*). This critique argued that the objectivity attributed to science was unjustified because observations were theory-laden. It claimed that science should be seen as a social activity in which disciplines develop their own rules of practice because observations are not "given" but shaped by the observer's preconceptions and theoretical notions. Kuhn's book brought this view to the attention of social scientists, and as psychologists began to examine the implications of the paradigmatic critique for the standard view of science under which they had been operating, researchers in composition soon followed suit.

As I have already shown, research in composition before 1962 demonstrated the truth of Kuhn's claims. When the Harvard Committee and Fred Newton Scott could look at the same data and see very different things, they demonstrated that observations are theory-laden, are subject to individual interpretation. The difference was that after 1962 composition research openly acknowledged the theories inherent in "objective" observation. The sequel to *Research in Written Composition* appeared in 1978. Titled *Research on Composing: Points of Departure*, it took a very different stance from the Braddock et al. collection. Instead of offering a summary of previous research, editors Cooper and Odell departed from the Braddock collection in "not illustrating conventional methodologies" (xiii) and in not assuming that we already have "a thorough understanding of written products and processes" (xiv). They were, thereby, questioning some of the a priori categories of composition research and opening the way for a new empiricism.

Cooper and Odell put questions about composition first and methodology second. They began by condemning researchers' concentration on pedagogical questions of materials and procedures for improving writing, a concentration that assumed "an adequate understanding of the term *composition*" (xi). As an alternative, they proposed an agenda that includes questions such as these:

> What do we mean by competence in writing?
> How can we best categorize diverse pieces of written discourse?
> What are the practices that allow skillful students and professional writers to evolve successful pieces of written discourse?
> What can we learn by observing successful writing teachers?
> How can we draw upon other disciplines such as developmental psychology to help us refine and pursue the questions we are beginning to ask? (xii)

Their final questions dealt with methodology:

> What new procedures seem especially suited to our new questions?
> Are there methodologies that seem likely to be particularly helpful as we pursue new lines of inquiry? (xiii)

Not only do Cooper and Odell subordinate methodological questions by placing them last in the series, they also frame the questions in a way that indicates consonance with the paradigmatic approach. Instead of insisting, as did Braddock et al., that composition researchers adhere to experimental design compatible with the traditional view of science, they acknowledge that researchers in composition may need to seek new methodologies, may need to develop their own ways of proceeding.

Like their editors, the authors included in this collection ask fundamental questions about writing and about the intellectual demands posed by various types of writing. Where they are concerned with methodology, it is not a methodology consonant with the standard view of science. Rather, they urge studies that consider the significant as well as the measurable. Barritt and Kroll, for example, write:

> At present, the best course for research in composing is probably eclectic: choosing from a diversity of methods and combining various research paradigms. Because composition research is young, there is need for meta-research theory: for the proposal and exploration of new models and procedures. . . . (57)

Richard Young's "Paradigms and Problems: Needed Research in Rhetorical Invention," one of the articles contained in this collection, articulates the paradigmatic critique for composition research. Young describes the "current traditional paradigm" as emphasizing:

> the composed product rather than the composing process; the analysis of discourse into words, sentences, and paragraphs; the classification of discourse into description, narration, exposition, and argument; the strong concern with usage (syntax, spelling, punctuation) and with style (economy, clarity, emphasis); the preoccupation with the informal essay and the research paper. . . . (31)

and claims that research's emphasis on application, specifically pedagogical application, demonstrates the dominance of this paradigm in research as well as in instruction (31–32).

The current traditional paradigm as Young articulates it has much in common with the priorities established by the Harvard Report of 1892; Young identifies four theories of invention as challenges to the paradigm and advocates theoretical, metarhetorical, and historical research. He goes on to recommend research that enables judgments about theories of invention and offers two guiding questions:

> 1. Does it do what it claims to do? That is, does it provide an adequate account of the psychological processes it purports to explain? And does it increase our ability to carry out these processes more efficiently or effectively?
> 2. Does the theory provide a *more adequate* account of the processes and *more adequate* means for carrying them out than any of the alternatives? (40)

Underlying these questions is a paradigmatic assumption that composition research must develop its own rules of practice, that it is a social activity in which disciplines develop their own ways of proceeding.

Just as the Braddock monograph helped shape composition research in its decade, so the Cooper and Odell collection has contributed to composition research in recent years. Discussions of composition's paradigmatic status (or lack thereof) continue to appear in journals (see Connors and Hairston), and composition researchers have responded to the paradigmatic mandate by developing a variety of new methodologies. As Lucy Calkins explains in the next chapter, case studies, descriptive studies, ethnographic work, and other new methodological approaches have been employed to answer fundamental questions about writing. In addition, new populations have become involved in composition research. Elementary and secondary teachers have joined the ranks of researchers, and the establishment of a funding category for teacher researchers by the NCTE's Research Foundation signifies the institutionalization of this new group.

The Cooper and Odell collection is not, however, so much responsible for the shift in empirical research in composition as a reflection of it. As noted earlier, composition research responded to the paradigmatic critique at the same time that it shifted priorities by moving terms such as "writing" out of a priori status. This shift has many benefits for composition research, but there are also some potential liabilities. Manicas and Secord, in their critique of both the standard view of science and the paradigmatic critique, note that neither approach can sustain the distinction between theory and application. As they put it:

> More generally, then, the dominating view of science, logical empiricism and the newer Kuhnian perspective cannot sustain the distinction, implicit in the practices of the well-established natural sciences, between the development of theories representing the structures of nature (including the experimental test of our theories about the structures of nature) and the application of these theories to explain, diagnose, and predict those particulars and events of interest to us. (403)

Because composition research has for so many years been primarily practical (and therefore concerned with application), it is particularly vulnerable to this confusion of theory and application. The emergence of teacher researchers provides a concrete illustration of how far this confusion may extend. The benefits of teacher-researcher investigations are considerable, and I have written on them myself ("Teacher Researcher"). But they pose an epistemological problem because they conflate theory and application. Can the practitioner, whose daily life centers on application, look at issues of composition in purely theoretical terms?

Manicas and Secord offer the "realist view of science" as an alternative. This view, derived from the work of Michael Scriven, Michael Polanyi, and Rom Harre, accepts the Kuhnian view that knowledge is a social and historical product but goes on to assert that the "things" of the world are nonreductive. The implication of this statement is that the Humean analysis of causation and lawfulness, one that assumes that events or classes of events occur no matter what obtains, is refuted. Instead, claims the realist view, scientific explanation is causal explanation and demands that we show how a particular causal configuration led to a specific result. This means more, say Manicas and Secord, than simply looking at complex interactions among variables through ANOVA or multiple regression analysis; it means looking at the multiple natural mechanisms that underlie behavior. In other words, specific behaviors "cannot be explained as the simple manifestation of some single law or principle. What we have is interacting levels of stratification. Indeed, the acts of persons are open-systemic events in which a wide variety of systems and structures are involved, systems that are physical, biological, psychological, and, as we shall argue, sociological as well" (405).

The implications of the realist view for composition research are both promising and frightening. Promising because this view gives cognizance to the immense complexity of the activities subsumed under the term "writing." It acknowledges that descriptions of writing processes cannot be applied to all writers, that the amount of revising done may not have any direct relation to the quality of the resulting writing. Frightening because such complex analysis will make composition research even more difficult. Work in this field was much simpler (even if less productive) when the standard view of science prevailed and written products were the major focus of analysis. Despite its difficulties, however, the realist view holds great promise for composition research because it opens the way for even more careful attention to the intricacies of writing and teaching writing.

Tracing the changing nature of empirical research in composition, then, leads not to a single point but to a description of a field growing ever more complex. The emergence of the paradigmatic approach and the realist view of science has not eliminated the standard view. It is possible to pick up a contemporary collection of research articles and find a study employing traditional experimental design next to one that acknowledges the paradigmatic critique by adapting ethnography and collecting participant-observer field notes, and next to that an article that moves toward the realist perspective by noting the limitations inherent in existing approaches. This multiplicity of approaches combined with the recently emerging questions about writing guarantee the continuing vitality of empirical research in composition.

Forming Research Communities among Naturalistic Researchers

Lucy McCormick Calkins

There is a contradiction at the heart of what we as composition researchers do. We urge teachers to focus on the process as well as the product of writing, but *our* focus continues to be on the topics of research, and we give only cursory attention to methods. Courses titled Research in Composition are typically structured according to topical units: error analysis, writing development, computers, and so forth. If one peruses a stack of anthologies of writing research, each bearing a broad and definitive title such as *Writing, New Approaches to Composition*, or *Research on Writing*, one will predictably find that these texts deal with subjects rather than methods of research, with products rather than processes. Research articles usually devote, at best, a few paragraphs to explicating methodology. And although every composition researcher probably owns a host of books in which notable writers have described the heartache and euphoria, strategies and dead ends of their craft, most of us do not own a single book that gives similar treatment to *our* craft.

There is another contradiction we fail to see. We are quick to warn student writers against relying exclusively on composition textbooks, with their decontextualized definitions and rules, encouraging them to read personal accounts of writers and their writing, accounts that have the texture and complexity and tentativeness of reality (John Gardner, Welty, Paris Review *Interviews*, Murray, Elbow). We encourage teachers and students to keep similar accounts of their writing processes, sharing these with one another and in this way not only developing a vocabulary for talking about writing but also engaging in an ongoing dialogue with themselves and others about what works and what does not work for them as writers. Yet, as researchers, we rely on decontextualized definitions and rules about research methods and on snippets of generalized information such as one finds in the methodology section of research articles. We do not interview skilled researchers, observe them at work, or study novice and expert researchers so as to differentiate one from another. We do not ask prominent researchers in our field to provide personal, honest accounts of their research processes (accounts with the texture and complexity and tentativeness of reality), nor do we keep such accounts of our own emerging methods. Although research in composition is what we do, we rarely read or write about the process of research.

Until recently, writing received similar treatment, probably because we assumed that good writing flowed magically from talent, inspiration, and the poetic muse. But wheareas it once was the writing process that was shrouded in mythology, now it is the research process that is in need of demythologizing. Just as writers do not sit down, wait for inspiration, and then proceed automatically to produce perfect prose, so, too, researchers do not define a question and then proceed as day follows night to the obvious research method. This linear model of research—like the linear model of the composing process—is an oversimplification. And although many people still subscribe to the adage that research methods are determined by research questions, in the field of composition it is more accurate to say that research methods are created, combined, adapted, invented, and stumbled on—and that ideally they are chosen based on the researcher's personality and belief system. For this reason Harste argues, "Eclecticism in research and teaching is not only an illusion, but also dangerous" (223). Harste is not arguing against the eclecticism of technique in which researchers gather information through a combination of interview, survey, questionnaire, experiments, field observations, and the like, but he is arguing instead that beneath any research project there is an attitude about language and learning. How we do research, like how we teach, reflects our underlying assumptions about human nature and learning. This means not only that the decisions each person makes about research are deeply personal ones but also that widespread changes in research methodology signify fundamental changes in a field. This has certainly been true in composition research, where there has been, over the past fifteen years, a dramatic shift towards holistic, field-based, descriptive research. Few would argue that this shift both reflects and creates substantial changes in the field. Kenneth Kantor, Dan Kirby, and Judith Goetz, in an issue of *Research in the Teaching of English* devoted specifically to ethnography, begin their lead article saying:

> Whether you align yourself with the cynics who view the current popular ethnographic studies as one more passing research fad or with the ethno-evangelists who see field investigations as a panacea for all educational problems, you certainly cannot ignore its growing impact on research in education. . . . (293)

I have chosen to devote this chapter to a discussion of research methods because I believe this is a time of vulnerability as well as of potential for the new, variously titled holistic research methodologies. Those of us who care about these methods (and yes, I do believe one can care about methodologies) must rally to their cause. Then, too, I hope the chapter encourages others to open the shutters that have been so tightly closed around the real, human dramas of research, and I hope the taxonomy I suggest helps to forge learning communities among composition researchers.

Having said that researchers choose methodologies based, in part, on their belief systems, I must also say that researchers have been drawn to a naturalistic approach as much because of what it is not as because of what it is. In his influential article "Meaning in Context: Is There Any Other Kind?" Elliot Mishler looks critically at the traditional positivist methodology, with its search for universal, context-free laws and its use of context-stripping methods in which subjects are removed from their natural settings, roles, and social networks. Mishler suggests that this model is more appropriate for experiments testing different strains of corn or alfalfa than for studies of how children learn. Many English educators agree, and they suggest that the early reliance on positivist methodology grew from the educational research community's insecure efforts to achieve status among the hard science and laboratory psychologists. Farr and Weintraub support this belief by asking, "Who could possibly look down his scholarly nose at a field which employs 4-way multivariate analysis of variance in randomized Latin-Square designs?" (2).

Now, however, even experimental researchers in English education are questioning the uses and abuses of the positivist paradigm. In a recent critique of methodologies used in composition research, Bereiter and Scardemalia criticize variable testing research on a number of fronts ("Levels of Inquiry"). They point out, for example, that in order to test the premise that students who read good literature write well, one must specify a procedure for measuring "writes well" and "reads good literature." This means that if findings do not support the original premise, one cannot know whether it is the premise that does not hold or whether the procedures for determining "writes well" and "reads good literature" were faulty. Even if the findings do support the premise, one cannot know whether the implied causal relationship (for instance, good reading causes good writing) may in fact have resulted from some untested variable.

Perhaps the most forceful argument against the positivist paradigm, however, is that it has failed to have a lasting impact on classroom practices (Kantor, Kirby, and Goetz 294; Harste, Woodward, and Burke 222). Graves summarizes by saying:

Devoid of context, the data become sterile. One of the reasons teachers have rejected research information for so long is that they have been unable to transfer faceless data to the alive, inquiring faces of the children they teach the next morning. Furthermore, the language used to convey these data has the same voiceless tone that goes with the projection of faceless information. . . . This research is written for other researchers, promotions, or dusty archives in a language guaranteed for self extinction. ("A New Look" 918)

The enemy within our gates: A call for clarity

Naturalistic researchers are good at saying what we are not. We are vocal and clear in our opposition to the traditional positivist paradigm and, I want to argue, this has become our greatest weakness. We know what we oppose, but we do not know what we support. Our confusion is evident even in the labels used for our inquiry paradigm: it is variously titled humanistic, phenomenological, field-based, case-study, qualitative, descriptive, longitudinal, participant-observationist, holistic, ethnographic, hermeneutic, naturalistic, and so forth, and the decision of which title to use often appears to be random. For example, in Beach and Bridwell's anthology *New Directions in Composition*, the term "case study" is used to describe Cooper's analysis of the writing samples of four hundred freshman writers in terms of cohesion, end-stop punctuation errors, mean clause length, and the like (19–52) as well as to describe Newkirk's detailed description of the changes in one student's perceptions of good writing as gleaned from eight weeks of interviews, classroom observations, and product analysis. Then, too, Graves claims that his Atkinson study, "How Children Change as Writers," was not contextual enough to be labeled ethnographic, even though it involved three full-time researchers in two years of daily classroom observations, combined with extensive interviewing of children, their teachers, and sometimes their parents (*Writing* 72–95). Kantor, by contrast, defines ethnography through extensive references to his "ethnographic case study" in which he described himself as a poet-in-residence and in which he acted as "both a co-teacher and a co-student," collecting data for only two hours a week for one semester (78).

This confusion over terminology is not a superficial one, for it illustrates a deeper and significant confusion over methodology. Perhaps we have expended so much energy defending ourselves against "the enemy" outside our gates that we have failed to realize that the only real enemy is that which lurks within. If we do not know what it means to do a case study or an ethnographic study, how can we distinguish the good from the mediocre? At this point, we do not have rigorous standards or accepted examples of excellence and, as a result, the humanistic-naturalistic, case-study paradigm is earning itself a bad reputation. Indicative of this is Kantor et al.'s assumption that their readers view ethnography as either a research fad or a panacea for every educational woe ("Research in Context" 293). Even if we overlook this remark, it is hard not to notice when Alan Purves, a past president of the National Council of Teachers of English, makes a spurious reference to "so-called ethnographers" in his description of the tote-bags and T-shirt mentality of today's NCTE leadership (694). And unless precautions are taken, the current emphasis on teacher-as-researcher will probably fuel the problem as more anecdotal "research reports" are written in celebration of one teacher's classroom practices and of the way several students responded. This format has already become standard for articles in *Language Arts* (see the Nov. and Dec. 1984 issues). I am suggesting not that these articles are unimportant (I have, in fact, written a few myself) but only that we need to distinguish personal narratives from research and one category of humanistic–case-study–field-based research from another. Within each category, we need goals and examples of excellence. We need these not only to promote excellence but also to promote a sense of community.

Interestingly, in their prize-winning study *In Search of Excellence*, Peters and Waterman found that the most successful American companies were characterized by a strong, shared sense of mission and by several clear, succinct goals. It is unusual to suggest parallels between a company and a research method, for one is a working community and the other a way of working. But in his important book *Patterns of Discovery in the Social Sciences*, Diesing writes from the assumption that a research method can be described as a subculture—a company—involving people who interact regularly, using and arguing against one another's ideas. He states that within the subculture of a research method, people have common friends, acquaintances, intellectual ancestors, and opponents. Their interaction is facilitated by shared beliefs and values—goals, myths, terminology, self-concepts—and by impermissible errors, the proper subject matter, the heroic exemplars, and the unfortunate failures or pseudoscientific villains (18).

The humanistic–case-study researchers in our field belong to such a subculture only to the extent that we agree to disagree with the experimental tradition. They are the villains; theirs, the impermissible errors. Our common ancestors tend to be only those persons who forcefully disagree with the experimental tradition (Graves, "A New Look"; Guba, Mishler) or those who made the breakthrough from analyzing written products to describing writing processes (Emig, *Composing*; Graves, "Examination"; Stallard; Sommers, "Revision"; Perl, "Composing"; Flower and Hayes, "Cognition" and "Cognitive Process"). But within the tradition of descriptive case-study research, we do not have heroes and villains, we do not have impermissible errors or shared goals. In these areas, we would do well to follow the example of the experimental researchers in our field. They have formed a subculture for themselves and they dialogue about research processes. During the 1960s and 1970s, they studied their own and one another's methods and gained a much-needed sophistication in employing the experimental-hypothesis testing approach (Beach and Bridwell 7).

A taxonomy

The task, then, is not only to open the shutters that have been closed around the real, human stories of our research endeavors but also to forge a learning community among humanistic-descriptive ethnographic researchers. A first step might be for researchers to classify themselves into subcategories that are homogeneous enough for there to be a shared sense of goals yet broad enough for the sort of dialogue that comes from important differences. In the remainder of this chapter, I want to suggest three such categories. First, a word of caution. I am *creating* as well as *uncovering* these categories. They are not integral to the field; they are, instead, one way of seeing things. Others will see different units with the changing flux of writing research. The question is not whether these categories are "right" but whether they are useful. I have found it helpful to look at humanistic-naturalistic methods for studying composition in terms of these three subcategories: (1) descriptive case studies, (2) ethnographically oriented case studies, and (3) teaching case studies.

In descriptive case studies, subjects are asked to solve a carefully designed problem or to do a preselected task. Data customarily are gathered on a limited number of occasions (perhaps four to six), in somewhat controlled settings (away from the classroom), and in such a way (with video or audio tapes) that they can be rigorously analyzed (often through content analysis, coding, and categorizing).

In ethnographically oriented case studies, researchers become participant observers in a natural setting, spending at least a semester (and often a year or two) as live-in observers. Data are gathered through a range of methods, with overlapping information coming from field-based observations, formal and informal interviews, questionnaires, and analyses of written products. During data analysis, researchers look for patterns and plot lines in the data and for interrelations between the setting and the events. Portions of the final reports are often written as narratives.

In teaching case studies, the practitioner-researchers usually begin with tentative theories that inform their practices, and they observe the results of those practices. These observations lead them to revise or develop their initial ideas, and the resulting theories are again translated into practices. These new practices are described, the resulting learning behaviors are observed and studied, and this information again leads practitioner-researchers to revise, refine, or expand their teaching ideas. The cycle continues. Sometimes it is a live-in researcher who engages in this sort of research; sometimes it is a teacher or a team composed of teachers and researchers. Always, the purpose is to affect practice for those within the setting and for a wider community of practitioners. I describe this third category in some detail at the end of the chapter.

To clarify these subcategories, I have compiled a tentative list of studies that seem to fit into each category. I say "tentative" because this is not easily done: the labels of some studies make classification difficult, and some studies straddle two or more categories.

Descriptive case studies
Applebee, *Child's Concept*
Emig, *Composing*
Flower and Hayes, "Cognitive Process"
Harste, Woodward, and Burke
Newkirk, "Anatomy"
Perl, "Composing"
Shaughnessy, *Errors*
Sommers, "Revision"

Ethnographically oriented case studies
Heath
Calkins, *Lessons*
Dillon and Searle
Freedman
Graves, "Examination"
Hickman
Kantor
Nelson
Perl, "Composing"
Scribner and Cole
Szwed

Teaching case studies
Atwell, *In the Middle*
Calkins, "Children Learn"
Giacobbe
Graves, *Writing*
Hansen and Graves
Harste, Woodward, and Burke
Macrorie, *Twenty Teachers*
Milz

It seems to me that the seeds of each approach were present in the late 1960s and early 1970s when Graves and Emig conducted their breakthrough studies (Graves, "Examination"; Emig, *Composing*). Although both researchers used the generic term "case study" to describe their research, the two studies were methodologically very different. Emig's study paved the way for what I now describe as descriptive case study and Graves's paved the way for ethnographically oriented case studies. With his references to medical and psychiatric case studies, Graves laid the groundwork for teaching case studies (see fig. 2).

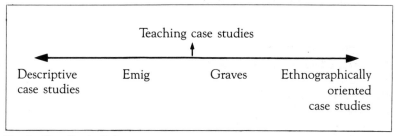

Fig. 2. Case-Study Relations

Descriptive and ethnographic case studies

Graves's and Emig's initial research projects continue to be important as breakthrough studies, as seeds for emerging research methods, but not as models. Researchers of both types—including Graves and Emig—have moved from these early studies to conduct more rigorous, more effective studies. I mention this because even today many doctoral students are "replicating" the methods of these early studies. This work is inappropriate, first, because case studies are meant to open the doors for other, broader-based studies rather than for replications, and second, because those early methods are no longer the best available models.

The strengths and limitations of today's ethnographic and descriptive case studies were evident even in the differences between Graves's and Emig's early studies. It is telling, for example, to note that although the two studies built on the same heritage, Emig's review of literature was approximately 8,000 words and Graves's a mere 1,000 words, more than half of which were devoted to summarizing Emig's study. While both Emig and Graves agreed that case-study research was new to the field of composition, Emig put her work into the context of accounts and correspondence by established writers, literary analysis, composing textbooks, empirical research on adolescents, and research into creative processes. Graves, by contrast, defended the case study as the method of choice for researchers venturing into unexplored territory. With this as the underlying rationale for his methodology, it is not surprising that in his review of literature, Graves does not stand on the shoulders of others but instead declares that there are no such available shoulders.

These differences, while striking, continue to be important today only because they illustrate an ongoing difference in emphasis between descriptive and ethnographically oriented case studies. Some—although by no means all—of the significant ethnographically oriented studies continue to be written as if there are no shoulders on which to stand. By contrast, the significant examples of descriptive case-study research are embedded in a strong theoretical context. For example, the authors of *Language Stories and Literacy Lessons* (which is based primarily on what I define as descriptive case-study work) spend almost as much time citing the work of other researchers as they do the work of their subjects. Harste, Woodward, and Burke introduce the book by quoting a reviewer who says, "This research is at once highly philosophical and enormously respectful of the concrete: observations of individual children, writings, drawings, conversations" (xviii). The authors are strong and clear in their emphasis on theory: "We wish to help educators get their theoretical act together; to move beyond cute, fun and soft" (xviii). It is characteristic, then, that in the chapter titled "Lessons from Latrice," Harste, Woodward, and Burke also include lessons from Halliday, Durkin, Applebee, Atwell, and other such scholars.

Similarly, Newkirk's descriptive case study of a freshman writer ("Anatomy of a Breakthrough") is set within the context of Calkins's study of children's revision ("Children's Rewriting") and Bereiter and Scardemalia's three-part model of revision ("Levels of Inquiry"). Newkirk relates his conclusions to the work of William James and Perry, includes a critical review of changes in research methodologies, and makes broad-reaching recommendations for the field: all this in an article-length case study of one freshman writer.

Although descriptive case studies that are not grounded in theory undoubtedly exist, these studies tend to be rather inconsequential. The same does not necessarily hold for ethnographically oriented case studies, where it is not unusual for researchers to give relatively little attention to placing their work within a theoretical context. This is true not only for composition researchers who employ the tools of ethnographers but also for some highly trained anthropologists. Powdermaker, in an autobiographical account of her four major ethnographic studies, never mentions studying related literature. In Liebow's ethnography of Negro street-corner men, the occasional footnotes are more apt to give street definitions of a word than to refer to another researcher's findings. Glazer's book *The Research Adventure* contains nine sections, none of which deals with theory building or with reviewing related literature.

It may not be surprising, then, that the only chapter that lacks a bibliography in Whiteman's anthology *Writing: Variation in Writing* is Szwed's "The Ethnography of Literacy." Similarly, Pettigrew, Shaw, and Van Nostrand do not place their study within a theoretical context but instead claim that there is no such context, that theirs is a pioneer work. This is their review of literature: "In the absence of an adequate historical data base, given these tasks, our research was necessarily exploratory. Lacking historical information, we formulated a few guiding questions and made decisions based on them" (330).

Although Kantor makes reference to research methods used by other ethnographers, once he moves from methodology to content, his references become scant and his theoretical framework thin. Neither of the books that are based on Graves, Sowers, and Calkins's two-year case study focus on the theoretical context for that study (Calkins, *Lessons*; Graves, *Writing*).

Some ethnographically oriented case-study researchers may argue that the inattention to theory is deliberate, that the goal of ethnography is "grounded theory" that comes bottom up from patterns in the data, rather than top-down from schema in the researcher's mind. However, there is not necessarily a contradiction between "grounded theory" and knowing related literature. A researcher *can* discover patterns in the data, drawing organizing concepts from the participant's own perceptions, while still seeing his or her work within a larger theoretical context. Shirley Brice Heath has done this in her book, and to a lesser degree, Dillon and Searle did this in their article. Some of the studies that have not done this have been criticized as being collections of anecdotes rather than research. Yet, there is no denying that, whereas a strong review of literature is essential for a good descriptive case study, even some of the best-known ethnographically oriented studies in composition have not given a great deal of attention to building a strong theoretical base. I am not suggesting that this should be so; I am only describing the reality as I see it. Of course, it would be ideal if every study did all things, but often there are trade-offs. Each form of research has its own ways of being contextual, and while descriptive researchers attend more to the theoretical context in which they work, ethnographic researchers attend more to the social, physical context in which their subjects work and live.

It follows then, that there are important differences in the data-collection methods used in descriptive and in ethnographically oriented case studies. Again, these differences were evident even between Graves's and Emig's early works. I have noted that while Emig's review of literature was approximately 8,000 words, Graves's was 1,000. A comparison of the length of Graves's and Emig's data-collection sections reveals an inverse relation. Whereas Graves devotes approximately 7,000 words to a section labeled "Data Collection," Emig does not have a section bearing such a title, and the closest equivalent is an 800-word section entitled "Design of the Study." The differences continue.

Researchers in the category of descriptive case study tend to gather slice-of-time data. Instead of observing her eight case-study subjects longitudinally and in natural settings, Emig gave each subject assigned writing tasks and then asked them to compose aloud. Although Harste, Woodward, and Burke (who sometimes describe themselves as ethnographers) would probably criticize Emig's methods as acontextual, I categorize the bulk of their research as descriptive case studies because they, too, collected slice-of-time data (52–53). They videotaped several children's problem-solving, problem-finding work on twenty predesigned "task settings." For example, each child was asked to draw his or her self-portrait and to write his or her name, and data were collected through two remote-control video cameras. Applebee's study of young children and their storytelling also falls into this category, for Applebee collected extensive data on children's responses to predesigned task settings.

Although these task settings may seem acontextual, researchers in this category go to great lengths to select purposeful and natural tasks. Harste et al. strongly advocate that researchers gather data through "open-ended real language situations" (51). They define real language situations as "functional instances of language where all language systems (graphophonemic, syntactic, semantic, pragmatic) in the event are allowed to transact with the other communication systems (i.e., art, music, math, gesture, drama, etc.) which naturally co-occur in the setting" (51).

Likewise, Newkirk is critical of the research tasks devised by Flower and Hayes, in which students are asked to "Write about your job for the readers of *Seventeen* magazine." Newkirk comments, "It is at least possible, though, that the assignment was so artificial that the inexperienced writers did not demonstrate the planning ability they normally use" ("Anatomy" 146). Of course, ethnographically oriented researchers might argue that the differences between Flower and Hayes's assignment and the assignments posed by Harste, Newkirk, and Applebee are minor and that in none of these instances are investigators in a position to understand the points of view and behavioral patterns of their subjects as they live and work in their natural settings. Clearly, the data-collection methods of ethnographically oriented case-study researchers differ markedly from those of the descriptive researchers.

While Graves, along with other ethnographically oriented case-study researchers, may gather some data through systematic slice-of-time interventions, these data become only one part of a kaleidoscope of converging data. For his dissertation, Graves spent five months collecting data from a study of written products, from 250 hours of unstructured classroom observations, and from formal and informal interviews with the eight case-study children and with their teachers. In the years since Graves and Emig did their breakthrough studies, researchers in both groups have extended data-collection methods. There have been several different lines of advancement in descriptive case study. Some researchers have been refining data-collection methods so that the information is more detailed and precise. Flower and Hayes, for example, have developed sophisticated ways to use protocol analysis, a technique borrowed from cognitive psychology, to understand the problem-finding, problem-solving behavior of writers. Perl developed an elaborate coding scheme for recording sequence and length of every minute behavior in a composing episode. Berkenkotter has found ways to adapt Flower and Hayes' use of composing-aloud protocols so that the information is gathered in natural settings. Harste et al. offset one kind of data with another, so that data gathered through "task settings" are balanced by data gathered through longitudinal observations in classroom settings.

In ethnographically oriented case studies the single greatest change in data-collection methods comes because researchers are deliberately employing tools of ethnography. Let me clarify. Although I have spoken of Graves's dissertation as ethnographically oriented, it is more appropriate to talk of that study as a precursor to today's ethnographically oriented research projects. In the early 1970s, it was enough of a breakthrough for researchers to observe the act of writing; very few in the field of composition were consciously employing ethnographic tools.

Over time, studies within this sector have become more ethnographic.

Some identify with the title "ethnography," but many skirt it by claiming only to use ethnographic tools. Some, like Graves himself, avoid the word altogether. It is difficult to understand why some studies are labeled ethnographic and others are not. Perhaps labels are not important. What does seem important, however, is that especially because these researchers often choose not to draw on a theoretical framework, they would be wise to avoid also cutting themselves off from a methodological framework. Anthropologists have highly developed ways to learn about the points of view and the behavioral patterns of participants within a culture. It seems senseless for us, out of our respect for "purity," to refrain from borrowing the anthropologists' methods and adapting them to the constraints and purposes of our work.

Some claim that when composition researchers call themselves ethnographers they are putting on airs. This may sometimes be true, but could it not also be true that when composition researchers take ethnography as their goal, they provide themselves with needed standards for measurement and criteria for excellence? Although few composition researchers will conduct true ethnographies, because of the amount of time involved (usually one to three years of field study), it seems important that researchers conducting ethnographically oriented case studies look to rigorous ethnographies as their models and recognize the compromises they make on that model. Too often, ethnographically oriented composition researchers model themselves after other ethnographically oriented composition researchers, with each new study building on, and inheriting the limitations of, the previous studies. The results look like Xerox copies of Xerox copies of Xerox copies.

Ethnographically oriented composition researchers would do well, then, to use annotated bibliographies of ethnographic source books, such as that in Hammersty and Atkinson's recent *Ethnography: Principles in Practice*, and to read the classic references on ethnography, such as Agar's *The Professional Stranger* and Spradley's *The Ethnographic Interview*. Although methods for reviewing the relevant literature and for data collection in descriptive case studies differ from those in ethnographic case studies, data analysis is equally crucial in both research categories. It is no surprise that both Graves and Emig in their early work devote a great deal of attention to data analysis. If they had not done so, the studies would not be regarded as exemplary. Without this final part of the equation, there is no research at all.

Data analysis is particularly problematic in ethnographically oriented case studies. In descriptive and experimental research, many of the decisions are made before data collection begins. When the data begin coming in,

they fit easily into preordained categories. In ethnographically oriented research, fewer decisions are made beforehand, and the data arrive in a chaos
of shapes and sizes. Unfortunately, very little has been written to guide
ethnographic researchers in their data analysis and writing. Hammersty
and Atkinson comment:

> One of the noticeable features about textbooks on field methods is
> that, by and large, the further one progresses through the research
> process, the less explicit commentary and advice they have to offer.
> They usually have a good deal to say about pre-fieldwork stages and
> the critical phases of data collection: finding and "casing" a research
> setting, negotiating access, first days in the field . . . and similar
> topics are generously covered. Later stages of fieldwork are much less
> visible. . . . With one or two exceptions (Spradley and Lofland) most
> authors are all but silent on the activity of writing an ethnography.
> (203)

It is hardly surprising, then, that other than the constraints imposed by
conducting ethnography in haste, the second most common problem area
in the ethnographically oriented composition studies is the stage of data
analysis and writing. The problems are many. Frequently, researchers simply use their data as a pool from which to draw theories and supportive
anecdotes, never dealing with the data bank as a whole. When the data
bank is dipped into rather than dealt with, it is easy to ignore exceptional
cases and problematic loose ends. Researchers end up illustrating their
preconceived ideas rather than documenting patterns in the data. Furthermore, they miss out on opportunities to learn. Consider what Peter Elbow
has to say in *Writing with Power*:

> For this is how new and better ideas arrive. They don't come out
> of the blue. They come from noticing difficulties with what you be-
> lieved, small details or particular cases that don't fit what otherwise
> feels right. The mark of the person who can actually make progress
> in thinking—who can sit down at 8:30 with one set of ideas and stand
> up at 11 with better ideas—is a willingness to notice and listen to these
> inconvenient little details, these annoying loose ends, these embar-
> rassments and puzzles, instead of impatiently sweeping them under
> the rug. A good new idea looks obvious and inevitable after it is all
> worked out and the dust has settled, but in the beginning it just feels
> annoying and the wrong old idea feels persuasively correct. (131–32)

Then, too, many ethnographically oriented researchers seem to want the
final products to look as if they came from survey research. Their final
reports consist of broad categories, counts, and labels. Although it is appropriate for ethnographers to categorize their data, the goals of ethnogra-

phy should include finding interrelations and telling a story. Davis goes so far as to say, "I do think it is essential that you try somehow to find some kind of story" (209), and Hymes says, "Instead of thinking of narrative accounts as an early stage that in principle will be replaced, we may need to think of them as a permanent stage, whose principles are little understood, and whose role may increase" (16).

Geertz's description of Balinese cock fighting provides other ethnographically oriented researchers with a particularly strong model of the power of the narrative. Hymes describes what Geertz has done, saying:

> Through his narrative skill, Geertz is able to convey a sense (mediated by his personal involvement) of the quality and texture of Balinese fascination with cock-fighting. Evidence of the fascination is important. . . . A film might help too, but it would need something verbal from Geertz to teach us what we should learn from it. The narrative part of Geertz's article in effect paints, as the narrator of a film might do, and also in absence of a film, shows. It does so through texture and proportion. (16)

In the field of composition, only a few ethnographically oriented case studies contain a balance between concepts and concrete details, between universals and particulars. Only a few weave their findings into a strong narrative thread (Heath, *Ways*; Bissex; Calkins, *Lessons*).

Teaching case study

But what of the third category, the teaching case study? What are the norms and goals within this research tradition and how do the methods differ from those used by ethnographic and descriptive case-study researchers? What are the models of excellence and criteria for success in teaching case studies?

There are no agreed-on answers to these questions. Although investigators within each of the categories I have described differ on the priorities and norms of their research subcultures, this is particularly true within the category of teaching case studies. Within this one category, investigators operate under totally different interpretations of their research methods.

Some think that teaching case studies involve a stage of study (reviewing related literature, promising practices, and past research) through which tentative theories are developed. These are then put into practice and revised against incoming data. Others describe teaching case studies without mentioning either reviewing related literature or developing a theory.

Instead, they stress devising a teaching technique and field-testing it in the classroom, often by documenting several students' responses to it.

Although these interpretations of teaching case studies are radically different, there appears to be no discussion of the conflict. This may be because practitioner-researchers are more apt to analyze their teaching practices than their research methods. Then, too, practitioner-researchers may not identify with one another enough to recognize similarities and differences among themselves. Instead of seeing the teaching case study as a viable methodology, with its own history and traditions, these teacher-researchers often view themselves as approximations of more "pure and scientific" research traditions. What this does, in effect, is to isolate them from all research communities. It is as if these practitioner-researchers are saying, "You can't expect me to do real ethnography," and in saying this, they claim themselves to be without peer group, or models, or realistic standards. When practitioner-researchers take themselves, their research methods, and one another seriously, they will realize they have a peer group (one another) and exemplary models from both within and outside the field of composition. They also have controversies, for the group is a divided one.

The most obvious difference of opinion focuses on how strong a theoretical context teaching case studies must have. Currently in English education, it seems fashionable to downplay the need for practitioner-researchers to study related literature. Donald Gallehr, director of the Northern Virginia Writing Project and of a teacher-as-researcher funded project, reports in the project newsletter, "Graves confirms our inclination to pursue our research questions initially without an extensive reading of previously conducted research. Teacher/consultants already know an enormous amount about writing, students, and writing instruction, and their own intuitions and curiosity are their best point of departure" (6).

Similarly, in "The Classroom Teacher as Researcher" Odell omits reviewing literature from his list of the stages involved in practitioner research. Only once in this six-page article does Odell even mention the importance of reading related literature, and this reference does not have the ring of conviction: "Sometimes a little reading or a conversation with a colleague can suggest new ways to proceed. But as often as not, we already know useful things for students to do, read, look at, talk about" (106). Although Mayher and Brause give some attention to the need for studying "multiple sources," the sources listed are introspective analyses of classroom approaches, reflection on processes involved in teachers' selection of vocabulary items, curriculum guides, teacher manuals, and so on, with no mention of the need for extensive reading of the best available published work on the topic (1008).

Many recent publications on teachers as researchers begin with the assumption that teachers do not read research—and the implication is that they are wise to avoid it. Graves states in his critique of educational research, "One reason teachers have rejected research information for so long is that they have been unable to transfer faceless data to the alive, inquiring faces of the children they teach. . . . Furthermore, the language used to convey these data has the same voiceless tone . . . " ("New Look" 918). Similarly, Odell's article begins:

> For some teachers—in public school and in college—the term *research* is almost a dirty word. It conjures up images of university types, secure in their ivory towers . . . providing equivocal answers to questions nobody was very interested in anyway. Moreover, the term reminds us of tedious prose. . . . Little wonder that both experienced and prospective teachers express some dissatisfaction at the suggestion that they read some research (106).

Mohr also begins similarly. Her second paragraph reads:

> I shared a general teacher prejudice against educational research. Teachers do not have much time to read research journals and when they do, they are too tired to plow through jargon, charts and statistics. . . . They read results from matched sets of controls and experimental groups and shrug, aware of the multitude of variables operating in any classroom.

Although it is certainly true that most teachers do not read educational research, it is wrong to assume that research in the field of composition has little to offer practitioner-researchers. Research in composition is not always written in tedious prose, filled with charts and numbers, nor is such research worthless. Practitioner-researchers would do well especially to read descriptive and ethnographic case-study research reports and to know the major scholars in their own areas of interest. Are we not patronizing teachers when we assume they will not study literature that relates to their field of study?

Curiously enough, pleas for a solid grounding in theory are coming not from the university but from the classroom. Nancie Atwell, for example, emphasizes that the link between the teacher-as-practitioner and the teacher-as-researcher is the teacher-as-scholar. She describes the teacher-as-researcher project she led in Boothbay, Maine, this way: "Working together to develop a theoretically sound, research based writing curriculum, we are writing, studying our writing, reading writing theory and research findings, . . . and conducting research" ("Class-Based" 84).

At Teachers College, the thirty teachers who have received research support from the Edwin Gould Foundation meet weekly to discuss exemplary articles written by other teacher-researchers, to compile a bibliography of readings that relate to their fields of interest, and to study the methodologies used by eminent composition researchers. A team of teacher-researchers from the Scarsdale public schools wrote a thirty-five-page review of literature before engaging in their study of students' perceptions of good writing.

Readers may want to conclude that some teaching case studies are more theoretically rigorous than others (as some studies will be in any research area), but I believe such a conclusion averages out a tension that is fundamental to teaching case studies. Within this category, two views coexist. These views are as different from each other as the experimental tradition is from the holistic case-study tradition. A large percentage of the studies conducted by teacher-researchers involves field-testing a teaching idea, and these projects are radically different from those that involve developing, implementing, and revising a theory.

In field-testing research, a practitioner develops a new idea (a method for teaching vocabulary, a way of responding to student writing, etc.), applies it in a classroom (usually his or her own), and documents the results. Proponents of this approach argue that in the traditional research-and-development process, in which researchers produce findings that are passed on to curriculum specialists or publishers who then create and field-test products, teachers are passive recipients only. Teachers are the receptacles at the end of a linear research-and-development process. When teachers conduct method-testing research, however, they produce the teaching ideas (the products) and field-test them in their classrooms.

This idea is appealing, for it enfranchises teachers. But does it enfranchise them as researchers or as curriculum specialists? Is this research or is it product testing? When publishers field-test a workbook series, we do not call what they do research. Why do we call it research when someone field-tests the notion of writing response groups and concludes they work? And if this is research, surely it is a poor version of the positivist methods that Mishler suggests are more appropriate for studies of different strains of corn and alfalfa than for investigations into how children learn. Granted, if practitioner-researchers choose to employ the experimental paradigm, there is no reason to argue against this decision, but more often than not, the method-testing studies are labeled "case studies" and statistical data are not collected. The studies, then, are neither experimental nor descriptive nor ethnographic. For field-testing "research" to be well-done, the investigators must truly begin with a question. More often, the investigator is already convinced that the teaching idea is an exemplary one, and the project becomes more like a show-and-tell session than research.

Finally, it seems to me that when practitioner-researchers merely field-test a technique (even one as child-centered as authors' circles or response groups) and then use examples to proclaim, "It works," they are taking the atheoretical stance of teachers who build lesson plans out of a hodge-podge of "neat ideas" picked up at exercise-swapping sessions. Each of these neat ideas "works" too — but toward what goal, for what reason, and with what implications for those of us interested in the teaching of writing? If research is to inform practice — and this is the goal of teaching case studies — then the guiding questions must be not only, "Does it work?" but also, "What are we working toward?" The goal must be not only method testing but also the development, assessment, and revision of theories that inform practice. If the ultimate goal is to learn to teach wisely and well, surely this research involves serious study.

It is ironic that in the field of composition, teaching case studies are often divorced from theory building. Historically, the method has been used to illustrate rich and broad-reaching theoretical schemes. When Graves pioneered the use of case study in composition research, he claimed that his methodology was borrowed from the fields of psychology and, in a sense, it was. Freud's work is conveyed through case study, as is the work of Erik Erikson and of Bruno Bettelheim. But their methods and goals did not resemble Graves's, or those of Emig, Stallard, Sommers, Perl, and so on. Instead, the work of these psychologists provides a grand and compelling model for the practitioner-researchers in our field.

Graves — and ethnographic and descriptive case-study researchers since him — raised a question, selected several subjects (students in someone else's classroom), and observed them systematically in order to describe what they do when they write. Freud, Erikson, and Bettelheim, by contrast, were practicing clinicians. Through working with patients and through related study they developed theories that informed their practices. They also acted as researchers, observing their own work and the results of it and letting these observations guide them as they studied. This constant interaction between practice, reflection, and study led them to flesh out and refine their theories. Then, in order to teach these theories to others, they wrote case-study reports. Each case report is used, finally, as a teaching device. Each case report provides a forum for integrating theory and practice. Just as case reviews in medical school prompt physicians to bring all they know to bear on a single patient's case, so, too, case reports in psychotherapy allow clinicians to integrate all they know and believe around the story of a particular person, a particular event. The goal of the case report is not only to learn but also to teach. Through focused, detailed reports, readers come to understand the theories that guide these practitioner-researchers.

What a contrast this theory-building approach presents to the product-testing model—and what a challenge it offers to practitioner-researchers in our field. Of course, we need not look only to psychotherapy and medicine for models of the teaching case study. We can look also to Vera Milz's work with first graders in Bloomfield, Michigan, to Marilyn Boutwell's work with third graders in Atkinson, New Hampshire, to Donald Graves's *Writing: Teachers and Children at Work*, to Ken Macrorie's *Searching Writing* and *Twenty Teachers*, to Nancie Atwell's work with eighth graders in Boothbay, Maine ("Class-Based"). Each of these practitioner-researchers is engaged in developing and illustrating theories that inform his or her practices. The researchers are asking not only, "What works?" but also, "What, ultimately, do I believe about language and learning?" For example, Nancie Atwell's forthcoming book *In the Middle* will begin with a chapter called "Learning How to Teach," in which she describes how her case studies of eighth graders led her to revise the assumptions that once governed her classroom practices. This chapter is followed by one titled "Making the Best of Adolescence," in which Atwell sets her beliefs about teaching and literacy into a developmental framework. The book continues in this way, with theory and practice woven together in the text just as they are in the work of Freud, Erikson, Bettelheim, and other practitioner-researchers.

Once Atwell has finished *In the Middle*, perhaps she will write another book, this one telling the real, human drama of what it is like to be in the middle, shuttling between research and practice, between scholar and teacher. Fifteen years ago, Graves and Emig created a tremendous breakthrough for the field of composition because they pulled their chairs alongside of students, in order to observe and understand how students learn to write. The time has come for another breakthrough.

Cognitive Studies and Teaching Writing

Andrea A. Lunsford

Two thousand years ago, Cicero directed one of his verbal volleys in the direction of the Platonic separation of thought and language, arguing that to send students to one teacher (the rhetor or orator) to learn how to speak well but to another teacher (the philosopher) to learn how to think well was patently absurd. In making this charge, Cicero was of course upholding the essentially interdisciplinary nature of classical rhetoric, but his arguments could not reverse the trend toward specialization of knowledge. Today, we see the results of our love of specialization: students now go to one department to learn to write, to another to read, to another to learn to speak, and to still others to learn to "think." Yet all is not well in the house that specialization built. Indeed, some signs now indicate that the house is at last to be renovated in a way that will encourage if not demand reestablishing and maintaining interdisciplinary concerns.

In a recent article, Robert de Beaugrande bemoans the fact that "scientific fragmentation has been the usual state of affairs in America. Psychologists believed that behavior could be explained with no regard to the human mind. Linguists asserted that language must be studied independently of everything else, . . . and so forth" ("Psychology and Composition" 211–12). But Beaugrande sees some reason for cautious optimism that the new interdisciplinary field of cognitive science might work against such fragmentation and, in fact, formulate a general theory of cognition and communication (see also Kintsch and Vipond; Schank and Abelson) on which instruction in discourse could build. Beaugrande further argues that interdisciplinary studies, or what he calls "interdependencies," are vital for the study of discourse processing and production (reading and writing). Of course, such an interdisciplinary enterprise will meet with considerable difficulties, since interdisciplinary research is arguably much harder to carry out than the more traditional kinds, which are also more widely accepted. As Kintsch, Miller, and Polson note in a recently published volume of essays, "Effective cooperation across disciplines takes more patience, tolerance, and good sense than scientific cooperation always does. . . . But . . . cognitive science is based on the belief that crossing the boundaries of traditional disciplines is not merely possible but indeed essential in the study of cognition" (ix).

Cognitive science thus holds out the hope of meeting the challenge posed by Cicero to reunite the arts of thinking and discoursing and hence holds great potential interest for those of us who teach writing and reading. But just what does this new field comprise? Miller, Polson, and Kintsch say that "the conglomerate that makes up cognitive science includes portions of psychology, artificial intelligence, and linguistics, as well as anthropology, philosophy, and neuroscience" (1), and I would add rhetoric and composition studies as well. Since this is not the place for a discussion of the origins of cognitive science or for an analysis of the considerable opposing forces within the field (see Beaugrande, "Psychology and Composition"; Miller, Polson, Kintsch), suffice it to note George Mandler's contention that "the various disciplines became 'cognitive' more or less simultaneously and in parallel, and . . . the Artificial Intelligence field emerged— independently—at about the same time. The time was the second half of the sixth decade of the twentieth century" (305–06).

The last twenty years have thus seen the emergence of a group of cognitive sciences that build bridges between disciplines in order to work toward a general theory of cognition and communication. It is no coincidence, I think, that the same twenty-year period has witnessed a remarkable revival of interest in rhetoric, with its ancient interdisciplinary framework relating thought, language, and action (see Lunsford and Ede, "Classical Rhetoric"), as well as the tremendous growth of computer studies and work in artificial intelligence, all of which demand interdisciplinary work.

Indeed, the importance of an interdisciplinary perspective can hardly be overemphasized, because such a perspective by definition broadens horizons and expands parochial or extremely narrow methodological and philosophical points of view. While strong disagreements, particularly over methodologies, do exist, some equally strong epistemological assumptions currently serve to unite disciplines. Primary among these is the recognition, in fields as diverse as anthropology, physics, philosophy, linguistics, and artificial intelligence, that shared social construction of reality takes place through a complex matrix of peculiarly human activities, which are linked by the interplay of thought and language. Also uniting the various disciplines that fall under the general heading of cognitive sciences is the search for answers to the following questions: how does human cognition develop? what is the relation among language, social interaction, and knowledge? how is knowledge represented in various symbolic modes?

In establishing a firm interdisciplinary base, current cognitive and rhetorical studies have simply confirmed what writing teachers have always intuitively known: that writing *must* be related to thinking, speaking, and reading and that the communicative arts simply cannot be neatly divided up in the classroom. This intuitive knowledge I believe accounts for writing teachers' intense interest in cognitive studies and for at least some of the impact such studies have had on our field. But theoretical and methodological differences, as I noted earlier, abound, and so many issues are unresolved that simply following, much less assessing, the contributions of cognitive studies presents a formidable task for writing teachers. The effort is worthwhile, however, and in the remainder of this chapter I wish to review the theories of representative cognitive developmentalists before turning to the work of several contemporary researchers who are applying work in cognitive studies to writing and reading. I close by setting out some implications for teaching and by outlining areas for further research.

Cognitive-developmental theorists

The work of Swiss psychologist Jean Piaget is of particular significance to our field in that it represents a turning away from the rigid focus of behaviorism and logical empiricism and toward the ways in which people "know" the world and hence construct both knowledge and reality. For Piaget, knowing is an action or, more explicitly, an *inter*action between the self and its environment, and development occurs as we alter mental structures in order to make sense out of the world. Piaget categorizes this mental development basically into four "stages": the sensori-motor stage, the preoperational stage, the concrete-operational stage, and the formal operational stage, which is characterized by the ability to abstract, synthesize, and form coherent, logical relations (*Construction of Reality, Language and Thought, Six . . . Studies*). At the stage of concrete operations, the child's thought is still closely linked to concrete data; completely representational, hypothetical thought still eludes the child. As the child moves through the stages of cognitive development, he or she relies less and less on such concrete data and direct physical experiences and more and more on general, abstract, representational systems (Inhelder and Piaget). Accompanying the child's reorganization of mental structures is the process of "de-centering," a process further defined by Lee Odell as "getting outside one's own frame of reference, understanding the thoughts, values, feelings of another person; . . . projecting oneself into unfamiliar circumstances, whether factual or hypothetical, . . . learning to understand why one reacts as he does to experience" ("Teaching" 455). Although a child first begins to "de-center" as early as the preoperational stage, egocentricity is still strong in the concrete stage, and, indeed, we apparently continue the process of "de-centering" throughout our lives as we move into unfamiliar tasks and environments. Learning, according to Piaget, occurs when the child is "de-centered" enough to resolve discrepancies between old and new information and thus to break "disequilibration" through assimilation and accommodation.

Although the Russian psychologist Lev Vygotsky reacts against a number of Piaget's conclusions, he agrees that children move through identifiable stages of cognitive development: the initial syncretic stage, in which "word meaning denotes nothing more to the child than a vague synthetic conglomeration of individual objects that have . . . coalesced into an image"; the "thinking in complexes" stage during which "thought . . . is already coherent and objective . . . although it does not reflect objective relationships in the same way as conceptual thinking"; and the true concept-formation stage (59–61). Vygotsky cautions, however, that

> even after the adolescent has learned to produce concepts, . . . he does not abandon the more elementary forms; they continue for a long time to operate, indeed to predominate, in many areas of his thinking. . . . The transitional character of adolescent thinking becomes especially evident when we observe the actual functioning of the newly acquired concepts. Experiments specially devised to study the adolescent's operations bring out . . . a striking discrepancy between his ability to form concepts and his ability to define them. (79)

Vygotsky goes on to distinguish between "spontaneous" concepts, those that are formed as a result of ordinary, day-to-day experiences, and "scientific" concepts, which are formed largely in conjunction with instruction. The student described by Vygotsky is able to formulate spontaneous concepts but not able to remove him- or herself from them, abstract from them, or define them into scientific concepts.

The relation of Vygotsky's "thinking in complexes" stage and "spontaneous-concept formation" stage to Piaget's concrete stage is clear, as is the movement from concrete to more abstract, general forms of concept formation. The work of Piaget and Vygotsky is highly provocative for those interested in the teaching of writing, because writing demands the ability to think abstractly and "formally" and because their work suggests that instruction is indeed a significant factor in development. On the whole, the influence of the Piagetian approach to language learning on our field has, I think, been positive, primarily because it clearly links thought, language, and action and because it is constructive. That is to say, Piaget recognizes that development must include constructing our own realities.

It is not yet clear, however, whether such developmental stages are universal or how directly applicable such developmental frameworks are. In *Children's Minds* Margaret Donaldson demonstrates, for example, that children's developmental levels are not static, that they vary according to the task undertaken as well as to the familiarity or unfamiliarity of that task. In *Frames of Mind* Howard Gardner notes that the

> undeniable strengths, which have made Piaget *the* theorist of cognitive development, cohabit with certain weaknesses that have become increasingly clear over the past two decades. First of all, while Piaget has painted a redoubtable picture of development, it is still only one sort of development. Centered on the intellectual agenda addressed by the young scientist, Piaget's model of development assures relatively less importance in non-Western and pre-literate contexts and may, in fact, be applicable only to a minority of individuals, even in the West. (20)

In our own field, Mina Shaughnessy cautioned that while teachers of writing should read Piaget, they should also realize that "no effort has yet been made to determine how accurately the developmental model Piaget describes for children fits the experience of the young adult learning to write for college" ("Basic Writing" 166). In particular, Shaughnessy pointed to Robert Selman's 1975 review of Furth and Wach's *Thinking Goes to School*, in which he describes the difficulties inherent in applying Piaget's theory to education (166).

Others, such as J. Kurfiss, argue that Piaget's work is indeed applicable to college-age students, who are often not yet

> formal thinkers, capable of using purely verbal, symbolic, abstract process to understand what is presented to them. . . . [The] use of formal operations by entering freshmen, at least as measured by traditional Piagetian tasks, may be the exception rather than the rule. Many freshmen . . . may reason formally in limited areas, in areas which interest them and where they have experience, or they may use a mix of concrete and formal strategies. ("Intellectual" 9–10)

Kurfiss's work ("Sequentiality and Structure") as well as that of McKinnon and of McKinnon and Renner support the applicability of the Piagetian model, the McKinnon and Renner study reporting that in 1971 fifty percent of the entering students at an Oklahoma university were operating only at Piaget's concrete level of thought.

In spite of this controversy, or perhaps because of it, writing teachers and researchers have not worked out any systematic application of Piagetian theory, and such a systematic application would have to overcome

problems noted by Shaughnessy as well as the fact that Piaget's work focuses primarily on skills associated with the natural sciences and
mathematics. Articles by Odell ("Piaget") and Lunsford ("Cognitive Development") make limited extrapolations from Piaget's theory, however, and
the work of Barritt and Kroll sets out a rationale for applying Piaget's theory to composition research. The concept of "de-centering," with its obvious relation to rhetorically based concerns for audience, has perhaps
generated the most discussion among teachers of writing. In "Cognitive
Egocentrism and the Problem of Audience Awareness in Written Discourse,"
Kroll makes the connection between Piagetian theory and composition
teaching explicit, as do articles by Rubin and Piche and by Scardemalia,
Bracewell, and Bereiter. But a theory capable of describing identifiable stages
of writing development *during the college years* eludes us, a fact to which
I will return.

While not exclusively concerned with cognitive development, the works
of William Perry and Lawrence Kohlberg deserve mention here because
they are often linked with Piagetian "stage" theory and because they have
provoked a great deal of discussion among those interested in higher education. In *Forms of Intellectual and Ethical Development in the College Years*,
Perry posits nine developmental "positions" through which we move on
our way to intellectual and ethical maturity: dualism and its modification
(positions 1–3), the realization of relativism (positions 4–6), and the evolution of commitment (positions 7–9). In "Cognitive and Ethical Growth:
The Making of Meaning," Perry includes figure 3 as illustrative of his
scheme.

As Perry's figure reveals, students at the dualist position tend to divide
meaning into two categories: good and bad, right and wrong, and so on.
They believe that right answers exist somewhere "out there" and posit
agency in others, especially in authorities. At the multiplicity position, students believe that everyone has a right to his or her own opinion and accept this diversity of values uncritically, while at the relativism positions
they engage in comparison, analysis, and evaluation of values or opinions.
By the time students reach the commitment positions, they can affirm
choices or decisions while still aware of relativism; they now posit agency
within themselves (89–95).

Like Piaget's stages, Perry's positions move from the concrete to the increasingly abstract, and while his original student sample has been criticized (Harvard students, all male), Perry at least studied college-age students,
and his original findings have been generally validated both by his own
further studies as well as by Kurfiss ("Late Adolescent Development") and
Clinchy and Zimmerman. Relatively few attempts have been made to ap-

Fig. 3. Scheme of Cognitive and Ethical Development

Dualism modified | **Relativism discovered** | **Commitments in relativism developed** (left margin vertical labels)

Position 1	Authorities know, and if we work hard, read every word, and learn Right Answers, all will be well.
Transition	But what about those Others I hear about? And different opinions? And Uncertainties? Some of our own Authorities disagree with each other or don't seem to know, and some give us problems instead of Answers.
Position 2	True Authorities must be Right, the others are frauds. We remain Right. Others must be different and Wrong. Good Authorities give us problems so we can learn to find the Right Answer by our own independent thought.
Transition	But even Good Authorities admit they don't know all the answers *yes!*
Position 3	Then some uncertainties and different opinions are real and legitimate *temporarily*, even for Authorities. They're working on them to get to the Truth.
Transition	But there are *so many* things they don't know the Answers to! And they won't for a long time.
Position 4a	Where Authorities don't know the Right Answers, everyone has a right to his own opinion; no one is wrong!
Transition *(and/or)*	But some of my friends ask me to support my opinions with facts and reasons.
Transition	Then what right have They to grade us? About what?
Position 4b	In certain courses Authorities are not asking for the Right Answer; They want us to *think* about things in a certain way, *supporting* opinion with data. That's what they grade us on.
Transition	But this "way" seems to *work* in most courses, and even outside them.
Position 5	Then *all* thinking must be like this, even for Them. Everything is relative but not equally valid. You have to understand how each context works. Theories are not Truth but metaphors to interpret data with. You have to think about your thinking.
Transition	But if everything is relative, am I relative too? How can I know I'm making the Right Choice?
Position 6	I see I'm going to have to make my own decisions in an uncertain world with no one to tell me I'm Right.
Transition	I'm lost if I don't. When I decide on my career (or marriage or values) everything will straighten out.
Position 7	Well, I've made my first Commitment!
Transition	Why didn't that settle everything?
Position 8	I've made several commitments, I've got to balance them — how many, how deep? How certain, how tentative?
Transition	Things are getting contradictory. I can't make logical sense out of life's dilemmas.
Position 9	This is how life will be. I must be wholehearted while tentative, fight for my values yet respect others, believe my deepest values right yet be ready to learn. I see that I shall be retracing this whole journey over and over — but, I hope, more wisely.

ply Perry's scheme to writing classes (see Hays, "The Development of Discursive Maturity"), though Krupa provides a rationale for doing so: "Perry's model of development matters to us finally as teachers of writing because it shows us how our work connects with the full human growth of our students. I think most of us have long been convinced that something important sometimes happens inside freshmen in our writing classes; what Perry gives us is the shape and features of that something" (20). Certainly, Perry's insistence that we deal with the whole student during his or her college years has influenced current thinking among composition researchers and teachers who are intent on using writing as a means of developing thinking and reasoning skills. But as Patricia Bizzell notes in a recent essay, such development is by definition value-laden, and we must ask *what* value systems are developing along with communicative skills. As Bizzell notes, Perry

> gives us a perspective on all college teachers as, in effect, rhetors [who] . . . persuade students to our values through our use of language, in lectures, textbooks, informal discussions, and writing assignments. . . . Some college teachers may not be comfortable with the view of themselves as rhetors, preferring to see themselves as investigators, reporters, value-neutral conveyors of truth. Perry's most important contribution to writing instruction may well be the critique he implies of this positivistic view of the teacher's role. ("William Perry" 454)

For his dissertation study, Lawrence Kohlberg gave student subjects brief "cases" and then analyzed the responses they gave to each one. Each "case" contained a classic moral dilemma: whether to support the practice of euthanasia, whether to steal a very expensive drug in order to save the life of a spouse, and so on. In analyzing the students' responses, Kohlberg identified three major stages in moral development: the preconventional stage, in which students begin by defining right and wrong in terms of whether an act is punished by an unquestioned authority and then move to a more utilitarian definition—whatever pleases me and accomplishes my goals must be right; the conventional stage, in which students begin to solicit approval by conforming to the expectations of parents or guides and then move to setting their standards of behavior by "majority rule" of the accepted legal and social system; and the postconventional stage, in which students begin by accepting the "social contract" while realizing that injustices should be challenged and then move toward a stand on universally ethical principles.

The relation of Kohlberg's theory to that of Perry and Piaget seems fairly clear: once again the student reportedly moves from concrete, egocentric responses toward increasingly abstract, general, and relative reasoning.[1] While the Kohlbergian scheme is certainly not without flaws (see Gilligan), it raises important questions for teachers of writing. The most obvious question concerns writing assignments and their sequencing. As I noted earlier, Kohlberg's situational dilemmas amount to brief cases, the use of which is increasingly popular in composition textbooks. But if Kohlberg's theory is at all applicable, then we must ask how such cases should be developed and, more importantly, how students' written responses to cases should be evaluated. Fundamental questions about the scope, subject, sequencing, and evaluation of writing assignments still remain to be answered (Lunsford, "Assignments"), and Kohlberg's findings may be of some help in answering them. At this point, the most provocative application of Kohlberg's work to composition occurs in Susan Miller's essay on rhetorical maturity, which questions some of our traditional assumptions about what constitutes such maturity and challenges us to redefine the term.

While the work of the developmental theorists I have briefly summarized is clearly of significance to writing instruction, it does not provide any firm answers to our questions concerning development during the college years. In fact, what Perry, Kohlberg, Piaget, and Vygotsky—as well as half a dozen others—have given us is a rich profusion of data, of particulars, without creating an acceptable general theory that will fit such rich and diverse data. In a recent article in the *New York Review of Books*, Jerome Bruner acknowledges this lack of a generally accepted developmental theory, but nevertheless concludes that

> it seems *much too soon* to despair about our ever understanding the universals of human development. Just because mind expresses itself through different modes, in different intellectual domains, in different settings, and by different instruments, it does not mean that mind is not to be distinguished from the instruments and occasions for its expression, that we will never be able to tell the dancer from the dance. Perhaps Piaget did not get it right—his specialized obsessive concern with parallels between the logic of the developing child and the history of science was too limiting. That the gap between the universal deep structure of mind in general and its expression across a variety of situations seems great is not surprising. *Unitas multiplex* may still be the best motto. (84)

But in the remainder of this essay, Bruner makes clear that in spite of our current limited understanding, he still believes we will eventually identify universals of human cognitive development.

Bruner's long-range optimism may be warranted, but it seems to me next to impossible to offer ontological "proof" of universal stages of mental development. In fact, the developmental theorists I have reviewed are most commonly criticized for their strong ethnocentrism and nongeneralizability. Let me go further to say that even if we could offer such proof of universal stages, doing so would not be of much immediate practical help to teachers of writing, because the mere existence of developmental stages will not bring the means of achieving or transcending those stages. The danger—and it is a very real danger—of the developmental perspective is that it will be used in unthinking ways by teachers and administrators who may wish to impose a rigid set of "stages" or "positions" on college students' development without recognizing the vital importance of context to that development. Joseph Williams makes this argument strongly in "Critical Thinking, Cognitive Development, and the Teaching of Writing," and he is supported in his contention by no less a light than Perry, who says that "Perhaps the best model for growth is neither the straight line nor the circle, but a helix, perhaps with an expanding radius to show that when we face the 'same' old issues we do so from a different and broader perspective" ("Intellectual" 62). Development, in other words, is not linear but recursive and context-dependent. Building on this concept, Williams proposes that instead of progressing through global stages of development, "we simply go through the same stages [which he calls "pre-socialized," "socialized," and "post-socialized"] over and over again . . . every time we confront a new universe of discourse" (14).

In spite of such caveats and in spite of the criticism mentioned earlier, the work of the cognitive developmental theorists should be important to writing teachers for the following reasons: all the theories take a constructivist perspective that relates thought, language, and action in creating meaning; and all shift our gaze from the traditional behavioristic, logical positivist one focusing solely on products or "outcomes" to a more complex attention to the processes through which we represent meaning and hence create our individual and social realities and selves.

Current applications of cognitive studies

At this point, we are brought neatly back to a consideration of the relatively new group of cognitive sciences, each of which in some way addresses the central theme or questions of process and representation (which most often takes the form of product). As George Mandler notes, the concepts of process and representation are "the primary foci of all the relative [cognitive] disciplines, and it is symptomatic of our acceptance and of their importance that we rarely hear anybody question these two foundations" (306). Certainly these dual foci have influenced composition research in very important ways. The early work of Emig (*Composing Processes*), with its careful attention to the writing process, its application of case-study methodology to composition research, and its insistence on the relation between thought, writing, and action, has profoundly influenced our field. Indeed, Emig's work has prompted, more directly than indirectly, an explosion of research on composing processes in the last decade. And throughout her career, Emig has persistently challenged us to realize just how important language (and particularly writing) is in representing the world in meaningful ways. The work of James Moffett, which grows out of developmental theory and also stresses process and representation, has influenced our teaching of composing in much the same way that Emig's work has influenced our research. In addition, Mina Shaughnessy's pioneering research on basic writing studied the complex ways in which students' representation of meaning is often confounded, ironically, by their writing processes.

Indeed, the concern with the concepts of process and representation is so pervasive in composition studies today that reviewing all such work lies beyond the scope of this essay, though such a review is badly needed. I have chosen, therefore, to focus briefly on three current attempts to understand the cognitive dimension of the writing process, attempts that are clearly representative of the most promising work being done today. Best known of this research is probably that of Linda Flower and John Hayes, whose cognitive-process model was derived through protocol analysis ("thinking aloud" reports of what is happening as a subject writes), a technique borrowed from cognitive psychology. Their provisional model (fig. 4) divides "the writer's world into three major parts: the task environment, the writer's long-term memory, and the writing process" ("Identifying" 10).

Flowers and Hayes advance their cognitive theory in a number of important articles (listed in the works consulted section), and they are cautiously optimistic that their research may provide data from which to derive a generally agreed on model of the writing process. In the short run, their research provides us with extremely valuable information on how writers set goals, how they solve problems, and how they represent meaning to themselves. Flower and Hayes's work has been criticized, sometimes harshly, primarily on the grounds that their "thinking aloud" protocols distort the very process they are trying to study. However, Flower and Hayes are generally cautious about drawing hard and fast conclusions from their research: "The data we garner is only a sample of the phenomenon we would study. But that is the nature of all research, and this window (on the act of think-

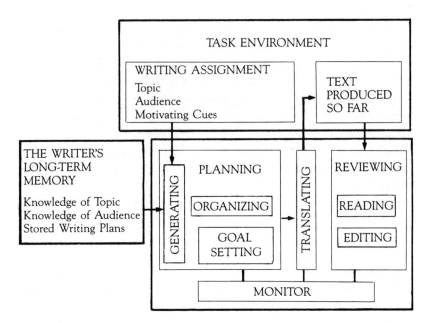

Fig. 4. Structure of the Writing Model

ing) is substantially larger than its alternatives . . . ("Images" 4). As far as most teachers of writing are concerned, *any* "window" is valuable. In opening their particular window, Flower and Hayes are helping writing teachers relate what students actually do to what we may want them to do.

Carl Bereiter refers to the Flower and Hayes work in his discussion of development in writing, noting that they have provided the beginning of a complete cognitive processing model of writing and citing the work of Nold and of Scardemalia, which amplifies our understanding of this process (77). Bereiter concludes that "a complete processing model would have to deal with . . . the cognitive moves that make up writing and their organization; with levels of processing, from the highly conscious and intentional to the unconscious and automatic; and with how processing capacity is deployed in these various functions in such a way as to enable writing to go on" (78). Drawing on current models of speech production (Fodor, Bever, and Garrett) and of language comprehension (Adams and Collins), Bereiter sketches in the necessary components of a model of written composition, arguing that our understanding of development of writing abilities depends on such a model (78). He then advances a provisional model of "stages in writing development" (82–84). Although this model is even more tentative than the Flower and Hayes model of the composing process and more seriously flawed, it focuses our attention not only on describing that process but on relating that process to instruction as it may or may not aid development of writing ability. Bereiter and his frequent coauthor Marlene Scardemalia pursue this notion of writing development and its relation to instruction in a number of other works, the most important of which for writing teachers is probably their "From Conversation to Composition: The Role of Instruction in the Developmental Process."

A third team of researchers whose work is beginning to have an impact on the field of composition is McGill University's Bracewell, Frederiksen, and Frederiksen. These researchers identify two broad categories of discourse processing: "framing" processes, which produce a "conceptual structure, or frame, for a text," and "regulating" processes, which "access language structures, translating conceptual structure into a text for production and regulating construction of the conceptual structure for comprehension" (146). The goal of their research is to develop a unified theory of discourse production (writing) and comprehension (reading). By linking the cognitive processes common to both reading and writing, Bracewell and the Frederiksens thus move in the direction Beaugrande's work calls for: a general theory of cognition and communication.

I have focused on the work of Flower and Hayes, Bereiter and Scardemalia, and Bracewell, Frederiksen, and Frederiksen because it emphasizes questions of process and representation and attempts to develop models that would identify and define the cognitive processes involved in reading and writing. As I have indicated, these models are all tentative and evolving. Thus teachers of writing can find no generally agreed on cognitive-process model, just as we can find no generally agreed on theory of intellectual and moral development.

I do not wish to suggest, however, that no agreement exists. In fact, most researchers and teachers today would agree that control of a full range of cognitive and emotive strategies characterizes mature writing and that certain cognitive strategies or sets of strategies are characteristic of certain writing—and reading—tasks. I would argue, then, that while universal developmental stages and completely elegant models elude us, we can identify certain cognitive strategies that can be taught and, incidentally, that doing so is as, if not more, important than identifying stages or models. Such an argument rests, of course, on my basic agreement with Vygotsky and others who say that instruction can foster development. In particular, I agree with Vygotsky's notion that a student's "zone of potential development" can be broadened and moved forward by the kind of instruction that "marches slightly ahead" of the student, thus allowing that student's reach only slightly to exceed his or her grasp.

If such instruction can be effective, if cognitive strategies can be not only

taught but learned, what are these strategies? I believe that the set of cognitive strategies including generalizing, abstracting, inferring, and synthesizing (by which I mean seeing patterns of "connections") can be learned and
that these strategies are crucial to both reading and writing. But while we
may discuss such strategies in general, we must remember that the range
and configuration of strategies necessarily shift from task to task, from one
rhetorical situation to another. Studies I have conducted over the last several
years, for instance, indicate that narrative and descriptive writing tasks typically elicit far fewer generalizations or abstractions than do argumentative
tasks. But in spite of the lower frequency of generalizations, these two cognitive strategies are necessary even to narrative and descriptive writing;
in fact, in comparing personal narratives written by basic writers with those
of skilled writers I have consistently found a higher number of generalizations in the skilled writers' narratives. A recent, unpublished study by Marilyn Sternglass corroborates the importance of generalizing, inferring, and
abstracting strategies in expository, argumentative, and speculative writing tasks. Across these three kinds of writing tasks, statements reflecting
inferences, generalizations, abstractions, and syntheses accounted for between seventy and ninety percent of all sentences produced.

It seems clear, then, that while combinations of strategies or the frequency
with which they are used will vary according to the writing task and the
rhetorical situation, the cognitive strategies of generalizing, inferring, and
abstracting are basic to writing and reading. Put most simply, learning to
be a skilled reader always involves going beyond the information given
on the page; drawing generalizations, inferences about motivations, underlying assumptions, and conflicts; and recognizing, and responding to,
motifs, image clusters, patterns of allusions—responding, in short, to the
conventions of the socialized literary community. Concomitantly, student
writers must be able to draw inferences from the wealth of materials, observations, and impressions at their disposal in order to conceptualize and
sustain even a very short piece of discourse. To rephrase this proposition
in the terms of cognitive psychologists Bracewell, Frederiksen, and Frederiksen, "the reader must use the text structure to infer a writer's conceptual
structure, and a writer must produce a text that is able to sustain a reader's
inferences about the underlying conceptual structure" (148–49).

In spite of the importance of such strategies to both reading and writing,
recent studies of the public schools in North America show that inferen-
tial reasoning skills are not taught until the last years of high school, and
then only sporadically and unsystematically taught at best. And we have
even more evidence to suggest that our students have difficulty using such
strategies successfully in academic reading and writing. After a long and

thorough study of basic writing and reading students, David Bartholomae reported that the inability to draw inferences and to generalize characterized the writing of his students even more than did a high level of error ("Facts"). For the last seven years, I have been studying the writing of beginning and advanced students. The data I have gathered in these studies generally support the argument Joe Williams makes against any arhetorical tendency to impose a rigid set of developmental stages on college students. My data also demonstrate, however, that while novice readers and writers do draw valid inferences and sustain generalizations about a family quarrel or the strange noise a motorcycle is making, they do not exercise such strategies with ease in academic discourse. In fact, in responding to academic writing tasks, my students often exhibit some of the characteristics that Linda Flower assigns to "writer-based" prose or that Bereiter and Scardemalia identify in their studies of younger writers: a tendency to order material as it occurs to the writer rather than in an order dictated by an overall structure or plan, failure to engage in whole-text planning or goal-directed planning, and a low level of generalization and inference, with a concomitant dependence on narrative and descriptive modes.

I hope I have provided at least partial evidence to support my contention that the cognitive strategies I describe are necessary to skillful reading and writing and that our students have great difficulty using these strategies effectively in analytic academic discourse. In terms of the conventions of our particular socialized community of discourse, I hope I have established that a problem exists. But if the problem is as significant and widespread as I have suggested, what can teachers of writing do? I have no easy answers to this question, and in spite of the promise shown by current work in cognitive studies, I would especially loathe to see our profession rush to embrace some new quick pedagogical cure or some simplistic "back to the basic thinking skills" movement, which has already happened in several states. I do, however, have some modest suggestions about how we may best address the issues I raise in my discussion of cognitive developmental theories and models.

Implications for teaching and research

1. We must strike a balance between attempts to map the cognitive processes of writing and reading and attempts to describe what Williams calls "socialized discourse communities." In other words, we must attend in our classes to both process and representation, or product.

2.   We must note the way the developmental theorists relate action to development, and we must try to apply that lesson to our own classes. Writing classrooms should thus be places where students write as well as learn about writing. In Gilbert Ryle's words, we must attend to both "knowing how" and "knowing that."

3.   We should recognize the significant role collaboration plays in all kinds of development and include collaborative learning in our repertoire of teaching techniques, remembering that in each developmental theory reviewed, learning occurs most often in conjunction with interaction.[2]

4.   We must establish an interdisciplinary framework for our courses that, at the very least, would make explicit connections among the discourse arts of writing, reading, and speaking. Such connections demand that we put assignments at the heart of our courses and that we structure our assignments so that students get conscious practice in the cognitive strategies necessary to successful completion of those assignments.

These steps that my review of cognitive studies has suggested are ones every writing teacher can take fairly easily. What is not easy at all is accepting the challenge of cognitive studies to encourage, develop, and maintain what Beaugrande calls "interdependencies" among disciplines. Yet only by doing so can composition studies hope to contribute to a general theory of cognition and communication that will provide answers for our most pressing questions:

1. What constitutes "development" in the college years, and how is that development related to development in reading, writing, speaking, and thinking skills?
2. What cognitive processes and strategies are basic to all types of writing? Which are basic to all types of reading? What processes are specific to particular contexts or communities of discourse?
3. How are cognitive processes related and correlated to affective aspects of reading and writing?
4. How are cultural constraints related to the development of reading and writing abilities?

Only when we have some answers to these difficult questions will we begin to understand what it means to be literate and how literacy develops in our society. As the field with the most clearly defined and most generally accepted interdisciplinary base, cognitive studies offers those of us in the field of composition studies a community of scholars with whom to collaborate in attempting to answer these questions. Most significantly, cognitive studies has the potential for providing us with a basis for the pedagogy Cicero called for two millennia ago, one that would unite thought, language, and action.

Notes

[1] The stage model developed by Andrew Wilkinson follows a similar pattern and provides the basis for Marilyn Sternglass's unpublished monograph "Fostering Cognitive Growth in Writing."

[2] The fact that much of the writing done on the job is collaborative strongly reinforces this recommendation. As this book goes to press, Lisa Ede and I are analyzing data gathered from a survey of the writing done by members of six professional organizations (two from the social sciences, two from the humanities, one from the hard sciences, and one from the government) in an attempt to define the various kinds of collaboration.

Research on Error and Correction

Glynda Hull

Attitudes and error studies

> As I Re-read my paper on my working experience, a lot of important people run throught my mind. I can see Ruth James the immigrate worker who lived by her wits. I can feel the depair of Kracha's Family struggling For a better way of Life. I can also see Roberto Acuna as a child who has climbed his way to a better way of Life. I feel that I am apart of all of these people. I have walk in their shoes, I have tasted thier Food and I also respect the way they have had to lived. In my working experiences I have had a chance to tuck poverty to one side. I don't mean Forget about it, I just mean that I have put it with my special thoughts. And Every Now and then my thougths are like a Fire that has been put out, but there's still a glance of a Flame still burning. I think Roberto is like me and I am like him. As a child he protects his Family. He is living in poverty, his conditions has made him a Fighter. He Fights back by getting a education; then he Fights back with union solidarity. I too have Fought back. . . . And I Feel that now I will Fight back in a very important way. Like Roberto I have my cap set For a higher Education. I might not make the total trip but I Feel it is the experience that counts. (An essay written in a composition class at the University of Pittsburgh, 1984)

In a recent essay called the "The Future of Testing," Robert Glaser recalls how educational tests once were selective, their purpose being to predict which students would get along in the present school system, which would need special help, and which should be discouraged from continuing. But now, he believes, things are beginning to change. "It seems clear," he writes, "that we are over the threshold in the transition from education as a highly selective enterprise to one that is focused on developing an entire population of educated people" (924). Instead of assessing which students are suited for whatever educational opportunities currently exist, we are becoming more interested in finding ways to help students take advantage of those opportunities, even to succeed at them. Instead of expecting students to assume most of the burden for learning, we are beginning to assign more accountability to our instructional programs, and we want to know just how helpful they are. "The requirement now," Glaser believes, "is to design a helping society in which we devise means for providing educational opportunities for all in equitable ways" (924).

Glaser's account of the changing purposes of educational testing mirrors, in macrocosm, the changes that have begun to occur in attitudes toward and treatments of error in writing. There was a time when a paper like the one above, with its misspellings and confused inflections and sentence-boundary mistakes, its missing apostrophes and its errors in agreement, its idiosyncratic capitalizations, and its word-boundary problems would have filled most of us with despair, would have suggested, even, that its author could find no place in our classrooms. Hers are the kinds of mistakes that, for a long time, we have considered evidence of ignorance, an ignorance that's been thought inexcusable. Harvard president Charles W. Eliot, speaking in 1873, complained that "bad spelling, incorrectness as well as inelegance of expression in writing [and] ignorance of the simplest rules of punctuation . . . are far from rare among young men of eighteen" (Hook 8). Over a century later, the National Assessment of Educational Progress could identify two distinct populations of seventeen-year-olds: one that "appears to have a general, though imperfect, grasp of written language" and another that "appears to be virtually lost" (*Writing Achievement* 1: 44). Sentence-level correctness has long seemed to us so rudimentary — representing the niceties, really, of scribal conventions — that not having internalized the correct forms has been tantamount to not having achieved something taken for granted as evidence of basic educability. (Robert Connors traces the history of this concern for correctness in "Mechanical Correctness as a Focus in Composition Instruction.")

Attitudes toward error in writing are now changing, and they are changing, in part, because we have come to value things other than sentence-level correctness in the writing of our students. There has been, to name the obvious example, a great flood of interest in revision as reformulation, where a writer returns to what he or she has written in order to rethink, reconceptualize, or resee and then to rewrite (rather than merely to correct). And he or she may produce, through willingness and ability to revise, a paper that is fundamentallly different from and better than the first attempt. In an effort to say how important this kind of revision can be to a writer, researchers and teachers have often contrasted it with what attention to editing or sentence-level correctness will buy. In "Revision in the Composing Process," Nancy Sommers complains that in typical handbooks "revision is equated with cleanliness; to revise is to groom, to polish, to order, and to tidy-up one's writing" (17). She goes on to describe, with sympathy, "the hapless student who is constantly exhorted to check his spelling, or check his grammar" (17) and to argue for an alternative definition of revision. Continuing Sommers's hygiene metaphor, Lester Faigley and Stephen Witte end a paper called "Analyzing Revision" with the admonition that only when we appreciate its "multidimensional nature" can we "teach revision as a rhetorical concern, bringing inexperienced writers to know revising as something other than a cleansing of errors" (412). And Donald Murray notes how professional writers spend most of their time revising in order to find out and develop what they have to say, while texts give attention to "the least part of the process, the superficial aspects of preparing a manuscript to be read" ("Internal Revision" 91).

So, on the one hand, we've come a great distance in our attitudes toward error. A new interest in revision, in what a writer has to say, signifies a new willingness to look beyond the surface features of texts like the one above and to discover that many writers who make numerous sentence-level errors are nonetheless writers who can compose sentences like, "In my working experiences I have had a chance to tuck poverty to one side." On the other hand, we've decided that correctness will not be the sole or most important virtue that we want to promote in our students' essays, nor its absence a reason for exclusion from educational opportunities. We've begun to appreciate how enormously difficult the process of editing can be for inexperienced writers. This realization has sprung from what has begun to be learned about why writers make errors and how they are able to detect and correct them. Instead of being content to tabulate the occurrence of various kinds of errors or to assess how well students perform on objective tests of grammar and usage and then to reason from such results that students need instruction and practice on those errors that occur (or are missed) most frequently, researchers and teachers are becoming concerned to discover the processes of mind that led to the errors in the first place and that finally govern their detection and correction. As we discover more about what motivates students' erroneous performance, as we construct an accurate picture of the misconceptions or faulty procedures that lead to an error and prevent its detection and correction, we put ourselves in a position to assess, refine, and build anew our instructional paradigms. This is the kind of educational research that Glaser was thinking of when he imagined how we might design a helping society. And it is the kind of research that has characterized the major scholarship on error and editing for the last ten years.

I don't want to suggest, however, because these new research trends have emerged, that error in writing is no longer a controversial topic, for it is, and it will remain so. Pleas to teach "basic skills" (or correctness in writing) are countered by quick rejoinders that surely there are skills more "basic" than sentence-level competence (Hillocks). Evidence that high school teachers respond most frequently to their students' essays by marking errors in "mechanics" is countered by other teachers who refer to "error-catching" as "that classroom blood sport which kills venturesome writing and response" (Ponsot and Deen 39–40). There is proof that professional people still have very conservative views on matters of grammar and usage, disapproving strongly of errors such as run-on sentences, superfluous commas, and nonparallel structures (Hairston, "Not All Errors"). Yet, Joseph Williams can also demonstrate that as readers we don't even notice many sentence-level errors—unless, that is, we're expecting them ("Phenomenology of Error").

Most of the controversy surrounding correctness in writing has finally to do with power, status, and class—whether, to call on the best-known example, we can be justified in asking all students to learn and use standard English. Sarah D'Eloia reviewed the long-standing arguments concerning this issue and concluded that we are, but other recent commentators on the social implications of literacy training have mixed feelings. Robert Pattison writes that common sense will tell anyone that the "inability to communicate in the linguistic style approved by the leadership of government, industry, and the professions increases the difficulty of joining these ranks or even attacking them in any effective way." Pattison's complaint is that the pragmatic value of using standard English in speech and writing isn't represented as such but is disguised as a moral or aesthetic imperative. Thus, when people don't conform to established language conventions, they run the risk of being considered "uncivilized, unreflecting cretins who offend against a culture merely by opening their mouths or applying pen to paper" (200). Pattison obviously has little patience for such attitudes, but he nevertheless recommends that students learn standard English—"all citizens should have access to the language of power" (169)—although as a kind of second language.

Richard Rodriguez also writes about the language of power, but from the perspective of one who has had to learn it. In *An Autobiography: Hunger of Memory* he describes his education, that of a Mexican-American who learned a public language at the cost of losing an intimacy with his past. He repeats the arguments of proponents of bilingual education (arguments similar, he reminds us, to those in favor of using black English in schools): if children can use their family language in school, they will be more comfortable, their learning will prosper, and they will also maintain their ties with their heritage. Rodriguez then continues:

Behind this screen there gleams an astonishing promise: One can become a public person while still remaining a private person. At the very same time one can be both! There need be no tension between the self in the crowd and the self apart from the crowd! Who would not want to believe such an idea? . . . If the barrio or ghetto child can retain separateness even while being publicly educated, then it is almost possible to believe that there is no private cost to be paid for public success. (34–35)

His argument is that there is a private cost, an alienation from old intimacies, at the same time that there is a public gain, an assimilation, and a growth. Rodriguez takes care to make clear, however, that the loss, "the diminished occasions of intimacy," was occasioned by a social change of which linguistic change was a mere sign: "*Intimacy is not created by a particular language,*" he writes; "*it is created by intimates*" (32).

The nettle of error in writing and, of course, in speech as well is that it points away from itself towards social issues. It is but a sign, a harbinger, of matters that have ramifications much broader than could exist in a decontextualized act of putting pen on paper, matters that have to do with the purpose and structure of educational systems. Seen thus, the position one takes on error and editing acquires political and social overtones. It is no wonder, then, that we are uneasy. (See also Elaine O. Lees's discussion of the sociological nature of error and editing in "Error-hunting, Fish and Game: Proofreading as Reading.")

There are, however, recent perspectives on error that can be viewed as walking a middle ground in the controversy, neither despairing that students must learn a privileged language nor grieving overlong that there is a cost. Mina Shaughnessy, in her introduction to *Errors and Expectations*, acknowledges the position of those who would argue that errors aren't important because, as mere conventions, they are arbitrary. However, she also points out how failure to abide by the conventions of written language is to intrude, with some risk, on a reader's consciousness: "all codes become codes by doing some things regularly and not others, and it is not so much the ultimate logic of these regularities that makes them obligatory but rather the fact that, logical or no, they have become habitual to those who communicate within that code" (12). And she also turns to imagine the effect of error, not on the sensibilities of readers but on the performance of basic writers. Shaughnessy's insights here are unusually important. She does not find students concerned that conventions are, after all, only conventions; rather, she documents their impulse, universal among language learners, to make sense of language data, "to seek out, either consciously or unconsciously, the underlying patterns that govern the language they are learning":

> At times variant and standard forms mix, as if students had half-learned two inflectional systems; hypercorrections that belong to no system jut out in unexpected places; idiosyncratic schemes of punctuation and spelling substitute for systems that were never learned and possibly never taught; evasive circumlocutions, syntactical derailments, timid script, and near-guesses fog the meaning, if any remains after the student has thus spent himself on the sheer mechanics of getting something down on paper. One senses the struggle to fashion out of the fragments of past instruction a system that will relieve the writer of the task of deciding what to do in each instance where alternative forms or conventions stick in the mind. (10)

Regardless of whether error shifts in status among composition specialists or teachers of English or the public, regardless of whether we support or decry the existence of a privileged language, beginning writers will appropriate or invent systems for spelling and punctuation and grammar and usage, for as Shaughnessy explains, "they are pressed by their language-learning faculties to increase the degree of predictability and efficiency in their use of language" (10). And for inexperienced adult writers, this activity, unless it is mediated by informed and helpful instruction, can be debilitating.

In a way this position can be seen as a sidestep, even a sleight of hand, since it shifts our attention from the overwhelming question of whether we ought sanction through our roles as teachers the existence of a privileged language, particularly when privileged means only arbitrarily approved scribal conventions. But it can also be seen as a compelling argument, both to provide instruction on error and to include editing among those aspects of writing worth our study. Such an argument is implicit in much recent research on error and editing, which has taken as its purpose not a delineation of the social and political implications of error and correctness but an investigation of those mental processes involved in making errors and correcting them. In the remainder of this chapter, I trace the evolution of such research, beginning with more traditional studies that preceded the new research and ending with the questions that remain.

Error counts and error categories

The most plentiful research on error in writing has, for a long time, been counts of its frequency. Rollo Lyman reported scores of such studies con-

ducted during the first quarter of this century—studies, for example, of
how many, and what kinds of, errors were made by children, high school
students, and adults and studies of which errors seemed to persist for particular students and in general. The purpose of such research was to "determine the 'common errors' in order to derive the minimum essentials
for a core curriculum in language-grammar" (71). And there was concern
to do so objectively, by looking to see what errors students actually made.
The method was simply to search writing samples for errors and to tabulate the errors according to a taxonomy of error types or a taxonomy developed from the data. For example, Roy Ivan Johnson, after examining
"50,371 words of composition from high-school freshmen of Kansas City
and 32,693 words of composition from high-school graduates of Kansas
City" (556), concluded that these students ought to study the mechanics
of English in this order of emphasis:

1. Mistakes in capitalization.
2. Mistakes in the use of the apostrophe.
3. Mistakes in punctuation.
4. Mistakes in the use of adjectives and adverbs.
5. Mistakes in spelling.
6. Mistakes in pronouns, *not including case*. Careless omission and
   repetition.
7. Mistakes in the use of verbs. Mistakes in the use of prepositions
   and conjunctions.
8. Sentence meaning not clear.
9. Sentence structure ungrammatical.
10. Mistakes in the use of quotation marks.
11. Mistakes in the *case* of pronouns. (578)

Recent tabulation studies have used similar procedures for related purposes. The National Assessment of Educational Progress, whose aim is to
describe the changes across grades in students' performance on certain writing tasks, has reported the results of its error tabulation research for nine-,
thirteen-, and seventeen-year-olds. NAEP's taxonomy, described in *Writing Mechanics*, includes:

1. Sentence Level Categorizations: Fused Sentence, On and On Sentence, Splice, Incorrect Sentence Fragment
2. Faulty Sentence Construction: Agreement, Awkward
3. Punctuation: Commas and Dashes, Colon, Semicolon, End
   Marks, Apostrophe, Quotation Marks
4. Word Level Categorization: Spelling, Word Choice, Capitalization

Among NAEP's findings are data showing that the number of errors that students make in punctuation, capitalization, and fragments does not appear to decrease from ages nine to seventeen but, rather, remains more or less constant. (See *Writing Mechanics* and John Mellon's *National Assessment*.)

The value of such frequency research depends to a great extent on the taxonomy that serves as its category system. (This limitation, however, is rarely noted in the literature, just as the taxonomies themselves are not usually discussed in much detail.) On the simplest level, constructing an error taxonomy requires one to decide what to count as an error. The distinction Strunk and White would maintain between "which" and "that" may be a subtlety that most readers don't recognize, for example, and thus might or might not need to be put in an error taxonomy, depending on how comprehensive or how strict a researcher wants to be. The problem takes on more seriousness, however, when one recalls how much disagreement there is (and has long been) about matters of usage among experts on language use. When T. J. Cresswell analyzed twenty works on grammar and usage, including the *American Heritage Dictionary*, all of which claimed "objectivity and authoritativeness in their evaluation of usage variants" (122), he found that they were almost never consistent in their treatment of the some 318 usage problems surveyed. Nor have individual grammarians been absolutely uniform in applying the rules they prescribe. In "Phenomenology of Error," Joseph Williams has shown how E. B. White, H. W. Fowler, and Jacques Barzun break on one page of their handbooks a rule that they state on another. Williams's point is that no one notices such lapses because no one expects to find them—a situation that reverses itself when the reading material becomes a student's essay. The findings of Cresswell and Williams argue for a less conservative conception of error, with greater tolerance of language variants than most handbooks show. (It is instructive to note, as John Brereton reminds us, that these findings were anticipated by Sterling Leonard's *Current English Usage* in the 1930s.)

A more serious difficulty accompanying error-tabulation research is that errors don't lend themselves so readily to cataloging as researchers have imagined. It is not so easy, that is, to devise a taxonomy whose categories are discrete—in Johnson's taxonomy given above, for example, "Sentence meaning not clear" might overlap with "Careless omission" or "Sentence structure ungrammatical"—yet if the aim of research is to figure out which errors deserve what emphasis in the classroom, the issue of overlapping or unclear categories becomes important. Similarly, it is often hard to reconstruct, with any assurance, what the writer had in mind when he or she wrote a particular sentence. And how we interpret a sentence, what meaning we assume the writer intended, will determine how we classify the error.

"Listing varieties of errors is not like listing varieties of rocks or butterflies," David Bartholomae reminds us. "What a reader finds depends to a large degree on her assumptions about the writer's intention" ("Study of Error" 259). If the errors we count and tabulate have no reality besides the interpretation we give them, if, that is, our counts can't inform instruction (or can inform it only wrongly), because the errors we see don't represent the errors students actually make, then tabulation research has limits we haven't yet considered. (See also the discussions of frequency counting by Braddock, Lloyd-Jones, and Schoer in *Research on Written Composition* and of error taxonomies by Hull in "Stray Dogs and Mermaids.")

Once we have a taxonomy that satisfies, however, and once we have tabulated the frequency of errors in students' writing across grades, we still do not know how such information should inform pedagogies and curricula. In Lyman's time, the assumption was that grammar and usage should be taught, and what tabulation research could do was provide an objective basis for determining what part of this instruction should be emphasized. There were attempts to be sophisticated in such assessments, to determine, for example, which errors persisted, as well as which were frequent, and the relation between errors made and actual opportunities for those errors, or what were called "error quotients." But for the most part, it was a given that students needed instruction on grammar points. In fact, although Johnson showed "in some instances a high degree of elimination of error" (580), he still urged teachers to give attention to error, recommending that they "fight old habit with new habit through the medium of drill—mechanical drill in the mechanics of writing" (579).

His findings wouldn't, I think, be interpreted the same way today. After noting that, according to NAEP data, error rates don't improve as students move through the grades, John Mellon takes care to argue against any increase in drill and practice on error correcting. He says, for example, that error rates aren't that high anyway, and besides, "older students will be experimenting with kinds and forms of language they could not have attempted at all when younger" and "naturally they will make errors in the process, errors which could not have been prevented by advance drill" (33). Aviva Freedman and Ian Pringle make a similar argument when they interpret the results of their error tabulation in grades 5, 8, and 12, as part of a project to measure writing quality in a particular school district ("Writing Abilities").

The recent tendency, clearly, is to deemphasize sentence-level correctness and to question the efficacy of drill and practice in improving it. This trend is healthy, coming as it does in reaction to evidence that English teachers have for a long time taught writing by reducing the enterprise to error eradication via exercises in grammar and usage. Albert Kitzhaber in *Themes, Theories, and Therapy* and Robert J. Connors in "Mechanical Correctness" note that composition instruction proceeded that way from the turn of the century through the mid-1900s. And according to Arthur Applebee, seventy-one percent of the high school teachers he recently surveyed still claimed to respond most frequently to their students' writing by marking errors in "mechanics"—usage, spelling, sentence structure (*Writing*). Perversely, not only has such a focus failed to provide students any help with other aspects of writing, like the reformulation of ideas, it has failed as well in what presumably was its primary aim, that of teaching students to produce error-free texts. (See, e.g., the review of research by Petrosky, "Grammar Instruction," the study by Elley and colleagues, and Patrick Hartwell's recent assessment, "Grammar, Grammars, and the Teaching of Grammar.")

Tabulation research of the sort I have described has seen its heyday; researchers who study error study it differently now. This shift in what constitutes interesting and valued research on error, what might be called a shift in paradigms, has occurred as part of a broadening of our notions of what constitutes acceptable scientific research. (See Anne Ruggles Gere's chapter in this volume.) It also reflects a movement away from a concern solely for correctness in writing and toward an interest in rhetoric. (See Connors, "Mechanical Correctness.") And it reflects, finally, new attitudes toward the role of error in language learning. In tabulation studies, the presence of error meant just the absence of correctness. Given this assumption, the essay that stands as the headnote to this chapter would stand only as testimony to a lack of learning or learning gone astray. Such notions have changed, however, and in the next section, I describe the changes that have occurred in how we think about error in writing and the research that accompanied and contributed to those changes.

Sources

Error has long been used outside the field of English as a window for learning about cognitive processes. Martin Nystrand points out the "error analyses have proved especially useful where the need for detailed theoretical explanations of psychological and linguistic phenomena has never been intuitively obvious" (58). That is, in order to understand behaviors that are normally taken for granted as natural or automatic, and thus are overlooked, it is helpful to study their failure or breakdown. Nystrand mentions Freud's discovery of associative thinking through analyses of slips of the tongue, Piaget's characterization of cognitive development based on his probing of children's errors in various problem-solving tasks, and Kenneth Goodman's studies of how readers "miscue" in their attempts to understand a text. Other examples can be found in mathematics research, where it has proven helpful to diagnose children's "bugs," the idiosyncratic algorithms by which they solve math problems incorrectly (Brown and Burton).

Another field in which error has been viewed as a window on cognitive processes is second-language learning. Partly in reaction to a once-dominant theory called "contrastive analysis" and partly under the influence of research on children's language acquisition, linguists have developed a theory and method called "error analysis" to guide the study of second-language error. (Jack C. Richards provides examples of this research.) Unlike constrastive analysis, which assumed that all errors in second-language learning could be attributed to differences in syntax and phonology between native and target languages, error analysis assumed several different causes for or sources of error. A particular aspect of a language might be intrinsically difficult to learn, for example, or language learners might "overgeneralize" particular rules, a common strategy for simplifying language data. The important departure here from traditional views of error is that error analysis, like language-acquisition research, posits an active learner, one whose mistakes can be analyzed to reveal the application of consistent, if erroneous, rules. Error is viewed as a necessary and healthy outcome of language experimentation, rather than merely as the absence of correctness.

Two recent influential works on error in written composition develop the implications of error analysis for error in composition: a much-cited article by Barry Kroll and John Schafer and Mina Shaughnessy's *Errors and Expectations*. Kroll and Schafer set out explicitly to apply error analysis to composition, demonstrating, for example, how an error analyst might investigate the omission of an *s* from verbs and the ambiguous use of *this*. The question they ask throughout is "Why does a student make this kind of error?" (245). Shaughnessy proceeds similarly. She groups error in broad categories—punctuation, syntax, common errors, spelling, vocabulary, and errors beyond the sentence—and then enriches her taxonomy by imagining sources for particular kinds of errors.

Here, for example, is her discussion of the troubled syntax in a sentence like "According to the list of jobs, you are basing whether or not to go to college, is a limited list."

> Like coordination, subordination requires that the writer add parts to his base sentence. These additions, however, serve different

purposes—either to qualify some element of the sentence, as an adjective or adverb might do, or to fill in (and fill out) the spot that a noun might occupy as subject, complement, or object of a preposition (apposition structures rarely occur at this stage). These consolidations require several things of a writer. If the dependent unit comes first in the sentence, the writer must suspend the independent unit in his mind while he qualifies it (as with introductory adverbial phrases and clauses). If the dependent unit comes between the subject and predicate of the base sentence (as with a relative clause after the subject), the writer must hold the main subject in his mind while he writes out the subject and predicate of the qualifying clause, and then he must return to the predicate of the base sentence. These operations require a memory for written words and grammatical structures that the inexperienced writer may not have. He hears what he says easily enough, but he does not as easily recall what he has written once his hand has moved on to another part of the sentence, and unlike the experienced writer, he is not in the habit of reviewing what he has written but instead moves headlong, as a speaker might, toward the open line, often forgetting the constraints he has set for himself a few words back. This difficulty with 'hearing' what has been written leads to bewildering and grammatically unworkable sentences that belie the writer's skill with the language. (58–59)

And thus, Shaughnessy imagines the difficulties that beset inexperienced writers at the sentence level and gives teachers a way to imagine such sentences as evidence of writers at work rather than of writers who are incapable or careless or dull. It would be hard to exaggerate the importance of Shaughnessy's book as an enactment of the kind of sympathetic and imaginative reading a teacher might give error-ridden papers. (See also Bartholomae's review of *Errors and Expectations*, "Released into Language.")

And indeed, much recent research on error has exemplified Shaughnessy's approach, although some of it arose apart from the study of basic writing. Researchers have begun, that is, to study error from the point of view of causation, attempting to understand the errors in writers' texts by reconstructing their probable sources. Instead of tallying the verb errors, for example, researchers try to infer why certain writers omit certain endings in certain linguistic contexts. Many of these analyses have been informal and anecdotal; a teacher who has noticed particular types of errors that tend to recur in several students' essays collects a corpus of these mistakes and then reasons ex post facto about their causes. Others have been more formal tests of hypotheses about the sources of particular errors.

There has been some interest in locating the source of some errors in what I'll call the human information-processing system—matters of faulty perception or limits on memory capacity. Patricia Laurence, for example, argues that perceptual difficulties prevent basic writers from seeing certain kinds of spelling or proofreading mistakes—and from seeing them "even after focused attention and seemingly effective grammatical instruction and practice" (26). The problems that she labels "perceptual" have a variety of sources: her students "do not focus on words in a structural way so there is little generalization about form and function; they have basic sound confusions because of second language/dialect interference or poor early training in phonics; they do not have strategies for approaching unfamiliar words which they must spell or read; they have a limited visual word storage" (24). Drawing on a psycholinguistic model of speech, Colette Daiute hypothesized that certain syntax errors in writing are caused by short-term memory constraints, and she found some evidence to support her theory. Specifically, she suggests that at the point of semantic recoding, when the exact wording of a clause fades from immediate memory and its meaning is stored in long-term memory, errors in syntax are likely to occur. She gives, as an example of an error signaled by such recoding, the sentence, "This waste of two intelligent women I know would still be active if their boss never had such policies at work" ("Psycholinguistic Foundations").

There have been many efforts to investigate the ways in which oral language patterns can be said to influence written language forms. In a recent study, Mary Epes hypothesized that certain errors, like inappropriate inflectional suffixes, and wrong whole-word verb forms, occur only in the writing of students who speak a nonstandard dialect but that errors having to do with written language conventions, like capitalization, spelling, and homophone confusions, occur equally in the writing of speakers of nonstandard and standard dialects. What she found was that nonstandard-dialect speakers made more errors in all the categories, even those where she hadn't expected a difference. But they made many more in the categories for which she had predicted a dialect-related difference. Epes would conclude, then, that certain errors in writing are indeed related to oral language patterns. However, in an attempt to study the relation between the oral and the written language of one speaker of Vernacular Black English, Marcia Farr and Mary Ann Janda concluded that the student's speech patterns could not account for his problems with written language. As Daniel Morrow points out in his review of the literature on dialect interference, there is a great deal of controversy and few clear findings concerning how oral language patterns influence written, controversy due in large part to methodological difficulties that mar data collection. (See also Hartwell, "Dialect Interference," which inspired a rebuttal from Morrow.)

Another source of written language errors might be thought of as a byproduct of language development. Lately, we've begun to attribute some errors to students' attempts to do things they can't handle. For example, Aviva Freedman and Ian Pringle found that when students wrote argumentative essays rather than narrative essays, they increased the number of errors they made. Error might be a symptom, Freedman and Pringle conclude, of "some other, and more fundamental, problem in the writing—greater rhetorical or intellectual or even moral difficulty" ("Writing Abilities"). Similarly, William Smith and colleagues have shown differences in the total numbers of errors that students make depending on the "structure" of the topic they are assigned. And Muriel Harris has demonstrated how one kind of sentence fragment might indicate not an error but rather college writers' use of "mature" syntactic structures, specifically Christensen's free modifier.

There is ample evidence, then, that the errors that occur in writing hail from a number of different sources: there are limits imposed on the language abilities of us all that may prove exceedingly disruptive to inexperienced readers and writers; there is the influence of oral language patterns; there are mistakes that fill essays as a kind of by-product of intellectual and linguistic maturation. Knowing sources, we should be in a better position to design a pedagogy. Kroll and Schafer claim that "when teachers understand the paths that lead to particular errors, they can more effectively show their students how they came to make a particular mistake" (247). And for some students, they suggest, this explanation of sources supplies sufficient motivation for careful editing. The claim that knowing why certain errors occur can inform a pedagogy is born out by the fact that different sources have already suggested different pedagogies. Mary Epes concluded from her investigation of oral language influences that the remediation of such errors requires direct instruction in the rules characterizing the dialect of standard English. On the opposite end of the continuum are those errors that are signs of intellectual growth, appearing in the process of learning and (the assumption seems to be) disappearing as a part of that process as well. On the middle ground might fall those errors that result from the difficulties of production, of holding one part of a sentence in mind while proceeding to the next part; these seem to require less systematic instruction in grammar than general encouragement to pay attention to the trail of one's sentences and to common patterns of derailments.

In summarizing the implications of causal analyses for instruction, I don't want to gloss over the complexities of carrying out such research and the care that should be exercised when such findings are incorporated into a pedagogy. As second-language researchers have noted, determining the source of an error isn't a straightforward matter (Schacter and Celce-Murcia).

Most obviously, it is not easy to say exactly why a particular writer has made a particular error. Brown and Burton point out in their analysis of math errors that the same "bug" can be accounted for in several ways, and David Bartholomae ("Study of Error") has illustrated something similar for writing. The same error can be caused by a lack of knowledge about a writing convention; it might be an accident, a slip of the pen; or it might represent an interaction of several causes. Nor is it clear, even if we feel certain that an error arises from a particular source, how causality is related to remediation. One assumption is that a writer who knows why he or she is making an error can avoid making it in the future. This assumption runs counter, however, to much classroom experience, where there is evidence that students continue to make errors and aren't able to correct them even after they can cite the rule they are violating and explain why they make the typical errors they do.

Some of the theoretical and methodological problems encountered in the study of error from the point of view of causation have begun to be addressed by research that focuses on the other end of the process, error detection and correction, or editing. These studies, unlike causal approaches, typically draw on the insights that can be gained not only from textual analyses but from protocols and interviews as well. Information on how writers locate and alter the errors they see in texts serves two purposes: it complements research on causes of error by providing evidence of how a writer responds to an error believed to arise from one source as compared to another, and it sheds light on other variables, those in addition to source, that can affect whether a writer notices and can correct an error in a text. I review this research in the next section.

Editing

Research on error sources is driven by a theory of how people learn language. If language learning occurs in stages of successive approximation, the theory goes, then the errors that learners make along the way will provide evidence of progress. Research on editing partakes of the same theory, expecting patterns of error in writing that are regular and systematic enough to be interpreted as evidence of stages in language learning. But research on editing can also supplement the theory. Given that errors occur in patterns suggestive of particular sources, the primary research questions become, how or by what mental processes does a writer recognize those patterns, and what accounts for failures to do so? Once we ask these questions, we necessarily broaden our focus to encompass not only error sources but other factors that might influence or characterize editing. From such a perspective, it won't be enough to name and interpret error patterns; we will also want to see what happens when a writer tries to locate and correct these patterns, and we'll want to understand his or her failures and successes.

One way to study the editing process is through product analyses: we devise an editing task, have a writer perform it, and then examine the results—the textual changes the writer made in order to correct whatever he or she perceived as an error. Another approach, and the one that has recently predominated among error studies, is to supplement what can be learned from product analyses with interviews and protocols. This development in methodology arose in part because scholars like Shaughnessy demonstrated how research on error can be informed by evidence other than frequency counts of the features of texts, evidence that takes into account a writer's motivations, for example. But, more generally, it reflects the shift that has recently occurred in psychological studies, a readmission of verbal data as acceptable experimental evidence (Ericsson and Simon). After decades of banning people's insights or explanations of their behavior as untrustworthy, psychologists have begun to analyze what people say as they perform a task—for example, as they solve physics problems or consider issues in economics—in order to construct models of what they know and how they think.

Similar procedures have been used to study the writing process as well, most notably by Flower and Hayes, but only recently has this approach found its way to studies of editing, and then it has entered through a back door. Perhaps because editing for errors in grammar and punctuation and spelling appears so automatic, requiring little time or attention or effort on the part of an experienced writer, it has been hard to think of it as an activity that can be observed, that has stages and operations, that requires attention and effort. However, researchers interested in studying the process of composing have necessarily studied the process of editing, for they have found editing high on an inexperienced writer's list of things to attend to while writing. Thus, some studies that address issues of error detection and correction have done so in the context of descriptive research on the entire composing process.

Among the first to examine the composing processes of unskilled writers was Sondra Perl, who tape-recorded five college students as they simultaneously wrote their essays and thought aloud. Using a clever and intricate coding system, Perl tabulated composing behaviors and their duration. One of the most frequent behaviors she observed was editing, which included "indicating concern for a grammatical rule," "adding, deleting, or considering the use of punctuation," "considering or changing verb form," and "considering or changing spelling" ("Composing Processes" 321). Perl concluded that editing occurs so frequently that it often "breaks down the rhythms generated by thinking and writing" (333). And she worried that teachers who stress correctness will reinforce writers' tendencies to be overly concerned with it, which in turn will cause writers to "begin to conceive of writing as a 'cosmetic' process where concern for correct form supersedes development of ideas" (334).

Perl's conclusions, like those of Sommers, have become something of a rallying cry for contemporary teachers and researchers who want good writing to mean more than correct writing. There is Perl's fear that students will, in attending to sentence-level matters, thwart their attempts to compose. And there is the concern, substantiated by Sommers's work, that students tend to neglect substantive kinds of revision in favor of the less crucial matters of correctness. Yet, the question that remains is what to do about students like those Perl observed, who struggle over editing so laboriously, with so little to show for their efforts. One approach is to study the editing process for clues that can suggest how to make learning to edit less burdensome. In a manner analogous to the way that error analysts look at patterns of errors and see evidence of a writer's consistent and rule-governed behavior, it's possible to look at the editing process for evidence of the procedures, choices, strategies, and behaviors that make up error detection and correction. Among the first to recognize the value of this approach for the study of error was David Bartholomae.

In "The Study of Error," Bartholomae reports how he asked a basic writing student to read aloud an essay written for a basic writing class and to stop and correct the errors he found. The student corrected almost every error in his paper, some forty mistakes, but he did not always recognize that there were errors on the page or that he had corrected them orally. The important aspect of Bartholomae's analysis is his use of the student's oral performance to learn about the student's editing ability. He notes, for example, that his student immediately noticed having written "chosing" for "choosing" in the sentence "This assignment calls on chosing one of my incident making a last draft out of it." Bartholomae points out that "while textual analysis would have led to the conclusion that he was applying a tense rule to a participial construction, or over-generalizing from a known rule, the ease with which it was identified would lead one to conclude that it was, in fact, a mistake, and not evidence of an approximative system" (264). This error, he would argue, was rooted in performance as opposed to competence.

Bartholomae's essay cleared a new path for error studies. It illustrated

that textual analyses can't always be trusted to identify error sources reliably and illustrated the value of students' oral reconstructions of their written texts as a diagnostic and instructional tool. It also helped move us from
a consideration of basic writers as merely thwarted and beleaguered in their
attempts to edit their writing to a recognition that students' editing behavior can sometimes be viewed as evidence of linguistic competence. This
is an important contribution, for so long as we observe a writer's attempts
to edit and see only a failure to do so, we are not far removed from the
error tabulators who saw errors in a text only as evidence of things done
wrong.

Having writers edit their essays aloud into a tape-recorder and analyzing their vocal corrections against their textual corrections seem to be means
of distinguishing between genuine errors, or those forms representing erroneous notions about what is correct in a given linguistic environment,
and accidental errors or slips of the pen. In such a manner, research on
editing can supplement research on error sources. Another technique Bartholomae used to study the editing process was to interview students, asking them to account for the changes they made or didn't make as they
edited. This approach can also help clarify the sources of errors, particularly errors resulting from erroneous rules. The reason that a paragraph
is full of comma splices seems wonderfully clear after a student has explained
that she never begins a new sentence until she begins a new idea.

Having students explain the changes they make in texts can also uncover what I have called editing "strategies." By means of a modified think-
aloud protocol—in which writers were asked to read silently until they
reached an error in a text and then to say how they might correct it—I
studied how college writers corrected and commented on the errors they
saw in several pieces of writing ("Editing Process"). The most interesting
finding from this research had to do with the strategies that writers used
to detect and correct errors. Sometimes they consulted their knowledge
of the conventions of written language: "It would look like—there should
be—a comma after 'very bad.' Inside the quotes. . . . Usually when you
have quotes, you have a comma too, especially at the beginning of a sentence." At other times they attended to semantics: "I don't know if I'd say,
'Dr. Lesgold's class was a study in confusion.' I'd say, 'which was confusing,'
maybe. . . . The writer here is acting like that's what they studied. I'm
not really sure how I'd word that. Maybe, 'Dr. Lesgold's class was quite confusing.'" And at other times they relied on a sense that something sounded
amiss, although they couldn't identify the problem precisely: "'Had gone'?
I don't know if that sounds right or not. But I think maybe, uh, 'However,
every year the biology class went to the anatomy lab.' I don't—you know,

it sounds better." Writers draw on various strategies in order to locate and correct errors, and basic writers, as the above examples illustrate, sometimes draw on wrong or unhelpful ones. Such evidence of erroneous strategies is a good reminder of how differently students and experienced writers view the activity of editing and also how actively students apply and develop a schema for editing.

Having writers explain their corrections uncovers a great deal of information about what motivates textual changes but doesn't, of course, reveal as much about those errors that writers fail to see. Here textual analyses and an experimental design can be helpful, as demonstrated by Elsa Jaffe Bartlett. Bartlett asked children to edit some brief paragraphs written earlier by other children as well as to edit their own writing; she reasoned that they would be better able to see particular kinds of errors in the texts of others. In part, she found that children were more likely to detect syntactic anomalies (left-out words) than referential ambiguities (mistakes in pronoun reference) in their own writing. They were better at detecting both types of problems in another's text, where they also could detect either problem equally as well. Bartlett's study shows that all errors are not equal when it comes to detecting them in one's own writing. That is, errors masked by what Bartlett calls "privileged knowledge," or the meaning writers bring to their texts, will be more difficult for children to detect than will errors that are not so masked. (See also Hull, "The Editing Process," for similar findings with college writers.)

If writers bring "privileged knowledge" to their texts, readers do also. In an effort to compare the knowledge about editing that a teacher brings to a text with that of a student, Elaine O. Lees and I have asked teachers to think aloud as they edit students' essays, and I have juxtaposed their readings of the text and the students'. These protocols show that teachers and students can have radically different approaches for going about the task of editing, knowledge systems sufficiently divergent to be barriers to teaching and learning, even when a teacher is aware of a student's particular approach ("Acts of Wonderment"). Such findings also suggest the usefulness of comparing how "experts" like teachers and "novices" like students go about the task of editing. This is a paradigm that, by throwing light on how experienced writers locate and correct errors, can contribute to what we know about those processes and can also locate some of the difficulties involved in teaching students to edit.

Such studies of the editing process are the most recent scholarship on error. They have shown us, thus far, how troublesome editing can be for students, stealing their attention and leaving them little energy for or interest in attending to other aspects of writing. But the research has shown us, as well, that within the apparent confusion and failure of editing as performed by beginning adult writers, there lie the beginnings of a competence. Even as students misplace commas and misspell words in an attempt to edit, they are learning to engage in the kind of reading that will finally serve their purposes as editors. They are, that is, actively employing the strategies that will finally allow them to imagine what might be wrong with the sentences of a text. The research has begun to tell us, too, a little about factors that influence editing other than a writer's lack of experience. Certain errors will prove more troublesome than others, for example, as will editing one's own writing as opposed to another's.

Research on editing has kept time with pedagogy, for many of the techniques used for gathering its data—having students read their papers aloud, for example—can double as tutoring stategies. Indeed, the research has often taken place in the context of a course on writing or a conference on editing, where students are learning to edit and the experimenter is teaching them. Because of this joining of research and teaching, notions of how a student can best learn to edit often come to the fore. Perhaps the most important pedagogical implication of these studies is that students can learn to edit through repeated acts of locating errors and imagining alternatives to them in contrast to learning about errors in the abstract in hopes of somehow inhibiting them.

Future studies of error

In a recent plea for commitment to achieve universal literacy, Jonathan Kozol writes that "not all dilemmas are equally important. Some count a little, some a lot, while others dwell within a separate kingdom of importance altogether." The dilemma that dwells apart for Kozol is adult illiteracy, and he argues that it ought to dwell apart for humanities professors, too: "If scholars do not choose to use their learning to face the need of those who never get within 10 miles of those [college] gates," he claims, "they may succeed in polishing the skills of those already in their own secure domain; but they cannot fail to drive a deeper wedge between the people who already have a fair shot at success and those who have no chance at all." The dilemma that still counts for many inexperienced writers in college classrooms is error. We can choose to make it count less by continued scholarship on the processes of mind that govern error commission and correction.

There is still much to be discovered about the sources or causes of errors in written language. In particular, there have been brief mentions of the erroneous rules that often guide a student's editing behavior—"you shouldn't begin a sentence with 'because'" or "always put a comma when there's a quotation mark"—and researchers like Sondra Perl and Nina Ziv and Mike Rose have documented students' reliance on such maxims. It would be useful to collect, through interviewing techniques, a set of such rules and then to trace their sources to partially learned usage prescriptions or to a student's inventiveness or to the rigid application of a rule that should be applied contextually.

Another neglected source for errors is what I'll call the writer's "rhetorical" aims, which govern those errors tied not to the production of a single sentence but to the larger structures and aims of discourse. There is, for example, a peculiar syntax error that seems rooted not in the problems of combining sentence constituents but in the problem of announcing that a writer is now beginning with a subject or a task: "My future employment, I want to advance myself in the clerical or business field." And in the following passage, the "although" and the "thus" indicate a coherence to the discourse that is not realized on the page: "Many people feel that there are great differences between generations. Especially in the area of ideals and morals. Although Rebecca West challenged this fact by acquiring an upholsterer. Thus, Rebecca West discovered there is hope between the generations because of the young girls' versatility in responces and actions." Here we begin to go beyond questions of editing to questions of revision, but there's a point at which the two kinds of activities overlap— where, that is, a student's discourse aims, inexpertly realized, are reflected in error in the sentence (it can no longer be accurately termed "sentence-level" error). I'm wondering, then, whether a writer's repeated attempts to get a sentence right, attempts we often discourage as an overzealous concern for correctness, might not represent something that we might want to praise; and I'm wondering how to tell the difference.

Thus far, most error studies have concerned themselves with particular kinds of error—errors in syntax or errors in spelling or errors that might be caused by oral language patterns. This is of course a reasonable way to proceed, to divide the universe so that it can be studied. But I look forward to the time when we'll be able to piece these individual efforts together so as to understand not just why students inflect infinitives, writing "I want to learned," and how they learn to correct such mistakes but also how prevalent such errors are and how long they persist and whether certain other errors accompany them and what other errors this particular one is most like. I'm suggesting, then, that the most useful grand category system would treat errors from a developmental perspective, would allow us, so far as possible, to describe a progression in the acquisition of writing skills, for basic writers and for writers in general. For a long time, one of the barriers to such longitudinal research has been the massive record keeping it would require. Computers ought to be the answer here, with their great storage capacities and with the search capabilities that clever programs provide.

There is bound to be interest, too, in the computer as an aid to error detection. Devotees of word processing have long claimed that the process of viewing text on a screen and the ease of altering it foster revision and editing. But there is also the possibility that we can devise programs to analyze the natural language texts of our students, providing feedback on the presence and location and perhaps even the correction of various kinds of errors. Two such efforts are underway: IBM's Epistle project and the University of Pittsburgh's basic writing project. (See Heidorn et al. and Hull, "Computer-Assisted Instruction.") And this feedback need not be limited to visual cues. Elaine O. Lees has recently demonstrated how speech synthesizers, or text-to-voice systems, can assist unskilled editors ("Proofreading"). There is also the possibility, mentioned by Hugh Burns in his chapter of this volume, that the research directed toward constructing intelligent machine tutors will shed light on human thought. In terms of error, this could mean that by creating programs that have the capability to detect errors in texts we gain insights about the correlate procedures in ourselves.

It will be interesting as well to see what new pedagogies emerge from the research on the sources of errors and editing. We'll want to ask ourselves, for example, how to define the relation between causation and remediation—which is another way of saying that it's time to join those studies whose theoretical pinning is locating an error's source to those studies that look mostly at a student's editing process. This undertaking will include research directed at finding out which errors respond to what kind of instruction and how we can provide that instruction while avoiding the pitfalls of previous attempts. In "Forward to the Basics," for example, Robert de Beaugrande has some suggestions about making grammatical principles accessible to students.

All this research needs a home, a context. That is to say, it needs a place within an account of how inexperienced adult writers learn not only to spell and to correct but to invent and to elaborate and to discover. And for such a theory to be sufficiently robust, for it to capture the complexity that is written language, it should, as Mike Rose reminds us, build on a broad conceptual research frame that includes attention to setting as well as to affect and cognition (*When a Writer*). One example of how we might imagine setting as an investigative frame is provided by David Bartholomae, who characterizes the activity of learning to write as the activity of learning to approximate the discourse conventions of particular disciplines and thereby learning to participate in those disciplines as an insider ("Inventing"). His image is of the student who, standing alone outside a closed community, gains entrance through the activity of writing, or learning that community's "specialized, privileged way of seeing and reporting on the world." Perhaps such a vision can suggest a schema, not only for thinking about the activities of learning to write (and to edit) but also for considering the kind of research that is most appropriate when our aim is to design a helping society where educational opportunities are distributed rather than meted out or withheld.

For many students, becoming an insider (like becoming "literate") will have, should have, little to do with learning to be correct; for them error is a minor matter. For other students, becoming an insider will, for a time, have everything to do with learning to edit; for them, error is a dilemma. The research that will aid the second group will pay respectful attention to a student's position as an outsider and will search for ways to ease his or her entry into the academic setting, even to make such a movement possible. It is such research that will, I expect, drive studies of error and editing for the next several years.[1]

Note

[1] Preparation of this manuscript was supported by the Learning Research and Development Center, which is supported in part by the National Institute of Education. I also wish to thank David Bartholomae, whose influence on my thinking about error and editing is apparent throughout, and Carolyn Ball, who provided helpful comments on several drafts.

The Competence of Young Writers

Thomas Newkirk and Nancie Atwell

Near the end of *Phaedrus*, Socrates begins to criticize methods of rhetorical instruction in use at the time. His catalog of miseducation is eerily familiar. He directs his sharpest attack against methods that focus on the "technicalities" of speechmaking, those that exhaustively classify formats for arguments or types of styles without connecting this information with the aims and contexts for speaking. These approaches, Socrates claims, are "threadbare," and he demonstrates their inadequacy by using a medical analogy:

> Socrates: Now if someone came to your friend Eryximachus or his father Acumenus and said that by the application of certain substances to the body of the patient he could induce at will heat or cold, or, if he thought fit, vomiting or purging, and so on, and by the virtue of this knowledge claimed to be a doctor or to be able to make a doctor of anyone to whom he imparted it, what would you think his hearers would say?
>
> Phaedrus: Obviously they would ask whether he also knew what patients should be subject to each of these treatments, and when, and to what extent.
>
> Socrates: Suppose he were to answer: "Of course not. I expect my pupil to be able to find out what you ask for himself."
>
> Phaedrus: Then no doubt they would say: "This man is mad. . . ."
> (*Phaedrus and Letters* 85–86)

Here we have one of the earliest and most devastating attacks on the "skills" approach to language instruction. The whole, Plato (through Socrates) argues, is more than the sum of its parts. It is the selection and ordering of these parts; it is the orchestration of these parts to achieve a purpose in a particular context.

This madness, to borrow Plato's term, characterizes much elementary school instruction in writing (and for that matter in reading). Donald Graves surveyed the instructional priorities concerning writing instruction in the most commonly used language arts texts and found that over seventy percent of the activities dealt with the "technicalities" of writing—grammar, punctuation, spelling, proofreading, and editing—all taught in isolation from actual composing. He recently replicated this survey ("Language Arts") and found few major changes; the "writing" activities that were added were generally unrelated to the process of writing, to the purposes for writing, or to the contexts of writing. Graves's blunt conclusion still holds: "Most writing instruction isn't instruction at all" ("Two-Year Case Study" 59).

Observational studies of classroom practice confirm this picture showing that far more time is spent on isolated skills activities than on sustained reading and writing (Durkin; Rosenshine and Berliner; Goodlad). Walk into the typical elementary school during reading or "language" time and you are likely to see students working away at faded worksheets, engaged in what David Pearson has called "purple education." And unless you come very near a major holiday, you are unlikely to see any sustained writing.

This must seem a somber beginning to a chapter on recent research in children's writing, certainly one of the most productive and happy areas of work in English education. Yet this brief account of current practice can serve as a counterpoint to the discussion that follows, for we are describing a bifocal phenomenon, with the gap between current knowledge and current practice becoming increasingly wider. To read a journal like *Language Arts* is really to read two journals. There is the message of the articles, and there is the message of the advertisements for skill-based texts. While the advertisers may attempt to use the language of process-based education, the products they sell are generally antithetical to that approach.

Research in the past two decades has challenged the assumptions of the skills model, in particular the view that children can be treated as "real" writers only when they have mastered a battery of discrete skills. We have picked two dates to bracket our examination of this challenge—1966 and 1984. The first was the date of the Dartmouth Conference, which rejected traditional assumptions about language learning in favor of a "growth model." We have picked 1984 because it is the year Jerome Harste, Virginia Woodward, and Carolyn Burke published *Language Stories and Literacy Lessons*, a comprehensive reformulation (and revision) of the growth model that synthesizes the body of research carried out since that pivotal conference.

The deliberations of the Dartmouth Conference were summarized in two books, John Dixon's *Growth through English* (1967) and Herbert Muller's *The Uses of English* (1967). But even more influential were the books of two of the conference participants, James Moffett (*Teaching the Universe of Discourse* [1968]) and James Britton (*Language and Learning* [1970]). The themes of these works—the emphasis on processes, on intentions, on the way language is used to know ourselves and our world, on the value of observing language users in natural settings—became the bedrock on which subsequent research would be carried out.

Emphases differed, to be sure. The British tended to stress "personal growth," the capacity of language to give shape to personal experience. For the child this use of language is spontaneous and uncalculating; in Britton's elegant phrase, language is "shaped at the point of utterance" ("Shaping"). The United States educators, and Moffett in particular, were more interested in "intellectual growth," and his developmental schema emphasized growth in the ability to form abstractions.

It was as if there were two uninvited guests standing behind the two groups and offering support. Behind the British group stood William Wordsworth, holding onto a copy of his *Prelude*. Echoes of Wordsworth appear in the British arguments for spontaneity, for the primacy of poetic (as opposed to transactional) language, for direct encounters with the natural world, and for an almost instinctive distrust of institutions – particularly schools – that shape, control, or even deny the possibility of such encounters.

Behind Moffett stood Jean Piaget. Moffett's scheme of development was an attempt to find analogues for the stages of cognitive development that Piaget claimed to have discovered. In addition there is the emphasis on conscious abstracting, and this issue of awareness – of metacognition – would lead to conflict between the British and the United States views.

This conflict recently came into the open with an article by Myra Barrs, an educational administrator in the London schools. Barrs sharply criticized Donald Graves and his associates for, among other things, their emphasis on revision, an emphasis, Barrs argued, that forced an adult model of composing on young children. For many of the British, this emphasis on the consciousness of composing (and recomposing) was contrary to fundamental cultural beliefs about childhood. Graves, like Moffett, views consciousness as empowering. In teaching students to revise, he would argue, we are not denying them their childhood; we are giving them power to control their language and by extension their world. Children may shape at the point of utterance, but they have the possibility of reshaping that utterance.

The seed of another dispute was planted at the Dartmouth Conference – and it had to do with the very concept of growth. To argue that children develop, grow, is to argue the obvious, but any attempt to define growth or development runs a risk. To justify any scheme the researcher must show the relative incompetence of the younger learner. Competence is acquired as the child develops. Because schemes of development must specify the relative incompetence of the young learner, the originators of such schemes may simply miss evidence of competence or evidence of the similarities between the performances of younger and older learners.

We contend that recent research on young writers has extended the map drawn by Moffett and Britton and has shown that parts of this map need to be redrawn. In particular, it has shown that both men underestimated the repertoire of young writers. Both viewed the young writer as dependent on the resources of speech and narrative—writing is initially similar to talk written down. By underestimating the influence of print awareness, of the capacity of children to master at an early age many of the conventions of written language, both claimed, inaccurately, that children begin from a narrow matrix. For Britton this matrix is "expressive writing"; for Moffett it is narrative writing.

The competent beginner

There is more than a hint of Calvinism in much literacy instruction. Schools were founded in the colonies so that children might learn to read the Bible and save their immortal souls. Reading, in other words, was serious business. Errors in writing also carry the whiff of damnation—to the lower ranks of society if not to the lower levels of hell. It is still common for school districts to pay lay readers to correct student errors; while this practice may have minimal value for the student, it does indicate to parents and the community that errors of any kind will not be tolerated. For any error tolerated is an error condoned.

Given this attitude, recent work in invented spelling is startling. Children (and some adults) have been inventing spellings for as long as they have written, but only in the early 1970s did researchers begin to study the systematic nature of children's inventions (Carol Chomsky, "Reading" and "Write First"; Beers and Henderson). In fact, children use a number of systems when they invent spellings. In *Gnys at Wrk* Glenda Bissex illustrates how children frequently begin with a letter-name system. She tells how her five-year-old son had tried unsuccessfully to get her attention and finally resorted to print. Selecting rubber stamps from his set, he wrote: "RUDF." He was, of course, asking, "Are you deaf?" To write this message her son matched the sounds of the words with the names of the letters. This strategy runs into major difficulty with some letters, and invariably one of them is *W*; we is usually spelled "ye" by students using this strategy. The confusion *W* causes is best illustrated by a conversation between two first-graders. One asked, "Do you know how to make a *W*?" "No," the other replied, "but I know how to spell it. It begins with a *D*."

Paul's message—RUDF—also illustrated another feature of invented spelling: the prominence of consonants in the child's perceptions of word sounds. Paul attends to the *D* and *F* sounds in deaf but not to the medial vowels.

This locus of attention is also evident in a sign Paul wrote and put on his door shortly after the note questioning his mother's hearing: "DO NAT DSTRB GNYS AT WRK." Again, most of the sounds represented are consonant sounds. The first vowel sounds to be represented are the long vowels because they are amenable to the letter-name strategy.

But inventive spellers rely on more than the sound of the word. Susan Sowers has noted that children also rely on the point of articulation; they attend to the way a word is formed in the mouth. For example a child sounding out the first sound in *pig* may be feeling the sound as well as hearing the sound. Another (and ultimately central) system is spelling from visual memory. At age six, Paul wrote *this* as "tihs" and *the* as "teh." The daughter of one of us wrote *house* as "huoes" at age five. Had either of these children relied on their sound-to-letter systems, they would probably not have had these sequencing problems. But Bissex notes that such errors are in the direction of progress because the sound-to-letter system can take them only so far in the mastery of English orthography. To advance to conventional spelling they must remember (and initially misremember) the look of words.

Children can also rely on word meaning to assist them in spelling. The most celebrated example, cited in *Language Stories and Literacy Lessons*, was written by Robert, an eight-year-old:

> (The king said to a subject) "I don't care how you do it just do it. I'm the ruler of this land, If you don't do it you will be axlacutted. . . . (Harste et al. 140)

To invent "axlacutted" Robert is probably seeing the word as composed of semantic units that contribute to the meaning of the intended "executed." "Executed" in this context probably means having one's head cut off with an ax, so "axlacutted" captures the meaning Robert sees in the word.

As students explore what they can do with written language they discover other conventions. Marie Clay has identified five principles that children learn concerning print: (1) the recurring principle—long messages are created by repeating a relatively small number of units; (2) the directional principle—language is written in two-dimensional space and it moves in prescribed directions; (3) the generating principle—messages are generated by combining known units in a variety of combinations; (4) the inventory principle—language can be used to array what one knows (see also Goody; Sowers, "Story"); and (5) the contrastive principle—language is made up of critical distinctions and contrasts that children can explore: pairs of letters often differ from each other by some key feature (e.g., *b* and *d*, *W* and *M*, *A* and *H*).

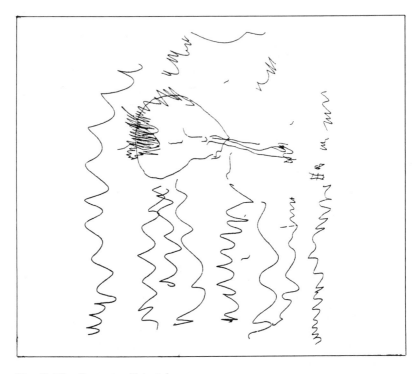

Fig. 5. The Recurring Principle

Fig. 6. The Directional and Contrastive Principle
The text reads: "My Dad works at night."

Children begin to explore these principles even before they attempt to write letters. Early on, in their scribbles, children discover the recurring principle. They find that they can make an extended line of writing by repeating one form again and again. In figure 5, a three-year-old is writing words to accompany one of her first representational drawings. She is able to create text by repeating the zigzag shape that will later be used to produce several letters (A, V, X, W, Y, M, N, Z, K).

In figure 6, written by an older child, there is also exploration of the directional principle. The text begins as a column with the writer trying to write "MY DAD." At the bottom right of the message he writes "WCS" (*works*) and then sends the message right to left "tn ta" (*night at*). The writer also explores critical contrasts between the letters *P*, *b*, and *Y*. If "MP" is not "MY" can he rotate the *P* and get it?

Clay contends that explorations like these have value not only for learning to write but also for learning to read. By "playing" with written language the child learns:

1. How to attend and orient to print.
2. How to organize one's exploratory investigation of printed forms.
3. How to tell left from right.
4. How to visually analyze words and letters.
5. How to study a word so as to be able to reproduce it.
6. How to direct one's behaviour in carrying out a sequence of movements needed in writing words and sentences. (Clay 75)

In addition, when children read their own writing, they have a prior understanding of the message just as they have a prior understanding of books that have been read to them many times. This understanding assists them in their analysis of words and sounds. Children have no such support when reading unfamiliar texts. It is like the difference between doing a jigsaw puzzle with and without knowing what the completed picture looks like (von Reyn).

Children also master the conventions for separating words. When beginning writers move beyond single words, their texts often look like this six-year-old's letter to his stepfather (fig. 7).

The text reads: "Tim I Love You. You are a good father. I am sorry I said go home." The letter is difficult to read because there are no spaces between the words. Indeed, the adult's sense of the word as a clearly defined unit is the result of familiarity with print. But children sense early on that there must be some way of segmenting this string of letters, and they invent strategies to deal with the problem. Many will experiment with a column system where words go across the page or down the page in columns.

Fig. 7. Child's Letter

Even more common is some form of dash or dot system. Sarah at age 4 experimented with dots to segment both letters and words when she wrote her first grocery list:

DOG.FOOD
S.h.n.PO
MEKBONS.

Bissex's son Paul made extensive use of the dot system at age 5. For example he wrote the following sign and put it on his door:

DO.NAT KM.IN.ANE.MOR.JST.LETL.KES. [Do not come in any more just little kids]

Bissex notes that children, when they use this dot system, are rediscovering a method of separating words used by manuscript writers in the Middle Ages.

One of the most critical principles that children learn is the alphabetic principle—that various letters combine to create the word. Young children frequently begin with a more global sense of what a word is. For example, a boy named John may be able to recognize his own name but would be unaware of the contributions each of the letters makes to the whole. Dyson has demonstrated how schools fail to connect with some students by automatically assuming that all children possess this alphabetic awareness. Her warning calls to mind the story of the teacher who, during a reading lesson, urged her children to listen to the sounds of the words—whereupon several of her students put their ears to the book pages.

The repertoire of functions

This research on the mastering of the conventions of print represents an extension—but not a revision—of the map drawn by the Dartmouth Conference. But research on the range of children's writing requires at least a partial redrawing of that map. Both Britton and Moffett viewed the writing of children as restricted in significant ways. Britton and his colleagues argued that writing was closely tied to speech: "Writing is likely to develop from that which relies most closely on the resources of speech (and story) to encompass an increasing range of different kinds" (20). Beginning writing, then, resembles "talk written down," language close to the self and language that will "only rarely . . . be in conformity with highly differentiated adult models" (Rosen and Rosen 95). The only adult writing that Britton and his colleagues acknowledge as important for the child is literature, particularly the story. The story clearly has a privileged place in the growth of the child as envisioned by these educators. Britton claims that he has known a number of children who have taught themselves to write at the age of five or six, and "in each case it was stories that they wrote" (Britton, "Spectator Role" 160). He concludes that this is evidence of the extraordinary ability of humans to succeed at doing what they want to do.

Underlying this view of development, we contend, is a distinctive view of childhood itself. Childhood is a privileged time that must be protected from the forms and demands of adult life and from the conscious rationality that characterizes adult intellectual activity. For in British schools the imposed rationality of the examination system will intrude into children's lives soon enough.

The limitations that Moffett places have somewhat different origins. Like Britton, he views writing as dependent on the resources of speech and story, but he also sees the young writer as working with cognitive limitations:

> Whereas adults differentiate their thought into specialized kinds of discourse such as narrative, generalization, and theory, children must for a long time make narrative do for all. They utter themselves almost entirely through stories—real or invented—and they apprehend

what others say through story. The young learner, that is, does not talk and read explicitly about categories and theories of experience. He talks and reads about characters, events, and settings. (49)

Moffett, then, has two major reasons for claiming this limitation. Since the story is an available extended form of oral language, children can use it while there are no available models of extended oral exposition or argument—oral exposition and argument occur primarily as dialogues. Furthermore, Moffett claims that most children lack the cognitive ability to relate propositions in the manner that is required in nonnarrative prose.

But recent studies of children's writing in home settings (Bissex; Gunlach; Denny Taylor; Newkirk, "Archimedes' Dream") and in school settings where a variety of writing is encouraged (Bonin; Matthews; Sowers) show conclusively that beginning writers do not make "narrative do for all." Furthermore, children begin to explore the various functions of written language from a very early age, often before they attempt to form letters. The differentiation of written language functions appears not to be one of the first things children attend to. For example, in figure 8 we reproduce a shopping list made by Alisha (age 4 years, 2 months).

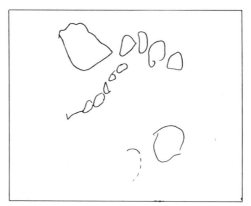

Fig. 8. Child's Grocery List: Cookies, Light Bulbs, and Money

Even though she does not try to represent the items on the list in words, she is showing that she knows what a shopping list is, a mnemonic device for aiding memory. Alisha is appropriating a differentiated model of adult written language, in this case, a model that is not closely related to oral language.

Another adult model that children find particularly attractive is the sign. Like the following advertisement for a booth at a lawn fair, their signs often show the rudiments of persuasive argument:

Desin-a-button
only 75 cents
the desin
cuc.E.Cheese
Unicon rainbows
and much much
more

it's better pric
tan last year
75 cents (age 6 years, 8 months)

Here there is an implied assertion (buy a design-a-button) coupled with reasons why this would be a good idea (the different kinds of buttons and the low price). The message is not expressive in the sense that it is directed to an intimate audience — nor does it resemble speech.

Other examples of nonnarrative forms can be found in children's letters. Take, for example, a letter quoted earlier:

Tim I love you
You are a good father. I am sorry that I said "Go home."
Love Ben

The statements in this letter are not unrelated. Ben begins by stating his love for Tim and then giving a reason. In the third statement he makes his affection more credible by saying that he is sorry for a previous action. This strategy is probably not conscious — awareness generally trails behind achievement — but it does seem evident in this text.

Moffett does admit that a child can write generalizations but they are generally so short as to blur the distinctions they are making; that is, they are so short that they fail to demonstrate that the child can carry on a sustained monologue in writing. But Moffett himself clouds this crucial issue and leaves us to ask how long a piece of nonnarrative writing must be in order to be considered discourse. Is, for example, the following letter from a five-year-old to her mother a true argument?

Dear Mom	Dear Mom
I CANTTACIT	I can't take it
ENEEMOR	any more
I WONT MION	I want my own
BEDROOM	bedroom
Love	Love
MARGOT	Margot

The child has written what Aristotle calls an enthymeme (Corbett, "Theory"), a syllogistic argument with one premise unstated (If I can't take it anymore I should have my own room).

It would seem far more profitable to take seriously the discursive writing that children choose to do, instead of denying its validity and assuming that "narrative must do for all." Work on story structure needs to be extended to look at the many structures children use in their writing. Story grammars need to be joined by list grammars, letter grammars, sign grammars, argument grammars, newspaper grammars. This examination will also suggest, we contend, that current models of writing development are far too simple.

Just as linear models of the writing process have had to be rejected in favor of more complex models that allow for a variety of paths in the production of texts, the models of writing development must evolve to account for the multiplicity of development. A term like "expressive writing"—if it must describe all the writing children do—simply sinks under the weight of the cargo it must carry. The argument for invariable stages of development becomes increasingly untenable in writing just as it has been soundly challenged in developmental psychology (Donaldson; Boden; Gardner). Attempts to find these developmental stages in writing have come up empty. When Graves proposed to the NIE his longitudinal study of children's writing, he fully expected to find "sequences of behavior along developmental lines," but in his final report—*A Case Study*—he notes that the variability of development became increasingly evident as his project continued. In "Development in Writing" Carl Bereiter similarly concludes that while children must integrate various "skill systems"—skills in social cognition, critical-literary judgment, rules of style and mechanics, and so on—children are not "yoked" to universal stages of development and, depending on educational experience (and presumably on individual temperament), they can master these systems in a number of different orders.

Toward a theory of competence

Margaret Donaldson's book *Children's Minds* is best known for its critique of Piaget's claims on the egocentricity of young children. But in the book she also challenges another giant, Noam Chomsky. Noting that children between the ages of two and five learn most of the syntax of human language, Chomsky suggests that human beings have a highly specific predisposition to understand language systems—a kind of language-acquisition device particularly attuned to using available bits and pieces.

Donaldson rejects the claims that the capacity to learn language is highly specific; rather, she claims, the child's ability to learn language is part of a more general ability to make sense of situations involving human interaction:

> The primary thing is now held to be the grasp of meaning—the ability to "make sense" of things, and above all to make sense of what people do, which of course includes what people say. On this view, it is the child's ability to interpret situations which makes it possible for him through active processes of hypothesis-testing and inference, to arrive at a knowledge of language. (33)

The child, then, can master language because he or she masters situations. Children learn to read texts because they can read contexts.

Donaldson's point is neatly illustrated in perhaps the best "language story" from *Language Stories and Literacy Lessons*:

> Joe, age 9, was shown a stop sign with the word "Ban" written on it as part of our efforts to explore the linguistic sign as formed by the relationship of print in context. We had found this particular Stop sign in a magazine advertising Ban Underarm Deodorant. In the context of the magazine advertisement the message was clear: "Ban stops wetness." By clever cutting, we were able to remove all other print and so managed to save the octagonal shape with the word "Ban" on it. We showed this print setting to Joe, a neighbor child, who not only knew of our interest in studying young children's writing and reading, but also knew our research quite well. Interrupting his play, we asked, "Joe, what do you think this says?" Joe paused a moment and said, "I suppose it says 'Stop' in German or something; that's just the sort of junk you'd carry around to pull out and ask unsuspecting kids about!" (Harste et al. 151)

Through stories—almost parables—like this, the authors develop a semiotic theory of language learning, a theory that places such learning in the wider context of learning to interpret signs. In the case of the Ban stop sign, its original meaning is signaled by its location and layout in relation to the articles in the magazine—readers of magazines instantly recognize it as an attempt to sell a product. The readers of the magazine ("readers" of traffic signs as well) also recognize the octagonal shape as signaling stop. When the researchers took this object and presented it to Joe in another context, Joe could not retrieve the original meaning but he could assign a meaning consistent with the new context. The object itself does not possess meaning; we assign meaning—we treat the object as a sign. Had Joe been shown this same advertisement in another context—in a frame in a modern art museum—he undoubtedly would have assigned it an entirely different meaning.

To read or write, then, we must rely on our awareness of how literacy communities operate, on the way communities use "signifying structures" to indicate various language intentions. This point was nicely illustrated at a recent conference where a presenter was giving a talk on "interpretive communities." Part of the way into the talk he asked the audience to read a text that he projected onto the screen. The projection failed to enlarge the text enough for the audience to read it, and there were those half-good-natured groans that accompany technical snafus. The speaker apologized and then asked, offhandedly, if we could tell him anything about the text. Someone volunteered that it was a poem because of the irregular right-hand margin. The speaker asked when it might have been written. Some-one else volunteered the nineteenth century because of the regular four-line stanzas. Did we have any idea what kind of poem? A lyric, someone guessed, because it was a relatively short poem. And by this time we recog-nized the trick. As members of an interpretive community that reads poems we could assign meaning to the various "signifying structures" of the text. The text, it turned out, *was* a nineteenth century lyric poem—written in Russian.

According to Harste, Woodward, and Burke, we learn about these sig-nifying structures by attending to "demonstrations"—to the processes of language users and to the products they produce. Take, for example, the diet plan drawn up by Sarah at age six. Her mother was beginning to diet after the birth of a third child and would regularly weigh out servings in accordance with the Weight Watchers' guidelines. Wanting to be part of the action, Sarah drew up her own plan for each day of the week. Tues-day's regimen is included as figure 9.

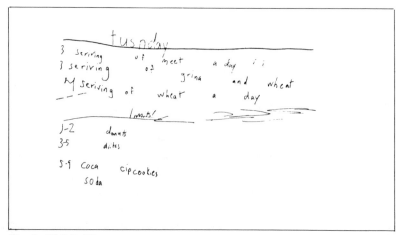

Fig. 9. Child's Diet

While diet plans are probably not included on any scope and sequence chart for first-graders, Sarah was able to pick up the conventions for setting a plan up—the indication of number of servings, the division of servings into food groups, the different diet plans for each day, the separation of food groups from sweets, and the limitations on the number of each sweet type. While her allowances for sweets may seem particularly generous, she clearly has mastered some conventions of indicating a diet plan because she had access to demonstrations of this form.

Children who also have access to a variety of types of letters quickly pick up the conventions of letter writing. We include as figure 10 an invitation to Ben's sixth birthday.

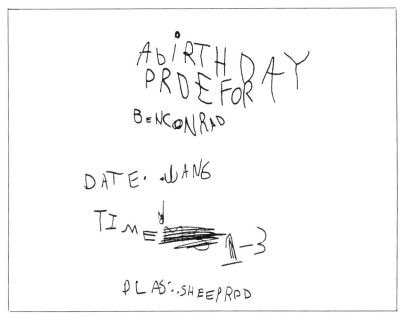

Fig. 10. Child's Birthday Invitation

Ben shows that he understands the order in which information should be included. He begins with the purpose for the invitation and then includes the three pieces of information that are necessary for the invitee to come—the date, the time, and the place. In writing this information he uses (appropriately) a column system rather than the connected text he uses in writing stories. He even understands that some form of punctuation should separate the category of information (date, time, place) from the specific information, and he experiments with dots and a colon-dot combination.

In neither of the previous two examples does the child seem to be relying substantially on oral language; rather, the children seem to have ap-
propriated written forms available in the home environment. But oral
language is clearly a resource that children draw on as well. One first-grade
teacher, bothered by the frequent interruptions during her writing conferences, told her students that she could be interrupted only by a written
note. This injunction spawned a wave of note writing. Here is one of the
longer exchanges:

> *Catrina*: I rot about I have a boy fan [friend] *Dont* Til [tell] Parks Do
> you no how [who] is may [my] *Boyfan?*
> *Teacher*: It must be Parks since you don't want him to see. Am I right?
> *Catrina*: Yes.
> *Teacher*: Well, he'll know as soon as you publish the book or read
> it to the class, won't he? What about that? You'll still be embar-
> rassed.
> *Catrina*: Yes [crossed out]. But [crossed out]. No I navr sat [thought]
> about that sut [should] I til him?
> *Teacher*: Well—which is more embarrassing? Telling him now or wait-
> ing for him to hear your story?
> *Catrina*: Telling him.

This language does sound very much like "talk written down"—like expressive language. But even this child is also relying on the demonstration
of a written form; that is, by writing back comments to the original note,
the teacher is showing the student how a written dialogue can work. To
sustain the written dialogue the child draws on both conversational skills
and on a knowledge of written forms made available by the teacher's demonstration.

The authors make a critical distinction between "demonstration" and
a term that is often used interchangeably with it, "modeling." Modeling
too often engages the student in imitating content or behavior without
understanding the relations or rules that underlie the model. The term
also suggests that the person doing the modeling has a complete conscious
awareness of the specifics to be picked up by the learner. Furthermore, it
suggests that these specifics are picked up in toto.

By contrast, the demonstration is made available to the learner so that
he or she might choose to appropriate features of the demonstration. Central to this view of learning is the "tacit" nature of most learning; relatively
little learning comes through direct instructions. Rather it occurs in situations where neither teacher nor learner is in full, conscious, articulate pos-
session of what he or she knows or learns. To borrow Michael Polanyi's
expression, demonstrations are essentially "mute acts of intelligence" (70).

If children are attuned to the various signifying structures in the texts that surround—or can surround—them, then it seems implausible to argue that any particular type of writing represents the starting point for all beginning writers. Indeed, the possibilities seem almost infinite:

> There is no sequence to the order in which the demonstrations involved are inherently learned. Which demonstrations are learned is a function of which demonstrations are highlighted. The context in which literacy occurs strongly affects the nature and direction of literacy learning. (Harste et al. 195)

The work of Harste, Woodward, and Burke also suggests the improbability of claiming that the writing of children will resemble speech and "only rarely . . . be in conformity with highly differentiated adult models." As readers of their culture, children seem particularly capable of appropriating differentiated adult models.

The implications of this work for future research are powerful as well. Not too many years ago context-based research (then called "action research," still a pejorative term among hard researchers) was seen as part of a continuum leading toward more controlled studies that isolated key variables. (See Bereiter and Scardemalia, "Levels.")

Harste, Woodward, and Burke reject this view. Ethnographic studies of literacy events are not part of a continuum leading to or from experimental studies. They represent an alternative "worldview," one in which phenomena are not reducible to components that can be "controlled" experimentally: "To 'control' a component is to distort the relationships which occur, and in the process, alter the event so that it is no longer an instance of what one is studying" (53). For this reason, the claim of experimental studies for generalizability is ultimately hollow: "From a semiotic perspective experimental research data are not generalizable because they deal with a distorted sign. How can studying nonlanguage instances, where key aspects of the process (which we have yet to identify) are not allowed to transact, help us understand real language?" (53). Context, in other words, is not a variable that can be swept aside.

But what does all this have to do with the classroom, with teachers caught in systems of skills instruction that they do not understand or that they feel powerless to challenge. Instead of promoting a *method* for teaching, these researchers offer a way of seeing. Harste, Woodward, and Burke claim that their research is grounded on an attitude of "I can find out," an attitude as important for teachers as it is for researchers:

The research attitude of "I can find out" is absolutely liberating, not only for teachers and researchers, but also for children. For us this new attitude allows a change from testing our language hypotheses to giving children an opportunity to test theirs. For children it allows a change from being tenants of our texts to owners of their own texts. (223)

For the teacher used to relying on a system that claimed to provide the answers, this shift can be a lonely one. But as teachers develop this capacity to *see*, to detect the intelligence that went into a scribble, they will break some of the barriers that have kept them aliens in their own profession.

Technical Communication in the Information Economy

Michael L. Keene

Technical communication—both inside and outside academia—is one of the most rapidly growing fields today. This growth and the factors causing it are producing research into the uses of language that may shape the work all of us will do in the coming years. The purpose of this chapter is to provide a definition of the field, a review of recent research and pedagogical developments in its academic side, and a look at current concerns and research initiatives in the applied, professional side of the field.

Technical communication today is alive and abundant with interesting scholarship. In 1984 our leading journal, *Technical Communication*, published a special issue on education in technical communication (vol. 31, no. 4). The largest professional organization solely for technical communicators, the Society for Technical Communication (STC), recently published a major bibliography, *An Annotated Bibliography on Technical Writing, Editing, Graphics, and Publishing, 1966-1980*. And a recent collection of essays by leaders in the field, *New Essays in Technical and Scientific Communication*, edited by Paul Anderson, R. John Brockmann, and Carolyn Miller, covers key issues in depth. Thus, whether one seeks information at the level of one chapter, one journal, or an entire book, the topography of technical communication and recent research is now readily accessible.

Definition of the field

First, let's settle a nagging question of terminology. The proper name of the field is "technical communication"; the leading professional organization and the leading journal both follow this usage. The field includes any number of smaller areas (and corresponding skills): technical editing, technical writing, technical speaking, science writing, popularized science writing, medical writing, publications production, graphics, design, information management, and (although this is debatable) business communication, to name but a few. Thus "technical communication" is a generic or umbrella term; around the fringes of the area it covers we should expect some disagreement over just what the term properly includes. David Dobrin of MIT provides a thorough philosophical discussion of definitions of the key subarea, technical writing, in "What's Technical about Technical Writing?"

No attempt to define the field of technical communication is complete unless it covers both sides of the field: on the one hand, the teachers and their students; on the other, the editors, writers, designers, artists, and managers who work for business, industry, and the government. Let's call the former group "the academics," the latter "the practitioners." A rough idea of the proportional sizes of the two groups is provided by the 1985 membership figures of the Association of Teachers of Technical Writing (just over 1,000) and of the STC (just under 10,000). The October 1984 *MLA Job Information List* advertised 16 openings for assistant professors specializing in technical communication. Soon after that MLA list came out, a Sunday issue of the *Boston Globe* advertised 46 technical communication positions.

The interplay between the two groups is considerable: academics and their students become practitioners, and practitioners become academics and students of academics. While one tends to see only the academics at the MLA convention and at the Conference on College Composition and Communication, the two groups mix freely and profit from each other's experiences at the STC's International Technical Communication Convention and the myriad of smaller meetings (such as the Practical Conference on Communication, sponsored by STC's East Tennessee chapter and held at the University of Tennessee, Knoxville).

In the introduction to the special issue of *Technical Communication* on education, Paul Anderson, who is with the master's degree program in technical and scientific communication at Miami University, finds four main points of contact between the two groups: (1) the basic service course, Technical Writing, taught at the junior or senior level in colleges and universities all over the country and frequently taken by current or future practitioners, (2) the role of educators in professional societies such as STC, which has always welcomed educators and prized academic training for practitioners, (3) the growing number of specialized programs for technical communication majors; programs typically created and steered with the assistance of the practitioners in that college's region, and (4) the mutual interest in research, which necessitates and encourages sharing between the academics and the practitioners. Though the demand for teachers of technical communication is growing rapidly, the demand and the salaries for practitioners seem to be growing faster.

Just as there has been debate over the best name for this whole field, so there has been debate over how broadly to construe the field. While there is a major umbrella organization, there are also a number of (not necessarily smaller) specialized organizations, such as the important Council of Biology Editors and the American Medical Writers Association. In "What Technical and Scientific Communicators Do," Paul Anderson presents a definition of the field that nicely pulls all its parts together; "the common aim of all technical and scientific communicators," he says, is to "solve problems that involve the management and communication of specialized information, where that information is to be used for practical purposes" (163).

So far we have been looking at technical communication from the outside in, so to speak; let us now look at its inside. What is there about technical communication that makes it different from other kinds of writing? Different answers focus on the strength of the message (if you have to describe a piece of machinery, much of what you say is dictated by that message), the varieties of audiences (from forklift operators to chief executive officers), or the special qualities of technical communication's purpose (it is always functional writing). A recent textbook by Charles Stratton of the University of Idaho describes the special qualities of technical communication in terms of the rhetorical triangle (writer, subject, and reader): creative writing focuses on the relation between writer and subject, expository on the relation between writer and reader, and technical on the relation between subject and reader (5–6). Put briefly, technical communication's special characteristic is the inherent tendency for the subject being discussed to overpower the other elements in the rhetorical situation.

The most cogent analysis of that special character of technical communication is restated by Mary B. Coney and James W. Souther, both of the University of Washington. Writing that lets the message have its own way they call "encyclopedic"; writing that takes into account purpose, audience, and situation (as well as message) they call "analytical." R. John Brockmann of the University of Delaware discusses the implications for teachers of technical communication.

Recent research and pedagogical developments

A number of bibliographies document recent research and pedagogical developments in the field of technical communication. In the *Technical Communication* special issue on education, Myra Kogen (of Hofstra University) and the CCCC Committee on Technical Communication have compiled an excellent short bibliography of one hundred important published sources. In addition, the Association of Teachers of Technical Writing also publishes a yearly bibliography in its journal, the *Technical Writing Teacher*. As mentioned earlier, the STC has recently published a major bibliography. Gerald Alred, Diana Reep, and Mohan Limaye take a historical approach in *Business and Technical Writing: An Annotated Bibliography of Books, 1880–1980*, and Jone Rymer Goldstein (of Wayne State University) and Robert B. Donovan survey key documents in *A Bibliography of Basic Texts in Technical and Scientific Writing*. Jack Selzer of Pennsylvania State University points out many ways that academics can find out more about technical communication besides consulting published sources—most notably, by seeking assistance from practitioners ("Resources").

"The teaching of technical writing is on the verge of a revolution," says Goldstein (25). She lists as sources for that revolution modern rhetorical theory, composition pedagogy, and empirical research. Modern rhetorical theory's contribution is the denial of the idea that language—especially scientific and technical language—is most properly viewed as a window through which objective reality is seen. When that objective reality is seen most clearly (that is, when the language does the least to obscure it), the document's purpose is fulfilled: others see what the author has seen. According to modern rhetorical theory, however, all language is rhetorical: language creates (as opposed to transmits) meaning—language is persuasive. Thus the readers and writers of reports require attention beyond that paid to the message. Composition pedagogy contributes to this revolution by its switch from "product" to "process" models of writing; new models emphasize the sequential and recursive elements of composing that lead to successful manuscripts. Empirical research contributes through sociological studies of the behavior of real writers and readers in the workplace and through cognitive studies of mental processes in writing and reading. Other areas Goldstein does not list as influences may be equally important, including two not originating from academia: the rapidly growing information economy (discussed later in this chapter) and the computer revolution. The growing influence of computers on the teaching of writing is explored in two recent NCTE books: *The Computer in Composition Instruction* (by William Wresch) and *Computers in the English Classroom* (by Sally Standiford, Kathleen Jaycox, and Anne Auten).

In more specific terms, perhaps the most significant pedagogical innovation in the teaching of technical writing (other than the growing use of computers) is the rapidly spreading case-study approach, described by R. John Brockmann, among others. Thomas Pearsall, professor and head of the department of rhetoric at the University of Minnesota, gives an example of the case approach at its simplest:

> You are a young executive in a firm in your professional field. You have been employed there for six months since graduating from the University. You realize that your department could profit by introducing a new procedure you learned at the University. You would like to persuade your boss to adopt this new procedure. Your boss seems satisfied with the way things are currently done in the department. He knows the field well, having graduated from the University 20 years ago in the same major you are completing. Also, he has personally introduced most of the current procedures himself. You realize it will be tricky, but you decide to write your boss a memo urging him to consider the new procedure. (23–24)

The advantage of this approach, says Pearsall, "is that teachers have a realistic way of evaluating the product that results. Would the finished product . . . meet its purpose? Would it convince the boss? . . . " (24).

Suppose, however, the imagined reader is an industrial engineer with twenty years' experience. Will the technical writing teacher, whose experience outside academia may not include much exposure to such people, be able to make a "realistic" reading of this report? As R. Scott Kellner of Texas A&M University points out, technical writing teachers do not necessarily have the backgrounds that would enable them to make such judgments accurately. Yet in front of a class of seniors and graduate students in engineering, the technical writing teacher who would use the case approach must know for a fact how engineering audiences respond. If a technical writing teacher does not know how the assigned audience will respond to the kinds of documents students may submit, that teacher will find the case method a perilous pedagogy.

Another significant curricular development that affects the teaching of technical writing is the already widespread movement known as writing across the curriculum. It appears in at least two varieties. In one, the various university departments build strong writing components—possibly even specialized writing courses—into each department's own curriculum. In the other, specific courses within the English department are tailored to allow students from the different disciplines to do writing appropriate to their disciplines. James Kinneavy of the University of Texas, Austin, describes these two varieties fully and thoughtfully in "Writing across the Curriculum." His conclusion places the movement's significance in perspective not just for technical writing teachers (who are typically intimately involved in it) but for the entire English department:

> Thus the writing-across-the-curriculum movement could, if properly pursued, place the English department at the center of the entire university community. But the price of this enviable and appealing prospect is for the English department to enlarge its interests from literary discourse to all discourse. English should be the study not just of literary artifacts and their production but of all language artifacts written in English, and especially of scientific and rhetorical artifacts. The department can then rightfully assume the title it usually takes: the Department of English. Such a department accepts as its province the scientific, the literary, the rhetorically persuasive, and the expressive texts of the language. (20)

A final factor that will be a powerful influence on the teaching of technical writing is the growing number of nonnative speakers of English in technical writing classrooms. The situation is nicely described by Carol Lipson, who leads the technical writing program at Syracuse University; her bibliographical approach will be especially useful for anyone who seeks to survey the literature of this field. She summarizes important published sources on "the cultural and historical influences that students from selected foreign cultures will bring with them" (233). She concentrates on students from three cultures: Arab, Japanese, and German. At the end of her article she also suggests texts that can be used for preparing classroom materials for such students. An especially important recent book in technical writing will make teaching nonnative speakers much easier. *English for Science and Technology: A Handbook for Nonnative Speakers*, by Thomas Huckin and Leslie Olsen of the University of Michigan, is an especially useful, major set of materials for teaching technical writing. Its chapters on connectives, countability and the indefinite article, the definite article, relative clauses, cohesion, modal verbs, verbs, and vocabulary building will be helpful to nonnative students (and their teachers).

Perhaps the most fertile area of current research in the academic side of technical communication is audience analysis and adaptation. Because audience provides an especially good example of an area in which academics and practitioners profit from (and share in) each other's research, I discuss it in the next part of this chapter.

Current concerns and research initiatives among practitioners

The overlap between academics and practitioners is increasingly filled by specialized programs in technical communication. Each year the *IEEE*

Transactions on Professional Communication compiles a list of such programs. According to Lionel A. Howard, Jr. (with Bell Communications Research, Inc.), in the 1984 list, a survey in 1975 found 15 bachelor's and graduate programs; the 1983 list names 128 institutions and 176 programs, and the 1984 list contains 177 institutions and 275 programs. The design of such programs has become a primary opportunity for practitioners and academics to work together, as demonstrated by Marcus Green and Timothy Nolan (both of Cincinnati Technical Institute). Their study of what technical communicators actually do resulted in these three conclusions:

> (1) The technical communicator is best described not simply as a writer or editor, but as a 'communicator' in a very broad sense. (2) Above the entry level, the job of the technical communicator involves a substantial amount of project management. (3) The entry-level tasks of the technical communicator's job focus very sharply on researching, writing, and editing (10).

In a study commissioned by the STC, Susan Feinberg of the Illinois Institute of Technology and Jerry Goldman of De Paul University polled a wide sample of practitioners and academics and used the Delphi method to discover the ideal design of a technical communication course.

The relation between teachers and practitioners can become touchy. Finding sufficient numbers of technical communication teachers with experience as practitioners is at times difficult for an English department. Some departments have taken to training their own teachers, a practice that can be very good or very bad, depending on whether the individuals involved succeed in finding experience as practitioners. R. Scott Kellner reviews this whole subject forcefully in "The Degeneration of Technical Writing." The supply and training of practitioners is also a problem. Although the importance of academic (as opposed to on-the-job) training for technical communicators is readily acknowledged, the value of the particular training some students receive is at times questioned. Fed by this concern and by the desire for members to be recognized fully as professionals (in the sense, say, of certified public accountants), the STC continues to consider either the certification of programs or the certification of practitioners (or both). Few issues generate so much heat within the profession, as witness this letter published in *Technical Communication* ("Correspondence"):

> There has been a lot of talk about STC accrediting technical communicators. It sounds nice, but in the end I believe STC would be cutting its own throat. I believe 90% of the technical communicators can be divided into two stereotypes:
> *Male, 40–50 years old, uneducated, and an ex-military technician

who is unable to write a correct sentence, but is knowledgeable in electronics. This person is often appointed head of a technical publications department because of his sex and age.

*Male or female English or journalism majors who state they can write and edit, and say they don't care if they understand what they are writing about and don't need to know what they are writing about.

I think both of the above stereotypes exist and make the worst technical communicators. The ideal technical communicator knows grammar, but is able to bend the rules when necessary to make something clearer or more friendly, and constantly reads and updates himself/herself technically. You cannot test these skills.

Hopefully, companies hiring technical communicators in the future will demand the traits of the ideal technical communicator, and the two stereotypes listed above will disappear, along with the dinosaur (without the help of an inaccurate accreditation test), because of their refusal to change. (Name withheld by request)

Significantly, the STC regularly profiles its membership. The "STC Membership Profile," by Shirley Carter (supervisory information management specialist with the Social Security Administration) and William Stolgitis (executive director of STC), shows that 90% of today's members have at least bachelor's degrees and 33% have masters or PhDs, figures that belie (on the surface, anyway) the stereotypes the letter describes. But who the technical communicators are, where they work, and what they do—not to mention what the significance of their work is—are subjects insufficiently addressed in the literature.

The concerns mentioned here are perhaps inherent in any field. A major concern more special to technical communication is the ongoing technological revolution, centered on computers. While in the next chapter Hugh Burns discusses the promise of artificial intelligence for writing, computers have already had a great impact on the publication and dissemination of technical information. Out of a myriad of discussions, the 1983 *Technical Communication* special issue on word processing and computerized composition (vol. 30, no. 4) is notable for its coverage of many important areas. The issue's editor, Patricia Caernarvon-Smith (vice-president of Firman Technical Publications, Inc.) summarizes the articles:

> Interestingly, each paper carries a common thread: automation is coming. Automation's most obvious symbol is still the acquisition of hardware. How we plan for it, purchase it, and use it are important issues. Less obvious but of more lasting importance is how we deal with all this hardware: by being involved in the decision-making process, in training, in security, and in the use of such systems, we professionals will have a strong influence on the eventual outcome of automation.

Practitioners as well as academics can feel threatened by this flood of technology. In its extreme form, this flood can make people fear for their very jobs. Marketing analyst William Houze, in "Today's Technical Writers/Editors in Tomorrow's 'Electronic Mega-Cottage Industry' World of Work: Will They Survive?" presents a disturbing future in which the substance of editorial functions has been taken over by computers.

Beyond computerized text management and production systems, computers are affecting both the face of technical documents and their audiences. As it becomes easier and easier for an editor to arrange words and visuals on a screen and then transfer precisely that image onto paper, the psychology of design gets more complex and more critical. A good review of recent problems in this area is provided by Annette Norris Bradford, senior associate information developer with the IBM Corporation in Kingston, New York.

Computers are having an equally significant effect on the audiences for technical information. One manifestation of this is the "electronic journal," whose primary availability to readers comes via on-line computer network. In areas such as medicine, where the timeliness of information is critical, electronic journals are especially attractive. The background and early stages of this phenomenon are reviewed by Jacques G. Richardson, editor of the *Impact of Science on Society*, a UNESCO journal.

The computer revolution's new audiences are not only producing new media such as the electronic journal but also bringing major changes in the way traditional documents look. These changes range from the tone and style of technical documents to the way individual pages look. David Bradford, manager of distributed systems programming publications with the IBM Corporation in Kingston, New York, explains the developing persona in technical communication. He contrasts the "typical technical persona" (suppression of first-person pronouns, use of passive voice) with the new, user-friendly persona (characterized by such conventions as humor, irony, cartooning, reinforcement, personification, personal pronouns, analogy and metaphor). Bradford concludes that, "In many cases we may be able to persist in adopting the traditional technical persona, but since that option can no longer be the default value for the practicing technical writer who seeks to address this audience, our newer role is much more likely to fall somewhere within the vaguely defined realm of the user-friendly" (66).

In user's manuals and other documents, the face of technical communication is changing as well. Such techniques as Robert Horn's "information mapping" (the term is copyrighted by Horn) emphasize breaking the text into coherent, concise units known as "information blocks," using marginal labeling for internal indexing, grouping related blocks together as single-page "maps," and providing exercises and questions after each unit to aid comprehension and recall. Horn's book, *How to Write Information Mapping*, describes the technique in detail. Although the profession has been slow to adopt Horn's techniques, the new pressures and changing information environment (described, e.g., by David Bradford) may well make information mapping or something very much like it the wave of the future.

Both of these last topics—the ways computers affect the face of technical documents and the changing audiences for those documents—are key factors in establishing the readability of any text. Of course readability is an especially important factor in technical documents. An excellent recent review of this complex subject is the special issue on readability of *Teaching English in the Two-Year College*, with Gary Olson of the University of North Carolina, Wilmington, as guest editor (Winter 1984). Part 2 of Anderson et al.'s *New Essays* ("Reassessing Readability") contains two thoughtful contemporary views on the subject: "What Constitutes a 'Readable' Technical Style?" by Jack Selzer and "A Cognitive Approach to Readability" by Thomas Huckin.

If technology provides the single biggest area of innovation in the field, the most important area of research is the concept of audience, especially the recognition of different audiences and of the accommodations those audiences demand. Perhaps the fullest treatment of this subject is Patricia Caernarvon-Smith's *Audience Analysis and Response*.

Research into audience also provides one of the most fertile areas of partnership between academics and practitioners. The recent research by Thomas Pinnelli (of NASA Langley Research Center) and others on preferences of readers of NASA reports provides a case in point. NASA funded original research on this subject because it needed to know how readers respond to the technical information it produces. Yet the results of the research are a feast for academics. Too much that has been written about audience in this field is based on introspection or anecdotal information and too little on solid research.

The last set of topics I discuss in this chapter is also potentially the most important (and also ripe for academic-practitioner partnerships). A salient fact of life for technical communicators has been the growth of the information economy (documented early on by Daniel Bell and by Marc Porat). While the United States economy may be said to have its historical bases in agriculture, manufacturing, and commerce, information has become a fourth major source of economic activity. Persons directly involved in the economics of information, such as Joshua Smith, chief executive officer and chairman of the board of Maxima Corporation, estimate this sector's percentage of the gross national product to be as high as seventy percent. Because of the attention given this topic, the dollar value of the information produced in government, business, and academia has become a subject of study. This study may concern how the information's value compares with its cost, how value may be added to the information, or how such value should properly be measured.

A landmark study in the first area is *Value of the Energy Data Base* by Donald King of King Research, Inc., under subcontract to Maxima for the Department of Energy. That study finds a ratio of about 2.2 to 1 between the value and the cost of such information. That is, "the DOE paid $5.8 billion for the research, information processing, and use which in turn has been found to be worth at least $13 billion" (1). Robert Taylor of Syracuse University provides a full discussion of problems associated with determining both value and value added. Writers and editors will find worth in being able to demonstrate the value of their skills in terms of value added to a particular document. Just as the teaching of writing is expensive because it is labor intensive, the technical editor's services are similarly expensive. As editors begin to demonstrate in dollars and cents the value of their work (see, e.g., Post), so too will writing teachers. In demonstrations of the worth of those services lies a more secure future for academics and practitioners alike. The key issues currently being researched by technical communicators—computers, training for writers, the characteristics that mark different sorts of discourse, the problems inherent in different sorts of discourse, the factors that make a text more readable, the way a given audience needs to shape a text, the information economy—will affect all of us who teach and study English. On each issue, the field of technical communication provides a valuable perspective.

The Promise of Artificial-Intelligence Research for Composition

Hugh Burns

So I said to the doctor, "I like computers, but I'm supposed to be a humanist. I read Arnold, Blake, Eco, Jarrell, Lowell. I teach Orwell, Aristotle, McPhee, Plath, Faulkner—still bytes, software, fifth-generation computers, and escape keys don't terrify me. Sure, most documentation scares me silly. But I don't mind teaching college freshmen how to craft argumentative essays; in fact, I enjoy watching them mutilate electronic draft after electronic draft. I like it myself—the tinkering, the moving here and there. Death to passives! But what really worries me, Doc, is that I am enjoying my research in artificial intelligence. I'm building expert systems and intelligent tutorial systems. I read Minsky, McCarthy, Schank, Anderson, DeKleer. I even think that part of my enjoyment comes because the many AI analogies to composition processes amaze me. I think there's a lot that any writer or writing teacher can learn from what's going on in artificial-intelligence research. What's wrong with me?"

The doctor said, "Did you say you don't mind teaching college freshmen? Is that what you said? You must be terribly ill. You'll need to come back more frequently."

"But you're missing the point, Doc. I'm a humanist who thinks some good will come from using machines in the humanities classroom, especially the composition classroom. I like computers."

"Artificial intelligence? A? I? Freshman composition? Yes, I'm beginning to understand now. I can see why you are worried."

Thanks to such therapy, I learned that I wasn't the only teacher befuddled by today's computer technology; however, I did verify I was one of the more optimistic.

I also learned through a series of personally financed ethnographies that most of us are pessimistically puzzled because visions of psychotic computers like Arthur C. Clarke's Hal from *2001* dance in our heads. Imagine that trapped in the vacuum of deep space—with stars reflecting off a plastic faceplate and heard, underneath, a soundtrack of deep, anxious breathing—a teacher confronts the 64K Hal Junior not far from the final frontier and thus speaks Zar Synthesizer: "I'm sorry, Hugh. I cannot let you write." No such electronic, synthesized wheeze in our classrooms.

Thank you very much, but no thanks. Never mind those laws of robotics we sometimes call writing assignments!

Nevertheless, our most human traits—intuition, imagination, wonder, hope—draw us toward the fascinating study of ourselves. How do we know? How do we create? How do we think? How do we feel? How do we write? How do we read? How do we remember? How do we forget? How do we learn? How do we teach? To me, artificial-intelligence research not only helps us address these enormous questions but also helps us start the investigation. This ambitious task alone is one promising feature of artificial-intelligence research for composition teachers.

Twenty-five years ago, if you had heard a conversation about intelligence and the emerging technology of AI among philosophers, psychologists, educators, and humanists, you would have heard an informative and entertaining discussion about the metaphysics of knowing, the beginnings of cognitive science, the formation of scholars interested in instructional theory, and many analogies drawn from art, music, dance, and literature for explaining the abstractions of intelligence. You would have heard little about implementing, imitating, or Lisp programming intelligent models for knowing, creating, thinking, feeling, reading, writing, remembering, forgetting, learning, or teaching. If instead you had listened to electrical engineers, computer programmers, mathematicians, and some youngsters who called themselves electronic engineers speculating about intelligence, the discussion would have substituted metaphysics for physics, complex information processing for data processing, and cybernetics for FORTRAN. Certainly more attention would have been given to the implementation of intelligence. How do we build a model of thinking? How do we build a model of creating? How do we build, test, and evaluate a model of learning? How do we build a model of writing? Twenty-five years ago, our professional paradigms were largely distinct.

Times have changed—what a surprise! As tubes yielded to transistors, cognitive psychologists at MIT, Stanford, Carnegie-Mellon, Yale, and elsewhere sought out programmers. As transistors yielded to integrated circuits, linguists and translators sought help from computer scientists. As integrated circuits now give way to very high speed integrated circuits (VHSIC), even rhetoricians collaborate with enlightened directors of instructional computing. In *The Soul of the New Machine* Tracy Kidder examines what seems to be at stake when we think about the sociology of computers and intelligence:

'Artificial Intelligence' had always made for the liveliest of debates. Maybe the name itself was preposterous and its pursuit, in any case, something that people shouldn't undertake. Maybe in promoting the metaphorical relationship between people and machines, cybernetics tended to cheapen and corrupt human perceptions of human intelligence. Or perhaps this science promised to advance the intelligence of people as well as of machines and to imbue the species with a new, exciting power. (241)

Most modern composition teachers fall into this first group and would agree that any machine analogy to the writing process is essentially a false one. For me, however, artificial-intelligence research is dissolving the artificiality of our twentieth-century specialities. What this preposterous pursuit called artificial intelligence may promise English educators, therefore, is a future-looking technological perspective on research and scholarship in composition, cognition, and computers. A sophisticated notion of how the mind works in the writing process may continue to elude researchers for a long while, but another gateway for understanding ourselves may come through such research. Far from corrupting writers' perceptions of human intelligence, these computing machines dedicated to artificial-intelligence research and application promise to imbue English language professionals with new, exciting powers. Despite the megahype (a computer as person of the year?) that incorrectly assumes computers are the great common denominator, we know the common denominator has been, is, and will continue to be human curiosity or, if you prefer, human ignorance. Today's computers enable our curiosity to explore our essential humanity in the hope that we simultaneously discover our ignorance and do something about it. We only have to remember Orwell's own experiences in Burma to realize that a computer would not shoot an elephant.

Toward rhetorical processing systems: Sublime or ridiculous?

What remains imprecise about many definitions of artificial intelligence is the precise ratio between the computer and the human mind. For Margaret Boden and some AI researchers—the ones for whom we are likely to have more empathy—artificial intelligence is "a symbolic and psychological model for representing and replicating intelligent human behavior." Boden defines artificial intelligence as the study not of computers but of "intelligence in thought and action." She cites Marvin Minsky's definition that "computers are its tools, because its theories are expressed as computer programs that enable machines to do things that would require intelligence if done by people" (*Artificial Intelligence* 3–4). Why should we as people interested in writing have empathy for this particular definition of artificial intelligence? First, people write. Second, writing is a symbolic and psychological process that derives from a mental model and ultimately generates a representation known as a text. Third, neither the model, the process, nor the text is threatened by the tool, by the computer. The rhetorical implication, however, is sublime: a theory of composition that is computationally precise and accurate would enable a computer program to follow the theory, build a model, and generate a text. Writing tools have not been able to do this before, have they? A quill was a quill was a quill. Writing tools have not seemed to remember before, nor have people thought so much about investigating those seams of experience, memory, and language before.

For other AI researchers—the ones who will seem a bit more practical—artificial intelligence means nothing more than complex information processing on sophisticated computers. In this context, AI is the use of computers to perform tasks typically considered to require human intelligence. Avron Barr and Edward Feigenbaum define artificial intelligence as "the part of computer science concerned with designing intelligent computer systems, that is, systems that exhibit the characteristics we associate with intelligence in human behavior—understanding language, learning, reasoning, solving problems, and so on" (1: 3). Why should practicality be appealing for researchers interested in the writing process and the teaching of writing processes? First, human energy is finite. Second, many tasks require intelligence but are only intelligent drudgery. An intelligent computer program that helps us solve the important problems is valuable for this reason alone. Third, such systems only are programmed to "exhibit" intelligent characteristics of human behavior.

The rhetorical implication here is merely beautiful: a computer system that exhibits those characteristics that we associate with writing should be able to identify features of our language use. These features, now represented as computational artifacts fragilely trapped on silicon, can be combined and analyzed in the performance of writing. We can define and capture an electronic protocol analysis if you will and, with some sound pedagogy and human inspiration, design an intelligent tutor for the writing process. Our teaching tools have not truly interacted before. Out of the human mind, therefore, comes a machined program that at once may mirror the human mind and perform some menial, intelligent tasks.

If these definitions are too broad and consequently imprecise, then perhaps stated goals of artificial-intelligence research will set up more of an operational definition and allow us to speculate on analogies in composition research. Dirk Hanson writes that the primary goal of AI "is to push back the limits on what computers can do, to make man's premier machine his intellectual equal" (307). We might find this idea overstated and too controversial because we may at first mistakenly believe that computers will be able to do everything if the limits are always being pushed back. Besides, what does "intellectual equal" mean? But what if I stated brashly that my goal as a composition researcher and teacher was to push back the limits on what people could write, could think, could arrange, could edit and, as a glorious consequence, to make them my intellectual betters? Would that idea frighten you? So many of our feelings about computers have to do with the unknown and therefore feared intention. In the "premier machine" case, the intention of the computer scientist or researcher is unknown, so we pose, unfortunately, as Caliban to some computer corporation's Prospero. There must be more than a single brave new world, for in the example of the computer teacher you probably assumed my intentions were good. Now I will assert that my goal of pushing back intellectual limits about writing processes is no different from yours – or else you wouldn't be holding this collection of essays. For us, AI research could articulate *how* to push the limits of our understanding *about how* we operate as writers, thinkers, arrangers, and editors. What an enormous challenge: understanding the billions and billions of conscious and subconscious decisions a writer makes.

Beyond the binary brain

You may have seen that poster of an auburn-haired chimpanzee with its long right arm twisted at incredible angles reaching over its puzzled head and cross-eyed countenance to scratch its left ear. The caption: "It isn't easy having a true-or-false mind in a multiple-choice world." Now take this wonderfully funny caption and paste it on any picture of a computer. What's left but – capital T – truth?

Another promising aim of AI research, therefore, is to represent those true-or-false decisions that – once assembled – resemble a single choice in a multiple-choice world. Douglas Hofstadter writes in *Gödel, Escher, Bach* that "the aim of AI is to get at what is happening when one's mind silently and invisibly chooses, from a myriad alternatives, which one makes the most sense in a very complex situation" (560). No one said writing research would be simple; in fact, it might be argued that the aim of research in writing is to get at what is happening when one's mind silently and invisibly chooses, from a myriad alternatives, which rhetorical decision makes the most sense. Both AI researchers and composition researchers must exploit each and every linguistic and rhetorical detail.

How can this intellectual scrutiny come about? The computational linguistics scholars who investigate an area called natural language processing have learned to focus microscopically on particular features of language, but a field called computational rhetoric or natural discourse processing has yet to emerge. At the risk of using too much jargon, I list a few of the major topics in computational linguistics: parsing algorithms, semantic constraints, slot grammars, semantic networks, cascaded augmented transition networks, pronoun resolution, and explanation generation. From the discoveries made at this admittedly minute level will emerge computational models of phrases, clauses, and sentences. Now at the risk of making up too much jargon and some absurdity, I list a few computational rhetoric topics beyond the sentence: persuasive algorithms, pragmatic constraints, slot texts, tagmemic networks, heuristic cascades, expository resolution scripts, and dramatistic motivation representations. Now you know why the doctor was so worried about me. I sometimes think I know what a heuristic cascade could be, and—perhaps worse yet—I think I could define it well enough for you to agree with me. Or vice versa.

When we understand the science of words well enough, then we can begin to use words with artful elegance. If we understand the science of sentences well enough, then Cicero's ornaments may even drift into our personal garden of eloquence. The act of composing takes us far beyond the word and beyond the sentence. Likewise, AI is a way of exploring issues far beyond any human-made, binary brain.

Perhaps the best key on this AI researcher's ring for understanding intelligence is the study of language in action: the study of the language arts— reading, writing, speaking, and listening. The next best key on the ring, however, is being used more frequently: the study of expert behaviors for designing performance and training aids called, respectively, expert systems and intelligent tutorial systems. Both expert systems and intelligent tutorial systems promise to influence the way English composition will be taught.

Expert systems and cognitronics

It startles me to realize how quickly expert systems have caught on in our industrial society. What should have been a cautious step in applying artificial-intelligence research is not, especially after some exaggerated claims in the seventies, such as the "automatic language translation system." But expert-systems technology as a particular artificial-intelligence application is gaining too much publicity too soon. The basic science in cognition, linguistics, and knowledge representation has not yet built a strong technology base. This intelligent computer application now proceeds in parallel with incomplete and perhaps "buggy" scientific findings. The electronics work may be complete enough, but the cognitive psychology and linguistics work has hardly started. Nevertheless, if this entrepreneurial enthusiasm can be tempered some, the industrial, business, and educational research communities may have a promising technology.

An expert system is a computer program that assists a human being by providing professional, humanlike expertise. Several prototype expert systems have been developed to assist in structural engineering, medical diagnosis, mineral exploration, and computer design. In medical diagnosis, a doctor looks for symptoms and, as they are discovered and as they correlate with the doctor's own experience, the doctor is able to properly diagnose the disease. An expert system operating in this way really assists in fault diagnosis; it helps you find the problem.

For the past two years, I have been investigating the issues of building expert systems, and the problem of so-called knowledge engineering is significant. A colleague likes to say that a lot of "cognitrons" have to fire if the entire domain of some closed system is going to be represented well enough to imitate a real expert. Imitation is the goal, and passing Turing tests provides the excitement—a Turing test being a procedure that pits human beings against computers programmed to seem human. An expert system under development attempts to imitate the troubleshooting process, and the first notion that evolves is an undeniable certainty about how terribly complex a human intelligence system is.

What does a knowledge engineer do? A knowledge engineer (1) writes if-then-else rules that accumulate evidence values for asserting that a certain state of affairs exists, (2) assembles and organizes these rules, frames, or scripts so that they are linked together in a common knowledge base, (3) writes sets of computer interaction screens that appear when the actual expert system is being consulted, and (4) throughout all this, hopes that the source of the expertise (a schematic, a technical document, an interview with an expert, a footnoted exception) is indeed true. When the knowledge-engineering work is complete, a knowledge base has been built. This warehouse of rules now can be searched by using any number of strategies, such as depth-first or breadth-first, to discover and report probable causes for a certain known situation. The computer program that searches the knowledge base is often called an inference engine—a term that makes many of my colleagues uncomfortable. Nevertheless, the inference engine finds promising causes and assembles a queue of tests that allow the expert system to interact with the user. What this system does is find "best guesses."

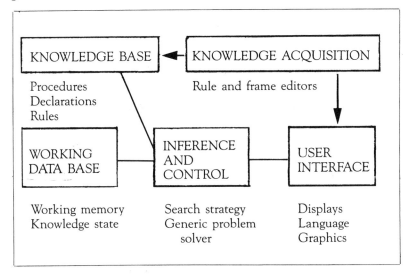

Fig. 11. Expert-Systems Architecture

In an expert system designed to help troubleshoot car engines, the following dialogue could occur:

> *ES (Expert System):* The purpose of this program is to help you isolate the problem with your car. Does your car start?
> *User:* Yes
> *ES:* Does your car run roughly?
> *User:* Yes. [With this information, the knowledge base is searched to find information that explains why cars run roughly. Once rules for "running roughly" are discovered, then the expert system will need more inputs from the user in order to "disambiguate" among the collected probable causes.]
> *ES:* A car that runs roughly suggests two probable causes. The problem could be a fuel problem or a carburetor problem. These can be checked rather easily. Please answer these questions; you may have to conduct a test and report a result. Has your gas mileage been low?
> *User:* Yes, it's been low.
> *ES:* Do you use high-grade gas?
> *User:* Yes.
> *ES:* Look inside the carburetor? Is it dirty?
> *User:* Yes.
> *ES:* Do you see any cracked hoses leading to the carburetor?
> *User:* No. [Now with this new information, the knowledge base is

again searched to find other causes and other tests that will enable this computational guessing machine to continue to solve the problem.]

Such a dialogue is, in fact, the state of the art. Underneath this dialogue are chains of rules, normally written in a version of a computer language called LISP (List Processing), that have asserted that the carburetor may be the culprit.

Fixing car engines is one thing, but writing is another. In composition, it is more difficult to isolate just what causes problems such as writer's block, loss of fluency, or poor coherence, because the symptoms are so difficult to recognize and describe let alone collect in a relational knowledge base. The problem with expert systems that identify the fault is that they too often stop there. "Dig for oil here" may be good advice to the chief executive officer of an oil company, but "Dig up another counterargument if rhetorical balance is important to you" may leave a writer cold. In the first case, the CEO knows how to dig for oil. In the second, the writer may not know how to dig up another counterargument. That writer would probably ask the computer to give a hint or two. Expert systems ought to be able to explain themselves, and some research is under way in this area.

If the first task in developing an expert system is knowledge engineering, then an appropriate first activity for language arts teachers would be to spend some time designing an expert system for their composition classrooms and going through the grueling articulation of knowledge bases, inference structures, and interfaces. Below I suggest a model for doing that and also suggest questions that may enable researchers in composition to weigh possible strategies for incorporating expert-systems analogies in their instructional repertoires.

In expert-systems technology, computer programs are developed to help novices demonstrate more expertise; such expert tools promise the evolution of automated writing aids, provided the knowledge engineer can articulate rhetorical expertise well enough to have a goal.

I am experimenting with an expert system that will help a writer decide which formal prewriting strategy would be the most effective depending on whether the writer wants to persuade, inform, or express. If a writer's goal is to persuade, then leading a writer to compare Aristotle's topics with his or her own topics or to compare Toulmin patterns with his or her own organizational pattern could be a promising consultation with an expert system. Likewise if a writer wants to inform, then invention and arrangement troubleshooting sessions comparing Kenneth Burke's dramatistic strategies or sequenced steps (process or time) in the draft stage could be useful. If a writer was writing to express, then an inference engine that could explore the text for analogies, image inventories, and clusters of ideas around a theme would be interesting. Unfortunately, it's not that easy even when it looks naive and oversimplified. The idea has yet to catch on in composition research because compositional expertise is much fuzzier, since few would state that writing can be circumscribed like an electronic circuit board, a car engine, or a five-paragraph theme. If, however, a knowledge engineer can divide the problem into finite parts by performing a thorough task analysis, then there is some hope that an expert system can be built.

The task analysis for inventing included top-level steps such as (1) has the writer studied the assignment? (2) has the writer discovered the appropriate materials? (3) has the writer defined an audience? and (4) has the writer set aside some time to write the paper? From this analysis, the rule building began. But, as you can predict, a "no" answer to any of these four questions would branch the student to advice such as, "The library may have some materials." Not good enough, but it still beats my saying that to sixty-seven freshman each semester.

The task analysis for inventing at deeper levels leads to more interesting questions, such as (1) has there been a court case? (2) is there a test for each inference against the counterargument? (3) has all relevant time been accounted for? and (4) do some clustered ideas appear to overlap too much in the text? The problem for the knowledge engineer at this level is deciding how to interpret the evidence so that the program will be able to make a best guess as to what the problem is. This inexact inferencing capability is one of the major benefits of an expert system. In chess, all the alternatives can be surveyed, and a grand-masterly move results. What does a grand-master of the essay do next? What has this expository genius seen as the next best step? How have the implications of that rhetorical move now changed the state of the emerging composition?

The promise that writers will become more experienced experts in the processes of troubleshooting composition and will see their compositions improve as a result is a fine and noble goal. If mechanics can isolate faults, so can writers. The development of expert systems has become a commercially attractive venture, and if the systems prove to be experts, they are bound to increase in number and quality. But the state of AI expert-systems technology today makes it safe for me to state unequivocally that I would have more success helping you change your car's spark plugs than helping you with those firing pins of your imagination. It would not be as much fun, but at least it would provide some reasonable service. What this means, however, is that some work in computational rhetoric remains to be done.

R-2-Fish-All instruction: More questions than answers

"Artificial" – my kindergarten daughter once spelled it "R-2-Fish-All" because it reminded her of one of the services R2D2 could perform for Luke Skywalker of *Star Wars* fame. And though she did not elaborate, what good pedagogy! Either this dumpy little robot can fish all the time, or it could teach someone to fish. Beware CP30, for the art of teaching may return once again to the memorable lessons Tom Sawyer taught us all at Aunt Polly's unwhitewashed fence in Hannibal, Missouri. Either the computers will write for us all the time, or the computers will help teach us to write. Which situation will AI research and development leave for the educational marketplace and, in particular, composition instruction? Will the legacy be a text-generating system complete with grammar checker and word-counting mechanism? Or, better, will the legacy be a human being with stimulating ideas, freshly rendered, who enjoys confronting the page? Which tactic leads us to this second alternative? In other words, how can composition teachers use their understanding of the applications of artificial intelligence in education to better design intelligent computer-assisted writing instruction? It's time to be involved.

Intelligent computer-assisted instruction has long been a goal of educational researchers and training developers. In intelligent computer-assisted instruction (ICAI) and in intelligent tutorial systems, computer programs adapt to demonstrated learning styles, instructional strategies, and diversified content simultaneously. An intelligent tutor is one class of ICAI that pays particular attention to the demonstrated performance of a particular task. The major difference between traditional CAI and ICAI is that ICAI adapts to the student based on the cumulative evidence derived from three separate modules. ICAI can change its instructional strategy, its representation of the student, and its content without affecting the "inference engine" that drives the program. Consequently, the goal for ICAI is to recognize what the student needs to know, when to intervene, and how to model the learning taking place. The pitfalls are deep and expensive, to be sure. The advantages of conducting composition research in this area, however, will be most promising.

Like expert systems, intelligent computer-assisted instruction will capitalize on research in knowledge acquisition and representation, inferencing heuristics or search strategies, and natural language understanding. The essential difference between ICAI and standard CAI is how the decision to branch is formulated and enacted. In standard CAI, the singularity of if-then drives the branching decision. As an example, if ten seconds pass, then print "Keep writing." If the characters S-T-O-P are recognized, then stop. In ICAI, the program branches after analyzing input from three sources—the content of the lessons themselves, the instructional strategy, and the demonstrated behaviors of the student. What exists then are at least three nested if-then statements. For example, if introductions for essays should have surprise value and if a model of an introduction with surprise value has been shown and if the student has imitated the syntax of that model opening at least twice, then ask the student to compare and/or evaluate two of five surprising openings written by professional writers. The instructional decision-making capability is more robust, more flexible, and more open-ended. And the fact today is that ICAI is unfortunately more of a goal than a reality.

Let's look at the three components in more detail. The first module is a rule-based representation of the expertise or the content, and the aim of the design of the expert module is to represent knowledge accurately and efficiently. The first goals of design will be to examine the procedures and how to represent step-by-step problem domains. Then the expert module should have multiple representations of the same content. More than likely, these meanings would be represented in a semantic network, networks of meaning that tangle intentionally around similar meanings, states, and goals.

The second module models the student's own learning strategy. These modules will be the complex set of algorithms for identifying learning styles and recognizing the motivational strategies that will work best for a particular student. At the center of this module will be the construction of pattern-recognition techniques that will capture the information being typed or, perhaps, even spoken by the student. These patterns could be implicit, that is, recognizing the keyboard behavior. The patterns could also be explicit in that prior knowledge could have been gained by the computer. For example, a machine could be programmed to ask for historical information about the student's writing habits. There should also be a structural bridge to the content and a subjective interface that would gauge some of the aptitude measures that will allow the program to infer how to branch this particular student in this particular content area.

The most problematic module to develop may be the instructor module. In this module, rules would have to be designed to (1) identify the goals for the lesson or the task, (2) decide on the feedback strategy—immediate or not, (3) adapt the amount of instruction appropriately, and (4) formulate the intervention tactics. Finally, all these matters are integrated with the other two modules. ICAI is nothing if not ambitious, but these programs do not have to run for a few years yet.

One of the best examples of an ICAI program is called Guidon. Guidon teaches medical students diagnostic problem solving of infectious diseases. William Clancey of Stanford University, the principal investigator, recounts a partial though specific interaction:

> [Guidon asks the student to state a hypothesis for a subgoal. The student may have volunteered to do this, or the program may be testing the student's understanding.]

> G: What is the type of the infection?
> User: Bacterial.

> [The program asks the student to support this hypothesis either because it is incorrect or, as in this case, because the student model indicates that the student may not know all the relevant rules.]

> G: What facts about this case tell you that the type of the infection
>   is bacterial? (Enter one factor per line.)
> User: PMNs.
> G: The percent of PMNs in the CbC is not relevant for determin-
>   ing the type of infection.
> User: PMNs in the CSF.
> User: Cerebral-fluid glucose value.
> User: Protein of the CSF.

> [These factors are related to the rules used to conclude that the infection is bacterial, and the student model is updated accordingly.]

> G: You're right about the CSF protein, the percent of PMNs in the
>   CSF, and the CSF glucose value; however, you should have men-
>   tioned the fact that the meningitis is partially treated, the WBC
>   from the CSF, and the fact that the simultaneous blood glucose
>   value is not known. (Barr and Feigenbaum 2: 273–74)

Obviously, this Guidon interaction is based on rules, evidence, and dimensions of a particular case. Could not an ICAI lesson be modeled on a composition case study—reporting a presidential press conference, persuading other students to vacation at Aspen over Christmas break, or writing Shakespearean sonnets rather than Italian sonnets? Perhaps the most intriguing possibility for composition will be the intelligent writing tutor or even a robust word-processing package.

The composition instructor who designs a series of intelligent computer-assisted instructions in advanced stylistics or an intelligent tutorial system for writing an expository essay will discover more unanswered questions about what writers do and what teachers understand about the act of writing. Some of the major questions are:

> When and how should computers intervene in the writing process?
> What are the most appropriate writing intervention strategies for invention, arrangement, and style?
> How could they be assembled as rules and linked to one another in a knowledge base?
> What other answers do we need as English educators about tutoring writing while writing is ongoing?
> How can master-apprentice roles in the composing process be computationally defined?
> How can writers be modeled as production systems?
> How can developmental writing assignments correspond to writers as production systems?
> How can AI-based composition become rich, robust, and flexible?
> What will the consequences of this kind of writing instruction be? Too much priming the pump? Never beyond a prototype? "R-2-Fish-All-ing"?

To note and improve the usefulness of such programs as Writer's Workbench, Wandah, Epistle, Topoi, Tagi, Burke, Maxthink, Think Tank, Brainstorm, Create, Seen, Compupoem, Dialogue, and Complab depends on noting and improving how these programs incorporate intelligent aiding and tutoring strategies. Every software designer I know agrees that instructional software for composition is imperfect. Every instructional software designer wishes for more memory, more processing speed, and more interactive feedback in order to be able to make the next version *seem* more knowing, more assertive, and more cooperative. Word-processing software such as Wordstar, Text Wizard, Bank Street Writer, Word, Perfect Writer, and MacWrite also will improve as more human-factors research is accumulated and intelligently engineered back into the next generation of writing software.

Knowing that this hardware and software marketplace is improving rapidly does not mean that composition teachers should avoid making an initial purchase of Brand X computers and Brand Y software just because "something better will be out in the next six months." Most hardware today can pass the "good enough" test in fine fashion though we all can quibble about a keyboard design, an optical mouse, a memory capacity, or a screen color. The word-processing software likewise passes most "good enough" tests. The instructional software for composition, though, is another matter. Much of it is not good enough, and some of it (including my own) is counterproductive if used indiscriminately. The intelligent writing tool will never be intelligent enough, and that is why composition teachers will need to stay in the instructional loop, following not only the research in writing but also the research in artificial intelligence.

The high road

Four years ago, not long after I stumbled officially into the field of artificial intelligence by writing pattern-matching subroutines to answer questions, I wrote an article entitled "Pandora's Chip." There I listed my concerns for developing quality computer-assisted instruction: "Developing quality computer-assisted instruction, to my mind, will have to become an inter-disciplinary activity." Little did I know that artificial intelligence researchers had formalized many of the interdisciplinary convenants I was describing and urging others to form. Today, although I think the stages of satura-tion, imitation, dissatisfaction, and assurance are useful concepts for un-derstanding the sociology surrounding instructional software design, I would not list as many variables for evaluating quality in software. Today, com-putational quality boils down to finding software that seems to understand us and our language. That means "designing in" more and more intelligence.

In order for us to do so, the programs will have to understand language, since intelligence is manifested in language. So who are the language arts experts? Today, computational quality in composition software simply means finding writers and teachers who seem to understand us and our language well enough to get involved in designing these tools. How will they be-come rhetorical-knowledge engineers? I am not sure I know the answer, but the direction we should move is not served by complaining that cyber-netics corrupts human perceptions of intelligence, by assigning essays robots could write, by isolating ourselves from the technology students carry in backpacks, or by fearing Hal Junior's electronic wheeze. English educators, composition researchers, and most of us in the humanities need to take the high road. Not that we give up offering constructive criticism of an emerging technology: we all must perform that role. The high road means accepting that science does not exclude art, research does not exclude prac-tice, and artificial intelligence does not exclude human intelligence. Rather art interprets science, practice defines research, and human intelligence promises sophisticated, "artificially intelligent" computer applications for composing and the teaching of composition. Yes, Doc, I like computers, but I like people who write well and teach well even more.

Works Consulted

Abercombie, M. L. J. *Anatomy of Judgement.* Harmondsworth: Penguin, 1960.

———. *Talking to Learn: Improving Teaching and Learning in Small Groups.* Soc. for Research in Higher Education. Surrey: U of Surrey, 1978.

Abrams, M. H. *The Mirror and the Lamp.* New York: Norton, 1958.

Adams, M., and A. Collins. *A Schema-Theoretic View of Reading Comprehension.* ERIC, 1977. ED 142 971.

Agar, Michael H. *The Professional Stranger.* New York: Academic, 1980.

Alred, Gerald J., Diana C. Reep, and Mohan R. Limaye. *Business and Technical Writing: An Annotated Bibliography of Books, 1880–1980.* Metuchen: Scarecrow, 1981.

Anderson, Freeman. *New Directions in English (Grades 1–8).* New York: Harper, 1973.

Anderson, Paul V. "Introduction." *Technical Communication* 31.4 (1984): 4–8.

———. "What Technical and Scientific Communicators Do: A Comprehensive Model for Developing Academic Programs." *IEEE Transactions on Professional Communication* PC-27.3 (1984): 161–67.

Anderson, Paul V., R. John Brockmann, and Carolyn R. Miller, eds. *New Essays in Technical and Scientific Communication: Research, Theory, Practice.* Farmingdale: Baywood, 1982.

An Annotated Bibliography on Technical Writing, Editing, Graphics, and Publishing, 1966–1980. Washington: Soc. for Technical Communication and Carnegie Library of Pittsburgh, 1983.

Applebee, Arthur N. *The Child's Concept of Story: Ages Two to Seventeen.* Chicago: U of Chicago P, 1978.

———. *Writing in the Secondary School: English and the Content Areas.* NCTE Research Report 21. Urbana: NCTE, 1983.

Argall, Rebecca S. "Sentence Combining: An Incisive Tool for Proofreading." Conference on College Composition and Communication. San Francisco. 18–20 Mar. 1982. ERIC ED 214 186.

Aristotle. *Rhetoric.* Ed. Lane Cooper. Englewood Cliffs: Prentice, 1960.

Arnauld, Antoine. *The Art of Thinking.* Trans. James Dickoff and Patricia James. Indianapolis: Bobbs, 1964.

Atwell, Nancie M. "Class-Based Writing Research: Teachers Learn from Students." *English Journal* 71 (1982): 84–87.

———. *In the Middle.* Stamford: Boynton. Forthcoming.

———. "Writing and Reading from Inside." *Language Arts* 61 (1984): 250–52.

Bailey, Richard W., and Robin Melanie Fosheim, eds. *Literacy for Life: The Demand for Reading and Writing.* New York: MLA, 1983.

Bain, Alexander. *English Composition and Rhetoric.* New York: Appleton, 1866.

Barnes, Douglas. *From Communication to Curriculum.* Harmondsworth: Penguin, 1976.

Barnes, Douglas, and Frankie Todd. *Communication and Learning in Small Groups.* London: Routledge, 1977.

Barr, Avron, and Edward A. Feigenbaum, eds. *The Handbook of Artificial Intelligence.* 3 vols. Los Altos: Kaufman, 1982.

Barritt, Loren, and Barry Kroll. "Some Implications of Cognitive-Developmental Psychology for Research in Composing." Cooper and Odell, *Research* 49–58.

Barrs, Myra. "The New Orthodoxy about Writing: Confusing Process and Pedagogy." *Language Arts* 60 (1983): 829–40.

Barthes, Roland. "From Work to Text." *Textual Strategies.* Ed. Josue V. Harari. Ithaca: Cornell UP, 1979. 73–81.

Bartholomae, David. "Fact, Artifacts, and Counter-facts: A Basic Reading and Writing Course for the College Curriculum." *A Sourcebook for Basic Writing.* Ed. Theresa Enos. New York: Random. Forthcoming.

———. "Inventing the University." *When a Writer Can't Write: Research on Writer's Block and Other Writing Process Problems.* Ed. Mike Rose. New York: Guilford. Forthcoming.

———. "Released into Language: Errors, Expectations and the Legacy of Mina Shaughnessy." *The Territory of Language: Linguistics, Stylistics, and the Teaching of Composition.* Ed. Donald McQuade. Forthcoming.

———. "The Study of Error." *College Composition and Communication* 31 (1980): 253–69.

———. "Writing Assignments: Where Writing Begins." *Forum: Essays on Theory and Practice in the Teaching of Writing.* Ed. Patricia Stock. Upper Montclair: Boynton, 1983.

———. "Yes, Teaching Grammar Does Help." *English Journal* 73 (1984): 66–69.

Bartlett, Elsa Jaffe. "Learning to Revise: Some Component Processes." *What Writers Know: The Language, Process, and Structure of Written Discourse.* Ed. Martin Nystrand. New York: Academic, 1982. 345–63.

Beach, Richard, and Lillian S. Bridwell, eds. *New Directions in Composition Research.* New York: Guilford, 1984.

Beaugrande, Robert de. "Forward to the Basics: Getting Down to Grammar." *College Composition and Communication* 35 (1984): 358–67.

———. "Psychology and Composition: Past, Present, and Future." *What Writers Know: The Language, Processes, and Structures of Written Discourse.* Ed. Martin Nystrand. New York: Academic, 1982. 211–68.

———. *Text, Discourse, and Process.* Norwold: Ablex, 1980.

Beaven, Mary H. "Individualized Goal Setting, Self Evaluation, and Peer Evaluation." Cooper and Odell, *Evaluating* 135–56.

Beers, James, and Edmund Henderson, eds. "A Study of Developing Orthographic Concepts among First-Graders." *Research in the Teaching of English* 11 (1977): 133–48.

Bell, Daniel. "The Social Framework of the Information Society." *The Microelectronics Revolution.* Cambridge: MIT P, 1981. 500–49.

Bennis, Warren G., and Herbert A. Shepard. "A Theory of Group Development." *Human Relations* 9 (1956): 415–37.

Bereiter, Carl. "Development in Writing." *Cognitive Processes in Writing.* Ed. L. Gregg and E. Steinberg. Hillsdale: Erlbaum, 1980. 73–93.

Bereiter, C., and M. Scardemalia. "From Conversation to Compositions: The Role of Instruction in the Developmental Process." *Advances in Instructional Psychology.* Ed. R. Glaser. 2 vols. Hillsdale: Erlbaum, 1982. 2: 1–64.

———. "Levels of Inquiry in Writing Research." Mosenthal et al. 3–24.

Berkenkotter, Carol. "Student Writers and Their Sense of Authority over Texts." *College Composition and Communication* 35 (1984): 312–19.

———. "Understanding a Writer's Awareness of Audience." *College Composition and Communication* 32 (1981): 388–99.

Berkenkotter, Carol, and Donald Murray. "Decisions and Revisions: The Planning Strategies of a Publishing Writer, and Response of a Laboratory Rat—or, Being Protocoled." *College Composition and Communication* 34 (1983): 156–72.

Berthoff, Ann E. *Forming/Thinking/Writing: The Composing Imagination.* Rochelle Park: Hayden, 1978.

———. *The Making of Meaning.* Montclair: Boynton, 1981.

———, ed. *Reclaiming the Imagination: Philosophical Perspectives for Writers and Teachers of Writing.* Montclair: Boynton, 1984.

Bissex, Glenda. *Gnys at Wrk: A Child Learns to Write and Read.* Cambridge: Harvard UP, 1980.

Bizzell, Patricia. "Cognition, Convention, and Certainty: What We Need to Know about Writing." *Pre/Text* 3 (1982): 213–39.

———. "Thomas Kuhn, Scientism, and English Studies." *College English* 40 (1979): 764–71.

———. "William Perry and Liberal Education." *College English* 46 (1984): 447–54.

Black, Janet K. "Those 'Mistakes' Tell Us a Lot." *Language Arts* 57 (1980): 508–13.

Bleich, David. *Reading and Feelings: An Introduction to Subjective Criticism.* Urbana: NCTE, 1975.

———. *Subjective Criticism.* Baltimore: Johns Hopkins UP, 1978.

Bobrow, D. G., and Allan Collins, eds. *Representation and Understanding: Studies in Cognitive Science.* New York: Academic, 1975.

Boden, Margaret. *Artificial Intelligence and Natural Man.* New York: Basic, 1977.

———. *Jean Piaget.* Harmondsworth: Penguin, 1980.

Bohm, David. *Cause and Change in Modern Physics.* London: Routledge, 1957.

Bonin, Sandra. "Beyond Storyland: Children Can Tell It Other Ways." Newkirk and Atwell 31–35.

Booth, Wayne C. "The Common Aims That Divide Us; or, Is There a 'Profession 81'?" *Profession 81.* New York: MLA, 1981. 13–17.

———. "'LITCOMP': Some Rhetoric Addressed to Cryptorhetoricians about a Rhetorical Solution to a Rhetorical Problem." Horner, *Composition* 57–80.

———. *Modern Dogma and the Rhetoric of Assent.* Chicago: U of Chicago P, 1974.

———. "Presidential Address: Arts and Scandals 1982." *PMLA* 98 (1983): 312–22.

———. *The Rhetoric of Fiction.* Chicago: U of Chicago P, 1974.

Borgh, Enola M. *Grammatical Patterns and Composition.* Oshkosh: Wisconsin Council of Teachers of English, 1963.

Bouton, Clark, and Russell Y. Garth, eds. *Learning in Groups.* San Francisco: Jossey, 1983.

Boutwell, Marilyn A. "Reading and Writing Process: A Reciprocal Agreement." *Language Arts* 60 (1983): 723–30.

Bracewell, Robert J. "Investigating the Control of Writing Skills." Mosenthal et al. 177–203.

———. "Writing as a Cognitive Activity." *Visible Language* 14 (1980): 400–22.

Bracewell, R., C. Frederiksen, and J. Frederiksen. "Cognitive Processes in Composing and Comprehending Discourse." *Educational Psychologist* 17 (1982): 146–64.

Braddock, Richard. "The Frequency and Placement of Topic Sentences in Expository Prose." *Research in the Teaching of English* 8 (1974): 287–304.

Braddock, Richard, Richard Lloyd-Jones, and Lowell Schoer, eds. *Research in Written Composition.* Urbana: NCTE, 1963.

Bradford, Annette Norris. "Conceptual Differences between the Display Screen and the Printed Page." *Technical Communication* 31.3 (1984): 13–16.

Bradford, David. "The Persona in Microcomputer Documentation." *IEEE Transactions on Professional Communication* PC-27.2 (1984): 65–68.

Brannon, Lil, and C. H. Knoblauch. "On Students' Rights to Their Own Texts: A Model of Teacher Response." *College Composition and Communication* 33 (1982): 197–222.

Brereton, John C. "Sterling Andrus Leonard." *Traditions of Inquiry.* New York: Oxford UP, 1985. 81–104.

Bridwell, Lillian S. "Revising Strategies in Twelfth Grade Students' Transactional Writing." *Research in the Teaching of English* 14 (1980): 197–222.

Britton, James. "The Composing Processes and the Functions of Writing." Cooper and Odell, *Research* 13–28.

——— . *Language and Learning.* Harmondsworth: Penguin, 1970.

——— . *Prospect and Retrospect.* Ed. Gordon Pradl. Montclair: Boynton, 1982.

——— . "Shaping at the Point of Utterance." Freedman and Pringle, *Reinventing* 60–65.

Britton, James, et al. *The Development of Writing Abilities, 11–18.* Schools Council Research Series. London: Macmillan Education, 1975.

Brockmann, R. John. *The Case Method in Technical Communication: Theory and Models.* ATTW, 1985.

——— . "What's Different about Teaching Technical Writing." *The Technical Writing Teacher* 10 (1983): 174–81.

Brod, Richard, and Phyllis Franklin. "From the Editors." *Profession 83.* New York: MLA, 1983. iii–iv.

Brown, John Seely, and Richard R. Burton. "Diagnostic Models for Procedural Bugs in Basic Mathematical Skills." *Cognitive Science* 2 (1978): 155–92.

Brown, Roger. *A First Language.* Cambridge: Harvard UP, 1973.

Bruffee, Kenneth A. "The Brooklyn Plan: Attaining Intellectual Growth through Peer-Group Tutoring." *Liberal Education* 64 (1978): 447–69.

——— . "Collaborative Learning and the 'Conversation of Mankind.'" *College English* 46 (1984): 635–52.

——— . *Short Course in Writing.* Boston: Little, 1980.

——— . "The Way Out." *College English* 33 (1972): 457–70.

——— . "Writing and Reading as Social or Collaborative Acts." *The Writer's Mind: Writing as a Mode of Thinking.* Ed. Janice N. Hays et al. Urbana: NCTE, 1983. 159–69.

Bruffee, Kenneth A., with Paula Beck, Thom Hawkins, and Marcia Silver. "Training and Using Peer Tutors." *College English* 40 (1978): 432–49.

Bruner, Jerome. "Language as an Instrument of Thought." *Problems of Language and Learning.* Ed. A. Davis. London: Social Science Research Council, 1975. 61–68.

——— . "State of the Child." *New York Review of Books* 27 Oct. 1983: 84–89.

———. *Toward a Theory of Instruction*. New York: Norton, 1968.

Bryant, Donald C. "Rhetoric: Its Function and Its Scope." *Quarterly Journal of Speech* 39 (1953): 401–04.

Budd, William C. "Research Designs of Potential Value in Investigating Problems in English." *Research in the Teaching of English* 1 (1967): 1–9.

Bunge, Mario. *Causality*. Cambridge: Harvard UP, 1959.

Burgess, C., et al. *Understanding Children Writing*. Harmondsworth: Penguin, 1973.

Burke, Kenneth. *Counter-Statement*. 2nd ed. Los Altos: Hermes, 1953.

———. *A Grammar of Motives*. Berkeley: U of California P, 1969.

———. *The Philosophy of Literary Form*. New York: Vintage, 1957.

———. *A Rhetoric of Motives*. Berkeley: U of California P, 1963.

Burns, Hugh. "Pandora's Chip: Concerns about Quality CAI." *Pipeline* 6.2 (1981): 15–16, 49.

Caernarvon-Smith, Patricia. *Audience Analysis and Response*. Pembroke: Firman Technical Publications, 1983.

———. "Introduction." *Technical Communication* 30.4 (1983): 4.

Calkins, Lucy McCormick. "Children Learn the Writer's Craft." *Language Arts* 57 (1980): 207–13.

———. "Children's Rewriting Strategies." *Research in the Teaching of English* 14 (1980): 331–41.

———. *Lessons from a Child: On the Teaching and Learning of Writing*. Exeter: Heinemann, 1983.

Campbell, Jeremy. *Grammatical Man: Information, Entropy, Language, and Life*. New York: Simon, 1982.

Carkeet, David. "Understanding Syntactic Errors in Remedial Writing." *College English* 38 (1977): 682–86, 695.

Carter, Shirley G., and William Stolgitis. "STC Membership Profile." *Technical Communication* 30.3 (1983): 17–19.

Cassirer, Ernst. *Language and Myth*. Trans. Susanne K. Langer. New York: Dover, 1946.

———. *The Philosophy of the Enlightenment*. Boston: Beacon, 1951.

———. *The Philosophy of Symbolic Form*. 3 vols. New Haven: Yale UP, 1955–65.

Chomsky, Carol. "Reading, Writing, and Phonology." *Harvard Educational Review* 40 (1970): 287–309.

———. "Write First, Read Later." *Childhood Education* 47 (1971): 296–99.

Chomsky, Noam. *Syntactic Structures*. The Hague: Mouton, 1957.

Christensen, Francis. *Notes toward a New Rhetoric*. 2nd ed. New York: Harper, 1978.

———. "The Problem of Defining a Mature Style." *English Journal* 57 (1968): 572–79.

Cicero. *De oratore*. Trans. E. W. Sutton and H. Rackham. 2 vols. Cambridge: Harvard UP, 1976.

Clark, Christopher M., and Susan Florio. "Understanding Writing Instruction: Issues of Theory and Method." Mosenthal et al. 236–61.

Clay, Marie. *What Did I Write*. London: Heinemann, 1975.

Clifford, John. "Beyond Subjectivity: Transactional Reading and Writing." *Teaching English in the Two-Year College* 6 (1980): 95–100.

———. "Composing in Stages: The Effects of a Collaborative Pedagogy." *Research in the Teaching of English* 15 (1981): 37–53.

———. "Using Intuition in the Composing Process." *English Record* 31.2 (1980): 6–9.

Clinchy, B., and C. Zimmerman. "Epistemology and Agency in Undergraduate Women." *The Undergraduate Woman: Issues in Education and Equity.* Ed. P. Perun. Boston: Heath, 1981.

Colvin, S. "Invention versus Form in English Composition: An Inductive Study." *Pedagogical Seminary* 9 (1902): 393–421.

Comley, Nancy R., and Robert Scholes. "Literature, Composition, and the Structure of English." Horner, *Composition* 96–109.

Coney, Mary B., and James W. Souther. "Analytical Writing Revisited: An Old Cure for a Worsening Problem." *Technical Communication* 31.1 (1984): 4–8.

Connors, Robert J. "Composition Studies and Science." *College English* 45 (1983): 1–20.

———. "Mechanical Correctness as a Focus in Composition Instruction." *College Composition and Communication* 36 (1985): 61–72.

———. "Review: Journals in Composition." *College English* 46 (1984): 348–65.

———. "The Rise and Fall of the Modes of Discourse." *College Composition and Communication* 32 (1981): 444–55.

Connors, Robert J., Andrea Lunsford, and Lisa Ede, eds. *Essays on Classical Rhetoric and Modern Discourse.* Carbondale: Southern Illinois UP, 1984.

Cook-Gumperz, Jenny, and John J. Gumperz. "From Oral to Written Culture: The Transition to Literacy." *Variation in Writing.* Ed. Marcia Farr Whiteman. Vol. 1 of *Writing: The Nature, Development, and Teaching of Written Communication.* Ed. Carl H. Frederiksen, Marcia Farr Whiteman, and Joseph F. Dominic. 2 vols. Hillsdale: Erlbaum, 1981. 89–110.

Cooper, Charles R., ed. *The Nature and Measurement of Competency in English.* Urbana: NCTE, 1981.

———. "Procedures for Describing Written Texts." Mosenthal et al. 287–313.

Cooper, Charles R., and Lee Odell, eds. *Evaluating Writing: Describing, Measuring, Judging.* Urbana: NCTE, 1977.

———, eds. *Research on Composing: Points of Departure.* Urbana: NCTE, 1978.

Cooper, Charles R., Roger Cherry, et al. "Studying the Writing Abilities of a University Freshman Class: Strategies from a Case Study." Beach and Bridwell 19–52.

Corbett, Edward P. J. *Classical Rhetoric for the Modern Student.* 2nd ed. New York: Oxford UP, 1971.

———. "The Theory and Practice of Imitation in Classical Rhetoric." *Rhetoric and Composition: A Sourcebook for Teachers.* Ed. Richard L. Graves. Rochelle Park: Hayden, 1976. 303–12.

"Correspondence." *Technical Communication* 31.4 (1984): 2.

Covino, William A. "Making Differences in the Composition Class: A Philosophy of Invention." *Freshman English News* 10.1 (1981): 1–13.

Cresswell, T. J. *Usage in Dictionaries and Dictionaries of Usage.* Publication of the American Dialect Soc. 63–64. University: U of Alabama P, 1975.

Crowhurst, Marion. "On the Misinterpretation of Syntactic Complexity Data." *English Education* 11 (1979): 91–97.

———. "Sentence Combining: Maintaining Realistic Expectations." *College Composition and Communication* 33 (1983): 65–72.

Daiker, Donald, Andrew Kerek, and Max Morenberg. *The Writer's Options: College Sentence Combining.* New York: Harper, 1979.

———, eds. *Sentence Combining and the Teaching of Writing.* Conway: L&S, 1979.

Daiute, Colette A. "Psycholinguistic Foundations of the Writing Process." *Research in the Teaching of English* 15 (1981): 5–22.

———. "Psycholinguistic Perspectives on Revising." *Revising: New Essays for Teachers of Writing.* Ed. R. A. Sudol. Urbana: NCTE, 1982. 109–20.

D'Angelo, Frank. *A Conceptual Theory of Rhetoric.* Cambridge: Winthrop, 1975.

———. *Process and Thought in Composition.* Cambridge: Winthrop, 1980.

Davis, F. "Stories and Sociology." *Urban Life and Culture* 3 (1974): 310–16.

Davis, Randall, and Douglas B. Lenat. *Knowledge-Based Systems in Artificial Intelligence.* New York: McGraw, 1982.

D'Eloia, Sarah. "Teaching Standard Written English." *Journal of Basic Writing* 1 (1975): 5–13.

Derrida, Jacques. *Of Grammatology.* Trans. Gayatri Chakravorty Spivak. Baltimore: Johns Hopkins UP, 1974.

Descartes, René. *Discourse on Method.* Trans. Lawrence J. Lafleur. Indianapolis: Bobbs, 1960.

Devlin, Frank. "Literature in the Freshman Writing Class." *Freshman English News* 13.2 (1984): 10–15.

Dewey, John. *Experience and Education.* 1938. New York: Collier, 1963.

Diederich, Paul B. *Measuring Growth in English.* Urbana: NCTE, 1974.

Diesing, Paul. *Patterns of Discovery in the Social Sciences.* Chicago: Aldine, 1971.

Dillon, David, and Dennis Searle. "The Role of Language in One First Grade Classroom." *Research in the Teaching of English* 15 (1981): 311–28.

Directory. Archives. Urbana: NCTE.

Dixon, John. *Growth through English.* Huddersfield: NATE, 1967.

Dobrin, David. "What's Technical about Technical Writing?" Anderson et al. 227–50.

Donaldson, Margaret. *Children's Minds.* New York: Norton, 1978.

Donovan, Timothy R., and Ben W. McClelland, eds. *Eight Approaches to Teaching Composition.* Urbana: NCTE, 1980.

Durkin, Delores. "What Classroom Observations Reveal about Reading Comprehension Instruction." *Reading Research Quarterly* 10 (1978–79): 481–533.

Dyson, Anne H. "Emerging Alphabetic Literacy in School Contexts: Toward Defining the Gap between School Curriculum and Child Mind." *Written Communication* 1 (1984): 5–55.

Eagleton, Terry. *Literary Theory: An Introduction.* Minneapolis: U of Minnesota P, 1983.

Ede, Lisa. "Audience: An Introduction to Research." *College Composition and Communication* 35 (1984): 140–54.

Ehninger, Douglas, ed. *Contemporary Rhetoric: A Reader's Coursebook.* Glenview: Scott, 1972.

———. "Dominant Trends in English Rhetorical Thought, 1750–1800." *Southern Speech Journal* 17 (1952): 3–12.

———. "On Systems of Rhetoric." *Philosophy and Rhetoric* 1 (1968): 131–44.

Elbow, Peter. *Writing without Teachers.* New York: Oxford UP, 1973.

———. *Writing with Power.* New York: Oxford UP, 1981.

Eliot, Charles W. *Educational Reform: Essays and Addresses.* New York: Century, 1898.

Elley, W. B., I. H. Barkham, H. Lamb, and M. Wyllie. "The Role of Grammar in a Secondary School English Curriculum." *Research in the Teaching of English* 10 (1976): 5–21.

Elsasser, Nan, and Kyle Fiore. "'Strangers No More': A Liberatory Literacy Curriculum." *College English* 44 (1982): 115–28.

Elsasser, Nan, and Vera John-Steiner. "An Interactionist Approach to Advancing Literacy." *Harvard Educational Review* 47 (1977): 355–59.

Emig, Janet. *The Composing Processes of Twelfth Graders.* Champaign: NCTE, 1971.

——— . "The Tacit Tradition: The Inevitability of a Multi-Disciplinary Approach to Writing Research." Freedman and Pringle 9–17.

——— . *The Web of Meaning.* Montclair: Boynton, 1983.

——— . "Writing as a Mode of Learning." *College Composition and Communication* 28 (1977): 122–28.

Epes, Mary. "Tracing Errors to Their Sources: A Study of the Encoding Processes of Adult Basic Writers." *Journal of Basic Writing.* Forthcoming.

Ericsson, K. A., and H. A. Simon. "Verbal Reports as Data." *Psychological Review* 87 (1980): 215–51.

Executive Committee Minutes. Archives. Urbana: NCTE, 1966.

Fahnestock, Jean. "What Makes a Text Coherent?" *College Composition and Communication* 33 (1983): 417–29.

Faigley, Lester. "Names in Search of a Concept: Maturity, Fluency, Complexity, and Growth in Written Syntax." *College Composition and Communication* 31 (1980): 291–300.

Faigley, Lester, and Stephen Witte. "Analyzing Revision." *College Composition and Communication* 32 (1981): 400–14.

——— . "Coherence, Cohesion, and Writing Quality." *College Composition and Communication* 32 (1981): 189–204.

——— . "Measuring the Effects of Revisions on Text Structure." Beach and Bridwell 95–108.

Falk, Julia S. "Language Acquisition and the Teaching and Learning of Writing." *College English* 41 (1979): 436–37.

Farr, Marcia, and Mary Ann Janda. "Basic Writing Students: Investigating Oral and Written Language." *Research in the Teaching of English* 19 (1985): 62–83.

Farr, Roger, and Samuel Weintraub. "Editorial: Methodological Incarceration." *Reading Research Quarterly* 10 (1975): 4–5.

Farrell, Thomas J. "Literacy, the Basics, and All That Jazz." *College English* 38 (1977): 443–59.

Feigenbaum, Edward A., and Pamela McCorduck. *The Fifth Generation.* Reading: Addison, 1983.

Feinberg, Susan, and Jerry Goldman. "Content for a Course in Technical Communication." *Technical Communication* 32.2 (1985): 21–25.

Feyerabend, Paul K. *Against Method.* New York: New Left, 1975.

Fish, Stanley. *Is There a Text in This Class? The Authority of Interpretive Communities.* Cambridge: Harvard UP, 1980.

Flower, Linda S. *Problem Solving Strategies for Writing.* New York: Harcourt, 1981.

——— . "Writer-Based Prose: A Cognitive Basis for Problems in Writing." *College English* 41 (1979): 19–37.

Flower, Linda S., and John Hayes. "The Cognition of Discovery: Defining a Rhetorical Problem." *College Composition and Communication* 31 (1980): 21–32.

——— . "A Cognitive Process Theory of Writing." *College Composition and Communication* 32 (1981): 365–87.

——— . "The Dynamics of Composing: Making Plans and Juggling Constraints." *Cognitive Processes in Writing*. Ed. L. Gregg and E. Steinberg. Hillsdale: Erlbaum, 1980. 31–50.

——— . "Identifying the Organization of Writing Processes." *Cognitive Processes in Writing*. Ed. L. Gregg and E. Steinberg. Hillsdale: Erlbaum, 1980. 3–30.

——— . "Images, Plans, and Prose: The Representation of Meaning in Writing." *Written Communication* 1 (1984): 1–28.

——— . "Plans That Guide the Composing Process." *Writing: Process, Development, and Communication*. Ed. Carl H. Frederiksen and Joseph F. Dominic. Vol. 2 of *Writing: The Nature, Development, and Teaching of Written Communication*. Ed. Carl H. Frederiksen, Marcia Farr Whiteman, and Joseph F. Dominic. 2 vols. Hillsdale: Erlbaum, 1981. 39–58.

——— . "Problem Solving Strategies and the Writing Process." *College English* 39 (1977): 449–61.

Flynn, Elizabeth A. "Composing Responses to Literary Texts: A Process Approach." *College Composition and Communication* 34 (1983): 342–48.

Fodor, J., T. Bever, and M. Garrett. *The Psychology of Language*. New York: McGraw, 1974.

Fort, Keith. "Form, Authority, and the Critical Essay." *College English* 32 (1971): 629–39.

Foucault, Michel. *The Order of Things: An Archaeology of the Human Sciences*. New York: Pantheon, 1970.

——— . "What Is an Author?" *Textual Strategies*. Ed. Josue V. Harari. Ithaca: Cornell UP, 1979.

Frederiksen, C. "Representing Logical and Semantic Structures of Knowledge Acquired from Discourse." *Cognitive Psychology* 7 (1975): 371–458.

Freedman, Aviva. "The Registers of Student and Professional Expository Writing: Influences on Teachers' Responses." Beach and Bridwell 334–48.

Freedman, Aviva, and Ian Pringle, eds. *Reinventing the Rhetorical Tradition*. Conway: L&S, for the Canadian Council of Teachers of English, 1980; Urbana: NCTE, 1980.

——— . "The Writing Abilities of a Representative Sample of Grade 5, 8 and 12 Students." Carleton Writing Project, part 2. Ontario: Carleton Board of Education, 1980. ERIC ED 217 413.

——— . "Writing in the College Years: Some Indices of Growth." *College Composition and Communication* 31 (1980): 311–24.

Freeman, Donald C. "Linguistics and Error Analysis: On Agency." *Linguistics, Stylistics and the Teaching of Composition*. Ed. Donald McQuade. Akron: C&S, 1979. 143–50.

Freire, Paolo. *Pedagogy of the Oppressed*. New York: Seabury, 1968.

Freud, Sigmund. *The Psychopathology of Everyday Life*. New York: Norton, 1965.

Fulwiler, Toby, and Art Young, eds. *Language Connections: Writing and Reading across the Curriculum*. Urbana: NCTE, 1982.

Gadamer, Hans-Georg. *Truth and Method*. New York: Seabury, 1975.

Gage, Nathaniel. "This Side of Paradigms: The State of Research on Teaching." *Research Design and the Teaching of English*. Champaign: NCTE, 1964. 22–33.

Gage, John T. "Conflicting Assumptions about Intention in Teaching Reading and Composition." *College English* 40 (1978): 255–63.

Gallehr, Donald R. "What Happens When Teacher Consultants Become Curiouser and Curiouser?" *National Writing Project Network Newsletter* 3.1 (1980): 6–7.

Gardner, John. *The Art of Fiction.* New York: Knopf, 1984.

Gardner, Howard. *Frames of Mind: The Theory of Multiple Intelligence.* New York: Basic, 1983.

Garrett, Marvin. "Toward a Delicate Balance: The Importance of Role-Playing and Peer Criticism in Peer Tutor Training." *Tutoring Writing.* Ed. Muriel Harris. Glenview: Scott, 1981. 94–100.

Gebhardt, Richard C., ed. *Composition and Its Teaching.* Findlay: Ohio Council of Teachers of Language Arts, 1979.

Gebhardt, Richard C. "Teamwork and Feedback: Broadening the Base of Collaborative Learning." *College English* 42 (1980): 69–74.

Geertz, Clifford. *The Interpretation of Cultures.* New York: Basic, 1973.

——— . *Local Knowledge: Further Essays in Interpretive Anthropology.* New York: Basic, 1983.

Genung, John Franklin. *Outline of Rhetoric.* Boston: Ginn, 1894.

George, Diana. "Working with Peer Groups in the Composition Classroom." *College Composition and Communication* 35 (1984): 320–26.

Gere, Anne Ruggles. "The Language of Writing Groups: How Oral Response Shapes Revision." *Evaluation, Response, Revision.* Ed. Sara Freedman. New York: Ablex. Forthcoming.

——— . "Teacher Researchers." *National Writing Project Newsletter* 7.1 (1984): 1–2.

——— . "Written Composition: Toward a Theory of Evaluation." *College English* 42 (1980): 44–58.

Giacobbe, Mary Ellen. "Who Says That Children Can't Write the First Week of School?" *Learning Magazine* Sept. 1981: 130–32.

——— . "A Writer Reads, a Reader Writes." Newkirk and Atwell 114–25.

Gilligan, C. "In a Different Voice: Women's Conceptions of Self and Morality." *Harvard Educational Review* 47 (1977): 481–517.

Giorgi, Amadeo. *Psychology as a Human Science.* New York: Harper, 1970.

Giroux, Henry A. *Theory and Resistance in Education.* South Hadley: Bergin, 1983.

Glaser, Robert. "The Future of Testing: A Research Agenda for Cognitive Psychology and Psychometrics." *American Psychologist* 36 (1981): 923–36.

Glazer, Myron. *The Research Adventure: Promise and Problems of Field Work.* New York: Random, 1972.

Golden, James, Goodwin Berquist, and William Coleman, eds. *The Rhetoric of Western Thought.* Dubuque: Kendall, 1976.

Goldstein, Jone Rymer. "Trends in Teaching Technical Writing." *Technical Communication* 31.4 (1984): 25–34.

Goldstein, Jone Rymer, and Robert B. Donovan. *A Bibliography of Basic Texts in Technical and Scientific Writing.* Washington: Soc. for Technical Communication, 1982.

Goodlad, John. *A Place Called School.* New York: McGraw, 1984.

Goodman, Kenneth S. "Analysis of Oral Reading Miscues: Applied Psycholinguistics." *Reading Research Quarterly* 5 (1969): 9–30.

Goody, Jack. *The Domestication of the Savage Mind.* Cambridge: Cambridge UP, 1977.

Goody, Jack, and Ian Watt. "The Consequences of Literacy." *Literacy and Traditional Societies.* Ed. Goody. Cambridge: Cambridge UP, 1968. 27–84.

Graves, Donald. *A Case Study of Observing and the Development of Primary Children's Composing, Spelling, and Motor Behavior during the Writing Process.* NIE Final Report, 1982. NIE G-78-0174.

——. "An Examination of the Writing Processes of Seven Year Old Children." *Research in the Teaching of English* 9 (1975): 227–41.

——. "Language Arts Textbooks: A Writing Process Evaluation." *A Researcher Learns to Write: Selected Articles and Monographs.* Ed. Graves. Portsmouth: Heinemann, 1984. 52–60.

——. "A New Look at Writing Research." *Language Arts* 57 (1980): 913–19.

——. "A Two-Year Case Study Observing the Development of Primary Children's Composing, Spelling, and Motor Behaviors during the Writing Process." Unpublished proposal submitted to the NIE, 1978.

——. *Writing: Teachers and Children at Work.* Exeter: Heinemann, 1983.

Green, Marcus M., and Timothy D. Nolan. "A Systematic Analysis of the Technical Communicator's Job: A Guide for Educators." *Technical Communication* 31.4 (1984): 9–12.

Guba, E. *Toward a Methodology of Naturalistic Inquiry in Educational Evaluation.* Los Angeles: Center for the Study of Evaluation, Graduate School of Education, University of California, 1978.

Gunlach, Robert. "Children as Writers: The Beginnings of Learning to Write." *What Writers Know: The Language, Process, and Structure of Written Discourse.* Ed. Martin Nystrand. New York: Academic, 1982. 129–47.

Guth, Hans. *English Today and Tommorrow.* Englewood Cliffs: Prentice, 1964.

Hairston, Maxine. "Not All Errors Are Created Equal: Nonacademic Readers in the Professions Respond to Lapses in Usage." *College English* 41 (1981): 794–806.

——. "The Winds of Change: Thomas Kuhn and the Revolution in the Teaching of Writing." *College Composition and Communication* 33 (1982): 76–86.

Halliday, M. A. K., and Ruqaiya Hasan. *Cohesion in English.* London: Longman, 1976.

Hammersty, Martyn, and Paul Atkinson. *Ethnography: Principles in Practice.* New York: Tavistock, 1983.

Hansen, Jane, and Donald Graves. "The Author's Chair." *Language Arts* 60 (1983): 176–83.

Hanson, Dirk. *The New Alchemists.* New York: Avon, 1982.

Harris, Muriel. "Mending the Fragmented Free Modifier." *College Composition and Communication* 32 (1981): 175–82.

Harste, Jerome, Virginia Woodward, and Carolyn Burke. *Language Stories and Literacy Lessons.* Portsmouth: Heinemann, 1984.

Hartman, Geoffrey. *Criticism in the Wilderness.* New Haven: Yale UP, 1980.

Hartwell, Patrick. "Dialect Interference in Writing: A Critical View." *Research in the Teaching of English* 14 (1980): 101–18.

——. "Grammar, Grammars, and the Teaching of Grammar." *College English* 47 (1985): 105–27.

Hashimoto, Irvin. "Toward a Taxonomy of Scholarly Publications." *College English* 45 (1983): 500–05.

Haswell, Richard H. "Minimal Marking." *College English* 45 (1983): 600–04.

Havelock, Eric. *Preface to Plato.* Cambridge: Harvard UP, 1963.

Hawkins, Nathaniel. "An Introduction to the History and Theory of Peer Tutoring in Writing." *A Guide to Writing Programs: Writing Centers, Peer Tutoring, Writing across the Curriculum.* Ed. Tori Haring-Smith. Glenview: Scott, 1984. 7–18.

Hawkins, Thom. *Group Inquiry Techniques for Teaching Writing.* Urbana: NCTE, 1976.

Hayes, J., and L. Flower. "Uncovering Cognitive Processes in Writing: An Introduction to Protocol Analysis." Mosenthal et al. 207–20.

Hayes-Roth, Frederick, Donald A. Waterman, and Douglas B. Lenat, eds. *Building Expert Systems.* Reading: Addison, 1983.

Hays, Janice. "The Development of Discursive Maturity in College Writers." *The Writer's Mind: Writing as a Mode of Thinking.* Ed. Hays et al. Urbana: NCTE, 1983. 127–44.

Healy, Mary K. "Using Student Writing Response Groups in the Classroom." *Teaching Writing.* Ed. Gerald Camp. Upper Montclair: Boynton, 1982.

Heath, Shirley Brice. "Toward an Ethnohistory of Writing in American Education." *Variation in Writing.* Ed. Marcia Farr Whiteman. Vol. 1 of *Writing: The Nature, Development, and Teaching of Written Communication.* Ed. Carl H. Frederiksen, Marcia Farr Whiteman, and Joseph F. Dominic. 2 vols. Hillsdale: Erlbaum, 1981. 25–43.

——— . *Ways with Words: Language, Life and Work in Communities and Classrooms.* Cambridge: Cambridge UP, 1983.

Heidorn, G. E., K. Jenison, L. A. Miller, R. J. Byrd, M. S. Chodorow. "The Epistle Text-Critiquing System." *IBM System Journal* 21 (1982): 305–16.

Hickman, Janet. "A New Perspective on Response to Literature: Research in an Elementary School Setting." *Research in the Teaching of English* 15 (1981): 343–54.

Hillocks, George, Jr. "English Programs under Fire." *The English Curriculum under Fire: What Are the Real Basics?* Ed. Hillocks. Urbana: NCTE, 1982. 1–10.

Hirsch, E. D. "'English' and the Perils of Formalism." *American Scholar* 53 (1984): 369–79.

——— . "Cultural Literacy." *American Scholar* 52 (1983): 159–69.

——— . *The Philosophy of Composition.* Chicago: U of Chicago P, 1977.

——— . "Reading, Writing, and Cultural Literacy." Horner, *Composition* 141–47.

Hitchcock, Alfred Marshall. *Composition and Rhetoric.* New York: Holt, 1906.

Hofstadter, Douglas. *Gödel, Escher, Bach: An Eternal Golden Braid.* New York: Basic, 1979.

Holland, Norman. *5 Readers Reading.* New Haven: Yale UP, 1975.

Holzman, Michael. "Scientism and Sentence Combining." *College Composition and Communication* 33 (1983): 73–79.

Hook, J. N. *A Long Way Together: A Personal View of NCTE's First Sixty-Seven Years.* Urbana: NCTE, 1979.

Horn, Robert E. *How to Write Information Mapping.* Lexington: Information Resources, 1982.

Horner, Winifred Bryan, ed. *Composition and Literature: Bridging the Gap.* Chicago: U of Chicago P, 1983.

——— , ed. *The Present State of Scholarship in Historical and Contemporary Rhetoric.* Columbia: U of Missouri P, 1983.

Houze, William C. "Today's Technical Writers/Editors in Tomorrow's 'Electronic Mega-Cottage Industry' World of Work: Will They Survive?" *Proteus: A Journal of Ideas* 1.1 (1983): 23–28.

Howard, Lionel A., Jr. "A Survey of Technical Communication Programs in U.S. Colleges and Universities—1984." *IEEE Transactions on Professional Communi-*

cation PC-27.3 (1984): 172–76.

Howell, W. S. *Eighteenth-Century British Logic and Rhetoric.* Princeton: Princeton UP, 1971.

———. *Logic and Rhetoric in England 1500–1700.* New York: Russell, 1961.

Huckin, Thomas N. "A Cognitive Approach to Readability." Anderson et al. 90–110.

Huckin, Thomas N., and Leslie A. Olsen. *English for Science and Technology: A Handbook for Nonnative Speakers.* New York: McGraw, 1983.

Hull, Glynda. "Acts of Wonderment." *Fact, Artifacts, and Counterfacts.* Ed. David Bartholomae and Anthony Petrosky. Upper Montclair: Boynton. Forthcoming.

———. "Computer-Assisted Instruction and Basic Writing: A Proposal." Martinez 125–36.

———. "The Editing Process in Writing: A Performance Study of Experts and Novices." Diss. U of Pittsburgh, 1983.

———. "Stray Dogs and Mermaids (or an Attempt to Categorize Error)." *Sourcebook on Basic Writing.* Ed. Theresa Enos. New York: Random. Forthcoming.

Hunt, Kellogg W. "Early Blooming and Late Blooming Syntactic Structures." Cooper and Odell, *Evaluating* 91–106.

———. *Grammatical Structures Written at Three Grade Levels.* NCTE Research Report 3. Urbana: NCTE, 1965.

Hunt, Russell A. "Toward a Process-Intervention Model in Literature Teaching." *College English* 44 (1982): 345–57.

Hymes, Dell. *What Is Ethnography?* Sociolinguistic Paper 45. Austin: Southwest Educational Development Lab, 1978.

Inhelder, B., and J. Piaget. *The Growth of Logical Thinking from Childhood to Adolescence.* New York: Basic, 1958.

Iser, Wolfgang. *The Implied Reader.* Baltimore: Johns Hopkins UP, 1974.

James, William. *The Varieties of Religious Experience: A Study in Human Nature.* New York: Collier-Macmillan, 1974.

Johnson, Nan. "Rhetoric and Literature: Politics, Theory, and the Future of English Studies." *ADE Bulletin* 77 (1984): 22–25.

Johnson, Roy Ivan. "The Persistency of Error in English Composition." *School Review* 25 (1917): 555–80.

Kagan, Dona M. "Run-on and Fragment Sentences: An Error Analysis." *Research in the Teaching of English* 14 (1980): 127–38.

Kail, Harvey. "Collaborative Learning in Context: The Problem with Peer Tutoring." *College English* 45 (1983): 592–99.

Kames, Henry Home, Lord. *Elements of Criticism.* 1762. 3 vols. Hildesheim: Olms, 1970.

Kantor, Kenneth J. "Classroom Contexts and the Development of Writing Intuitions: An Ethnographic Case Study." Beach and Bridwell 72–95.

Kantor, Kenneth J., Dan R. Kirby, and Judith P. Goetz. "Research in Context: Ethnographic Studies in English Education." *Research in the Teaching of English* 15 (1981): 293–309.

Kantor, Kenneth J., and Donald L. Rubin. "Between Speaking and Writing: Processes of Differentiation." *Exploring Speaking-Writing Relationships.* Ed. Barry M. Kroll and Roberta J. Vann. Urbana: NCTE, 1981.

Kellner, R. Scott. "The Degeneration of Technical Writing: A Question of Teacher Competency." *ABCA Bulletin* 45.3 (1982): 5–10.

Kennedy, George. *Classical Rhetoric and Its Christian and Secular Tradition from Ancient to Modern Times*. Chapel Hill: U of North Carolina P, 1980.

Kidder, Tracy. *The Soul of the New Machine*. Boston: Little, 1981.

King, Donald W., et al. *Value of the Energy Data Base*. Oak Ridge: Technical Information Center, 1982. DOE/OR/11232-1 (DE82014250).

Kinneavy, James L. "Contemporary Rhetoric." Horner, *Present State* 167–213.

———. "Restoring the Humanities: The Return of Rhetoric from Exile." Murphy 19–28.

———. "Sentence Combining in a Comprehensive Language Framework." Daiker et al., *Sentence Combining* 60–76.

———. *A Theory of Discourse*. Englewood Cliffs: Prentice, 1971.

———. "Writing across the Curriculum." *Profession 83*. New York: MLA, 1983. 13–20.

Kinnucan, Paul. "Computers That Think like Experts." *High Technology* Jan. 1984: 30–42.

Kintsch, W., and D. Vipond. "Reading Comprehension and Readability in Educational Practice and Psychological Theory." *Perspectives on Memory Research*. Ed. L. G. Nilsson. Hillsdale: Erlbaum, 1979. 329–65.

Kintsch, W., J. Miller, and P. Polson, eds. *Method and Tactics in Cognitive Science*. Hillsdale: Erlbaum, 1984.

Kitzhaber, Albert R. "Rhetoric in American Colleges 1850–1900." Diss. U of Washington, 1953.

———. *Themes, Theories, and Therapy: The Teaching of Writing in College*. New York: McGraw, 1963.

Kleine, William Michael. "Syntactic Choice and a Theory of Discourse: Rethinking Sentence Combining." Diss. U of Minnesota, 1983.

Kline, Charles R., Jr., and W. Dean Memering. "Formal Fragments: The English Minor Sentence." *Research in the Teaching of English* 11 (1977): 97–110.

Knoblauch, C. H. "Intentionality in the Writing Process: A Case Study." *College Composition and Communication* 31 (1980): 153–59.

Knoblauch, C. H., and Lil Brannon. *Rhetorical Traditions and the Teaching of Writing*. Upper Montclair: Boynton, 1984.

———. "Teacher Commentary on Student Writing: The State of the Art." *Freshman English News* 10 (1981): 1–4.

Kogen, Myra, et al. "Bibliography on Education in Technical Writing and Communication, 1978–1983." *Technical Communication* 31.4 (1984): 45–48.

Kohlberg, L. "Continuities and Discontinuities in Childhood and Adult Moral Development." *Human Development* 12 (1969): 93–120.

———. "The Developmental Modes of Moral Thinking and Choice in the Years Ten to Sixteen." Diss. U of Chicago, 1958.

Kozol, Jonathan. "Dehumanizing the Humanities." *Chronicle of Higher Education* 13 Mar. 1985: 88.

Kress, Flemming, and Robert J. Bracewell. "Taught but Not Learned: Reasons for Grammatical Errors and Implications for Instruction." *Teaching Writing Learning*. Ed. Ian Pringle and Aviva Freedman. N.p.: Canadian Council of Teachers of English, 1981. 59–66.

Krishna, Valerie. "The Syntax of Error." *Journal of Basic Writing* 1 (1975): 43–49.

Kroll, B. "Cognitive Egocentrism and the Problem of Audience Awareness in Written Discourse." *Research in the Teaching of English* 12 (1978): 269–81.

Kroll, Barry M., and John C. Schafer. "Error Analysis and the Teaching of Composition." *College Composition and Communication* 29 (1978): 243–48.

Krupa, G. "Perry's Model of Development and the Teaching of Freshman Writing." *Freshman English News* 11 (1982): 17–20.

Kuhn, Thomas S. "The Function of Dogma in Scientific Research." *Scientific Change.* Ed. A. C. Abercrombie. New York: Basic, 1963. 347–96.

———. *The Structure of Scientific Revolutions.* 1962. Chicago: U of Chicago P, 1970.

Kurfiss, J. "Intellectual, Psychological, and Moral Development in College: Four Major Theories." *Manual for Project Quality Undergraduate Education.* Washington: Council for Independent Colleges, 1983.

———. "Late Adolescent Development: A Structural Epistemological Perspective." Diss. U of Washington, 1975.

———. "Sequentiality and Structure in a Cognitive Model of College Student Development." *Developmental Psychology* 13 (1977): 565–71.

Lamberg, Walter J. "Self-Provided and Peer-Provided Feedback." *College Composition and Communication* 31 (1980): 64–69.

Langer, Susanne K. *Philosophy in a New Key.* Cambridge: Harvard UP, 1967.

Lanham, Richard. "One, Two, Three." Horner, *Composition* 14–29.

Laurence, Patricia. "Error's Endless Train: Why Students Don't Perceive Errors." *Journal of Basic Writing* 1 (1975): 23–43.

Lawlor, Joseph. "Sentence Combining: A Sequence for Instruction." *Elementary School Journal* 84 (1983): 53–62.

Lees, Elaine O. "Error Analysis and the Editing Behavior of Basic Writing Students." Conference on College Composition and Communication. New York. Mar. 1984.

———. "Error-hunting, Fish and Game: Proofreading as Reading." *Sourcebook on Basic Writing.* Ed. Theresa Enos. New York: Random. Forthcoming.

———. "Proofreading with the Ears: A Case Study of Text-to-Voice Performance of a Student's Writing." *Collegiate Microcomputer.* Nov. 1985.

Leonard, Sterling Andrus. *Current English Usage.* NCTE English Monograph 1. Chicago: Inland, 1932.

Lévi-Strauss, Claude. *Structural Anthropology.* Garden City: Doubleday, 1967.

Lewin, Kurt, and Paul Grabbe. "Conduct, Knowledge, and the Acceptance of New Values." *Journal of Social Issues* 1 (1945): 53–64.

Liebow, Elliot. *Tally's Corner.* Boston: Little, 1967.

Lindemann, Erika. *A Rhetoric for Writing Teachers.* New York: Oxford UP, 1982.

Lipson, Carol S. "The Effects of Culture on Prose Handling: Preparing for an Influx of Foreign Students in Technical Writing Courses." *Technical Writing Teacher* 10 (1983): 232–41.

Loban, Walter. *Language Development: Kindergarten through Grade Twelve.* Urbana: NCTE, 1976.

Locke, John. *Essay concerning Human Understanding.* Ed. Peter H. Nidditch. Oxford: Clarendon, 1979.

Lofland, John. *Analysing Social Sciences.* Belmont: Wadsworth, 1971.

Lubin, G. I., J. F. Magary, and M. K. Paulsen, eds. *Piagetian Theory and Its Implications for the Helping Professions.* Los Angeles: U of Southern California P, 1975.

Lunsford, Andrea. "Assignments for Basic Writers: Unresolved Issues and Needed Research." *Journal of Basic Writing* (Winter 1986).

———. "Cognitive Development and the Basic Writer." *College English* 41 (1979): 38–47.

———. "What We Know – and Don't Know – about Remedial Writing." *College Composition and Communication* 29 (1978): 47–52.

Lunsford, Andrea, and Lisa Ede. "Classical Rhetoric, Modern Rhetoric, and Contemporary Discourse Studies." *Written Communication* 1 (1984): 78–100.

———. "Why Write . . . Together?" *Rhetoric Review* 1 (1983): 150–57.

Lyman, Rollo L. *Summary of Investigations Relating to Grammar, Language, and Composition.* Chicago: U of Chicago, 1929.

Macrorie, Ken. *Searching Writing.* Upper Montclair: Boynton, 1980.

———. *Twenty Teachers.* Oxford: Oxford UP, 1984.

———. *Uptaught.* Rochelle Park: Hayden, 1970.

———. *Writing to Be Read.* New York: Hayden, 1968.

Mailloux, Steven. *Interpretive Conventions: The Reader in the Study of American Fiction.* Ithaca: Cornell UP, 1982.

Maimon, Elaine P. "Knowledge, Acknowledgement, and Writing across the Curriculum: Toward an Educated Community." *The Territory of Language: Linguistics, Stylistics, and the Teaching of Writing.* Ed. Donald McQuade. Carbondale: Southern Illinois UP. Forthcoming.

———. "Maps and Genres: Exploring Connections in the Arts and Sciences." Horner, *Composition* 110–25.

———. "Talking to Strangers." *College Composition and Communication* 30 (1979): 364–69.

Maimon, Elaine P., and Barbara Nodine. "Measuring Syntactic Growth: Errors and Expectations in Sentence-Combining Practice with College Freshmen." *Research in the Teaching of English* 12 (1978): 233–44.

Malmstrom, Jean, and Janice Lee. *Teaching English Linguistically.* New York: Appleton, 1971.

Mandler, George. "Cohabitation in the Cognitive Sciences." Kintsch et al. 305–16.

Manicas, Peter T., and Paul F. Secord. "Implications for Psychology of the New Philosophy of Science." *American Psychologist* 38 (1983): 399–413.

Markels, Robin. "Cohesion Paradigms in Paragraphs." *College English* 45 (1983): 450–64.

Martin, Nancy. *Mostly about Writing.* Upper Montclair: Boynton, 1983.

Martin, Nancy, et al. *Writing and Learning across the Curriculum 11–16.* Schools Council Writing across the Curriculum Project. London: Ward Lock, 1976.

Martinez, Thomas E., ed. *Collected Essays on the Written Word and the Word Processor.* Villanova: Villanova U, 1984.

Mason, Edwin. *Collaborative Learning.* New York: Agathon, 1972.

Matthews, Kathy. "Beyond the Writing Table." *Breaking Ground: Teachers Relate Reading and Writing in the Elementary School.* Ed. Thomas Newkirk, Jane Hansen, and Donald Graves. Portsmouth: Heinemann, 1985. 63–71.

Mayher, John, and Rita Brause. "Learning through Teaching: Teaching and Learning Vocabulary." *Language Arts* 60 (1983): 1008–16.

Mayher, John, Nancy Lester, and Gordon Pradl. *Writing to Learn/Learning to Write.* Montclair: Boynton, 1983.

McCulley, George A. "Writing Quality, Coherence, and Cohesion," Diss. Utah State U, 1983.

McCullough, Robert A., Thomas E. Pinelli, Douglas D. Pilley, and Freda F. Stohrer. *A Review and Evaluation of the Langley Research Center's Scientific and Technical Information Program. Results of Phase VI—The Technical Report: A Survey and Analysis.* Hampton: Langley Research Center, 1982. NASA Technical Memorandum 83269.

McKee, Macey Blackburn. "Sentence Combining—Not If or When, but How." *Selected Papers from the Illinois TESOL/BE Tenth Annual Convention.* Ed. John R. Boyd and John F. Haskell. Chicago, 1982.

McKinnon, J. "The College Student and Formal Operations." *Teaching and Learning within the Piaget Model.* Ed. J. Renner. Norman: U of Oklahoma P, 1976.

McKinnon, J., and J. Renner. "Are Colleges Concerned with Intellectual Development?" *American Journal of Physics* 39 (1971): 1047–52.

Mellon, John C. *National Assessment and the Teaching of English.* Urbana: NCTE, 1975.

——— . *Transformational Sentence-Combining: A Method for Enhancing the Development of Syntactic Fluency in English Composition.* NCTE Research Report 10. Champaign: NCTE, 1967.

Miller, J., P. Polson, and W. Kintsch. "Problems of Methodology in Cognitive Science." Kintsch et al. 1–20.

Miller, J. Hillis. "Composition and Decomposition: Deconstruction and the Teaching of Writing." Horner, *Composition* 38–56.

Miller, Susan. "Classical Practice and Contemporary Basics." Murphy 46–57.

——— . "How Writers Evaluate Their Own Writing." *College Composition and Communication* 33 (1982): 176–83.

——— . "Rhetorical Maturity: Definition and Development." Freedman and Pringle 118–27.

——— . "What Does It Mean to Be Able to Write? The Question of Writing in the Discourse of Literature and Composition." *College English* 45 (1983): 219–35.

Milz, Vera E. "First Graders Can Write: Focus on Communications." *Theory into Practice* (Summer 1980): 179–85.

——— . *Young Children Write: The Beginnings.* Tucson: Center for Research and Development, U of Arizona, 1982.

Mishler, Elliot G. "Meaning in Context: Is There Any Other Kind?" *Harvard Educational Review* 49 (1979): 1–19.

Mitchell, Richard. *Less than Words Can Say.* Boston: Little, 1979.

Moffett, James. *Teaching the Universe of Discourse.* Boston: Houghton, 1968.

Mohr, M. "The Teacher as Researcher." *National Writing Project Network Newsletter* 3 (1980): 4.

Moran, Charles. "Teaching Writing/Teaching Literature." *College Composition and Communication* 32 (1981): 21–29.

Morrow, Daniel. "Dialect Interference in Writing: Another Critical View." *Research in the Teaching of English.* Forthcoming.

Mosenthal, Peter, Lynne Tamor, and Sean A. Walmsley, eds. *Research on Writing: Principles and Methods.* New York: Longman, 1983.

Muller, Herbert. *The Uses of English.* New York: Holt, 1967.

Mullis, Ina, and John C. Mellon. "Guidelines for Describing Three Aspects of Writing: Syntax, Cohesion, and Mechanics." Report no. 10-W-50. Denver: National Assessment of Educational Progress, 1980.

Murphy, James J., ed. *The Rhetorical Tradition and Modern Writing*. New York: MLA, 1982.

Murray, Donald. "Internal Revision: A Process of Discovery." Cooper and Odell, *Research*. 85–103.

——. *Learning by Teaching*. Montclair: Boynton, 1982.

——. "Teaching the Other Self: The Writer's First Reader." *College Composition and Communication* 33 (1982): 140–47.

——. *Write to Learn*. New York: Holt, 1984.

——. *A Writer Teaches Writing*. Boston: Houghton, 1968.

Myers, Miles. *A Model for the Composing Process*. Berkeley: Bay Area Writing Project, U of California, 1980.

Nelson, M. W. "Writers Who Teach: A Naturalistic Investigation." Diss. U of Georgia, 1981.

Newcomb, Theodore M. "Student Peer Group Influence." *The American College*. Ed. Nevitt Sanford. New York: Wiley, 1962.

Newkirk, Thomas. "Anatomy of a Breakthrough: Case Study of a College Freshman Writer." Beach and Bridwell 131–49.

——. "Archimedes' Dream." *Language Arts* 61 (1984): 141–50.

——. "Direction and Misdirection in Peer Response." *College Composition and Communication* 35 (1984): 300–11.

——. "Looking for Trouble: A Way to Unmask Our Readings." *College English* 46 (1984): 756–66.

Newkirk, Thomas, and Nancie Atwell, eds. *Understanding Writing: Ways of Observing, Learning, and Teaching*. Chelmsford: NEREX, 1982.

Nold, Ellen. "Revising." *Writing: Process, Development, and Communication*. Ed. Carl H. Frederiksen and Joseph F. Dominic. Vol. 2 of *Writing: The Nature, Development, and Teaching of Written Communication*. Ed. Carl H. Frederiksen, Marcia Farr Whiteman, and Joseph F. Dominic. 2 vols. Hillsdale: Erlbaum, 1981. 67–79.

North, Stephen. *The Dynamics of Inquiry in Composition*. Upper Montclair: Boynton. Forthcoming.

——. "The Idea of a Writing Center." *College English* 46 (1984): 433–46.

Nystrand, Martin. "An Analysis of Error in Written Communication." *What Writers Know: The Language, Process, and Structure of Written Discourse*. Ed. Nystrand. New York: Academic, 1982. 57–74.

Odell, Lee. "The Classroom Teacher as Researcher." *English Journal* 65 (1976): 106–11.

——. "Piaget, Problem-Solving, and Freshman Composition." *College Composition and Communication* 24 (1973): 36–42.

——. "Teaching Reading: An Alternate Approach." *English Journal* 22 (1973): 450–63.

O'Donnell, Roy C., William J. Griffin, and Raymond C. Norris. *Syntax of Kindergarten and Elementary School Children: A Transformational Analysis*. Champaign: NCTE, 1967.

O'Hare, Frank. *Sentence Combining: Improving Student Writing without Formal Grammar Instruction*. NCTE Research Report 15. Urbana: NCTE, 1973.

Ohmann, Richard. *English in America: A Radical View of the Profession*. New York: Oxford UP, 1976.

Olson, David. "From Utterance to Text: The Bias of Language in Speech and Writing." *Harvard Educational Review* 47 (1977): 257–81.

Ong, Walter. *Orality and Literacy*. London: Methuen, 1982.

Onore, Cynthia. "Students' Revisions and Teachers' Comments: Toward a Transactional Theory of the Composing Process." Diss. New York U, 1983.

Paris Review *Interviews: Writers at Work*. 4 vols. Ed. George Plimpton. Harmondsworth: Penguin, 1965.

Parker, William Riley. "Where Do English Departments Come From?" *College English* 28 (1967): 339–51.

Pattison, Robert. *On Literacy: The Politics of the Word from Homer to the Age of Rock*. New York: Oxford UP, 1982.

Pearsall, Thomas E. "Situational Analysis of the Technical Writing Course." *Technical Communication* 31.4 (1984): 21–24.

Peitzman, Faye C. "The Composing Processes of Three College Freshmen: Focus on Revision." Diss. New York U, 1981.

Perelman, Chaim, and L. Olbrechts-Tyteca. *The New Rhetoric: A Treatise on Argumentation*. Notre Dame: U of Notre Dame P, 1969.

Perl, Sondra. "The Composing Processes of Unskilled College Writers." *Research in the Teaching of English* 13 (1979): 317–36.

——— . "Understanding Composing." *College Composition and Communication* 31 (1980): 363–69.

Perry, William. *Cognitive Ethical Growth: The Making of Meaning in Understanding Today's Students*. Ed. David DeCoster and Phyllis Mable. San Francisco: Jossey, 1981. 76–116.

——— . *Forms of Intellectual and Ethical Development in the College Years: A Scheme*. New York: Holt, 1970.

——— . "Intellectual and Ethical Forms of Development." *Pupil Personnel Services Journal* 6 (1977): 61–68.

——— . *Patterns of Development in Thought and Values of Students in a Liberal Arts College: A Validation of a Scheme*. HEW Report 5-0825, 1968.

——— . "Students' Use and Misuse of Reading Skills: A Report to the Faculty." *Harvard Educational Review* 29 (1959): 193–200.

Peters, Thomas J., and Robert H. Waterman, Jr. *In Search of Excellence*. New York: Warner, 1982.

Petersen, Bruce T. "Writing about Responses: A Unified Model of Reading, Interpretation, and Composition." *College English* 44 (1982): 459–68.

Petrosky, Anthony R. "From Story to Essay: Reading and Writing." *College Composition and Communication* 33 (1982): 19–36.

——— . "Grammar Instruction: What We Know." *English Journal* 66 (1977): 86–88.

Pettigrew, Joan, Robert A. Shaw, and A. D. Van Nostrand. "Collaborative Analysis of Writing Instruction." *Research in the Teaching of English* 15 (1981): 329–41.

Phelps, Louise Weatherbee. "The Dance of Discourse: A Dynamic, Relativistic View of Structure." *Pre/Text* 3 (1982): 51–83.

——— . "Dialectics of Coherence: Toward an Integrative Theory." *College English* 47 (1985): 12–29.

Piaget, Jean. *The Child's Conception of the World*. New York: Humanities, 1951.

——— . *The Construction of Reality in the Child*. New York: Basic, 1954.

——— . *Language and Thought of a Child*. Trans. Marjorie Bagain. New York: Free, 1965.

——— . *Six Psychological Studies*. New York: Random, 1967.

Pike, Kenneth L. "Beyond the Sentence." *College Composition and Communication* 15 (1964): 129–35.

Pinnelli, Thomas E., et al. "Report-Reading Patterns of Technical Managers and Nonmanagers." *Technical Communication* 31.3 (1984): 20–24.

Plato. *Gorgias*. Trans. W. R. M. Lamb. Cambridge: Harvard UP, 1975.

———. *Phaedrus*. Trans. W. C. Helmbold and W. G. Rabinowitz. Indianapolis: Bobbs, 1956.

———. *Phaedrus and Letters VII and VIII*. Harmondsworth: Penguin, 1973.

Polanyi, Michael. *Personal Knowledge: Toward a Post-Critical Philosophy*. 1958. London: Routledge, 1962.

Ponsot, Marie, and Rosemary Deen. *Beat Not the Poor Desk: Writing: What to Teach, How to Teach It, and Why*. Upper Montclair: Boynton, 1982.

Porat, Marc U. *The Information Economy*. 9 vols. Washington: GPO, 1977.

Post, Louis. "The Economics of Information." *Technical Communication* 31.4 (1984): 25–26.

Powdermaker, Hortense. *Stranger and Friend: The Way of an Anthropologist*. New York: Norton, 1966.

Priestley, Joseph. *A Course of Lectures on Oratory and Criticism*. Yorkshire: Scolar, 1965.

Purves, Alan. "NCTE: The House of Intellect or Spencer Gifts." *College English* 46 (1984): 693–97.

Purves, Alan C., and Virginia Rippere. *Elements of Writing about a Literary Work: A Study of Responses to Literature*. Urbana: NCTE, 1968.

Quintilian. *Institutio oratoria*. Trans. H. E. Butler. 4 vols. Cambridge: Harvard UP, 1969–79.

Rabinow, Paul, and William Sullivan, eds. *Interpretive Social Science: A Reader*. Berkeley: U of California P, 1979.

Ravitch, Diane. *The Troubled Crusade: American Education 1945–80*. New York: Basic, 1983.

Raymond, James C., ed. *Literacy as a Human Problem*. University: U of Alabama, 1982.

Read, Charles. *Children's Categorization of Speech Sounds in English*. Urbana: NCTE, 1975.

Reports of the Visiting Committees of the Board of Overseers of Harvard College. Cambridge: Harvard Coll., 1902.

Rhetorica ad herennium. Trans. H. Caplan. Cambridge: Harvard UP, 1954.

Richards, I. A. *Philosophy of Rhetoric*. New York: Oxford UP, 1936.

Richards, Jack C., ed. *Error Analysis: Perspectives on Second Language Acquisition*. London: Longman, 1977.

Richardson, J. Jeffrey. *Artificial Intelligence: An Analysis of Potential Applications to Training, Performance Measurement, and Job Performance Aiding*. Denver: Air Force Human Resources Laboratory, 1983. AFHRL-TP-83-28.

Richardson, Jacques G. "The Changing Role of Periodicals in Scientific-Technical Communication." *Journal of Technical Writing and Communication* 14.1 (1984): 1–12.

Roberts, Franklin C., and Ok-choon Park. "Intelligent Computer-Assisted Instruction: An Explanation and Overview." *Educational Technology* Dec. 1983: 7–12.

Roberts, Paul. *English Sentences*. New York: Harcourt, 1962.

Roche, Maurice. *Language, Phenomenology, and the Social Sciences*. London: Routledge, 1973.

Rodriguez, Richard. *An Autobiography: Hunger of Memory*. Toronto: Bantam, 1982.

Rohman, D. Gordon. "Pre-Writing: The Stage of Discovery in the Writing Process." *College Composition and Communication* 16 (1965): 106–12.

Rorty, Richard. *Philosophy and the Mirror of Nature*. Princeton: Princeton UP, 1979.

Rose, Mike. "Rigid Rules, Inflexible Plans, and the Stifling of Language: A Cognitivist Analysis of Writer's Block." *College Composition and Communication* 31 (1980): 389–401.

———. *When a Writer Can't Write: Studies in Writer's Block and Other Composing Process Problems*. New York: Guilford. Forthcoming.

Rose, Shirley. "Down from the Haymow: One Hundred Years of Sentence Combining." *College English* 45 (1983): 483–91.

Rosen, Connie, and Harold Rosen. *The Language of Primary School Children*. Harmondsworth: Penguin, 1973.

Rosenblatt, Louise M. *Literature as Exploration*. 1938. New York: MLA, 1983.

———. *The Reader, the Text, the Poem: The Transactional Theory of the Literary Work*. Carbondale: Southern Illinois UP, 1978.

Rosenshine, Barak, and David Berliner. "Academic Engaged Time." *British Journal of Teacher Education* 4 (1978): 3–16.

Rubin, Donnalee. "Evaluating Freshman Writers: What Do Students Really Learn?" *College English* 45 (1983): 373–79.

Rubin, Donnalee, and G. Piche. "Development in Syntactic and Strategic Aspects of Audience Adaptation Skills in Written Persuasive Communication." *Research in the Teaching of English* 13 (1979): 293–316.

Salvatori, Mariolina. "Reading and Writing a Text: Correlations between Reading and Writing Patterns." *College English* 45 (1983): 657–86.

Sapir, Edward. *Language*. New York: Harcourt, 1949.

Saussure, Ferdinand de. *Course in General Linguistics*. Trans. Wade Baskin. New York: Ronald, 1965.

Scardemalia, M., R. Bracewell, and C. Bereiter. "Writing and Decentered Thought: The Development of Audience Awareness." Symposium on the Writing Process. American Educational Research Assn. 1978.

Scardemalia, Marlene. "How Children Cope with the Cognitive Demands of Writing." *Writing: Process, Development, and Communication*. Ed. Carl H. Frederiksen and Joseph F. Dominic. Vol. 2 of *Writing: The Nature, Development, and Teaching of Written Communication*. Ed. Carl H. Frederiksen, Marcia Farr Whiteman, and Joseph F. Dominic. 2 vols. Hillsdale: Erlbaum, 1981. 81–103.

Scardemalia, Marlene, Carl Bereiter, and Hillel Goelman. "The Role of Production Factors in Writing Ability." *What Writers Know: The Language, Process, and Structure of Written Discourse*. Ed. Martin Nystrand. New York: Academic, 1982. 173–210.

Schacter, Jacquelyn, and Marianne Celce-Murcia. "Some Reservations concerning Error Analysis." *TESOL Quarterly* 11 (1977): 441–51.

Schank, Roger C., ed. *Conceptual Information Processing*. New York: American Elsevier, 1975.

Schank, R., and R. Abelson. *Scripts, Plans, Goals, and Understanding*. Hillsdale: Erlbaum, 1977.

Schank, Roger C., with Peter G. Childers. *The Cognitive Computer: On Language,*

Learning, and Artificial Intelligence. Reading: Addison, 1984.

Scott, Fred N. "What the West Wants in Preparatory Education." *School Review* 17 (1909): 10–20.

Scott, Fred N., and J. V. Denney. *Elementary English Composition.* Boston: Allyn, 1900.

Scribner, Sylvia, and Michael Cole. "Unpackaging Literacy." *Variation in Writing.* Ed. Marcia Farr Whiteman. Vol. 1 of *Writing: The Nature, Development, and Teaching of Written Communication.* Ed. Carl H. Frederiksen, Marcia Farr Whiteman, and Joseph F. Dominic. 2 vols. Hillsdale: Erlbaum, 1981. 71–88.

Selman, R. Rev. of H. Furth and H. Wach, *Thinking Goes to School. Harvard Educational Review* 45 (1975): 127–34.

Selzer, Jack. "The Composing Process of an Engineer." *College Composition and Communication* 34 (1983): 178–87.

——— . "Resources for Teachers of Technical Writing." *Technical Communication* 31.4 (1984): 39–44.

——— . "What Constitutes a 'Readable' Technical Style?" Anderson et al. 71–89.

Shaughnessy, Mina. "Basic Writing." Tate 137–68.

——— . *Errors and Expectations.* New York: Oxford UP, 1977.

Simon, Herbert A. *The Sciences of the Artificial.* 2nd ed. Cambridge: MIT P, 1981.

Sledd, James. "Doublespeak: Dialectology in the Service of Big Brother." *College English* 33 (1972): 439–56.

Sleeman, D., and J. S. Brown, eds. *Intelligent Tutoring Systems.* New York: Academic, 1982.

Smith, Adam. *Lectures on Rhetoric and Belles Lettres.* Ed. John M. Lothian. London: Nelson, 1963.

Smith, Frank. *Writing and the Writer.* New York: Holt, 1982.

Smith, Joshua. "Keynote Address." Eighth Annual Practical Conference on Communication. Knoxville. 22 Oct. 1984.

Smith, William L., et al. "Some Effects of Varying the Structure of a Topic on College Students' Writing." *Written Composition* 2 (1985): 73–89.

Sommers, Nancy I. "The Need for Theory in Composition Research." *College Composition and Communication* 30 (1979): 46–49.

——— . "Responding to Student Writing." *College Composition and Communication* 33 (1982): 148–56.

——— . "Revision in the Composing Process: A Case Study of Experienced Writers and Student Writers." Diss. Boston U, 1978.

——— . "Revision Strategies of Student Writers and Experienced Writers." *College Composition and Communication* 31 (1980): 378–88.

Sowers, Susan. "Six Questions Teachers Ask about Invented Spelling." Newkirk and Atwell 47–54.

——— . "The Story and the 'All about Book.'" *Breaking Ground: Teachers Relate Reading and Writing in the Elementary School.* Ed. Jane Hansen, Thomas Newkirk, and Donald Graves. Portsmouth: Heinemann, 1985. 73–82.

Spradley, James P. *The Ethnographic Interview.* New York: Holt, 1979.

Stallard, C. "An Analysis of the Writing Behavior of Good Student Writers." *Research in the Teaching of English* 8 (1974): 206–18.

Standiford, Sally N., Kathleen Jaycox, and Anne Auten. *Computers in the English Classroom.* Urbana: NCTE, 1982.

Stewart, Donald C. "Composition Textbooks and the Assault on the Tradition."

College Composition and Communication 29 (1978): 171–76.

———. "Some Facts Worth Knowing about the Origins of Freshman Composition." *CEA Critic* 44 (1982): 2–11.

Stewart, Murray F., and Cary H. Grobe. "Syntactic Maturity, the Mechanics of Writing, and Teachers' Quality Ratings." *Research in the Teaching of English* 13 (1979): 207–15.

Stotsky, Sandra. "Types of Lexical Cohesion in Expository Writing: Implications for Developing the Vocabulary of Academic Discourse." *College Composition and Communication* 33 (1983): 430–46.

Stratton, Charles R. *Technical Writing: Process and Product.* New York: Holt, 1984.

Strong, William. "How Sentence Combining Works." *Sentence Combining: A Rhetorical Perspective.* Ed. Donald Daiker, Andrew Kerek, and Max Morenberg. Carbondale: Southern Illinois UP, 1985. 334–50.

———. *Sentence Combining: A Composing Book.* New York: Random, 1973.

Strunk, William, Jr., and E. B. White. *The Elements of Style.* 2nd ed. New York: Macmillan, 1972.

Szwed, John G. "The Ethnography of Literacy." *Variation in Writing.* Ed. Marcia Farr Whiteman. Vol. 1 of *Writing: The Nature, Development, and Teaching of Written Communication.* Ed. Carl H. Frederiksen, Marcia Farr Whiteman, and Joseph F. Dominic. 2 vols. Hillsdale: Erlbaum, 1981. 13–25.

Tate, Gary, ed. *Teaching Composition: 10 Bibliographic Essays.* Fort Worth: Texas Christian UP, 1976.

Tate, Gary, and Edward P. J. Corbett, eds. *The Writing Teacher's Sourcebook.* New York: Oxford UP, 1981.

Taylor, Denny. *Family Literacy.* Exeter: Heinemann, 1983.

Taylor, Robert S. "Value-Added Processes in the Information Life Cycle." *Journal of the American Society for Information Science* 33 (1982): 341–46.

Thomas, Owen P. *Transformational Grammar and the Teacher of English.* New York: Holt, 1965.

Thorpe, James. *The Aims and Methods of Scholarship in Modern Languages and Literature.* New York: MLA, 1963.

Todorov, Tzvetan. *Théories du symbole.* Paris: Seuil, 1977.

Tompkins, Jane, ed. *Reader Response Criticism: From Formalism to Post Structuralism.* Baltimore: Johns Hopkins UP, 1980.

Toulmin, Stephen. *The Philosophy of Science.* New York: Harper, 1953.

———. *The Uses of Argument.* Cambridge: Cambridge UP, 1958.

Touretzky, David S. *LISP: A Gentle Introduction to Symbolic Computing.* New York: Harper, 1984.

Trimbur, John. "Literature and Composition: Separatism or Convergence?" *Journal of Teaching Writing* (1984): 109–15.

———. "Peer Tutors and the Benefits of Collaborative Learning." *Writing Lab Newsletter* 8 (1983): 1–3.

———. "Students or Staff: Thoughts on the Use of Peer Tutors in Writing Centers." *WPA* 7.1–2 (1983): 33–38.

von Reyn, Janet. "Learning Together: A Teacher's First Year Teaching Reading and Writing." *Breaking Ground: Teachers Relate Reading and Writing in the Elementary School.* Ed. Jane Hansen, Thomas Newkirk, and Donald Graves. Portsmouth: Heinemann, 1985. 29–35.

Vygotsky, Lev. *Thought and Language*. Cambridge: MIT Press, 1978.

Walmsley, Sean A. "Writing Disability." Mosenthal et al. 277–86.

Warnock, Tilly. "Preface 5: The Dreadful Has Already Happened; or, What Is a Rhetorician's Role in an English Department?" *Pre/Text* 4 (1983): 165–78.

Welty, Eudora. *One Writer's Beginnings*. Cambridge: Harvard UP, 1984.

White, Edward M. "Post-Structural Literary Criticism and the Response to Student Writing." *College Composition and Communication* 35 (1984): 186–95.

Whitehead, Alfred North. *Modes of Thought*. New York: Free, 1966.

Whyte, William Foote. *Street Corner Society*. 2nd ed. Chicago: U of Chicago P, 1955.

Wiener, Norbert. *The Human Use of Human Beings: Cybernetics and Society*. Boston: Houghton, 1950.

Williams, Joseph. "Critical Thinking, Cognitive Development, and the Teaching of Writing." Inst. on Higher Order Reasoning, U of Chicago. May 1984.

——— . "On Defining Complexity." *College English* 40 (1979): 595–609.

——— . "The Phenomenology of Error." *College Composition and Communication* 32 (1981): 152–68.

Winograd, Terry. *Understanding Natural Language*. New York: Academic, 1972.

Winston, Patrick. *Artificial Intelligence*. Reading: Addison, 1977.

Winterowd, W. Ross. "Black Holes, Indeterminacy, and Paolo Freire." *Rhetoric Review* 2.1 (1983): 28–35.

——— . "A Comment on Bruce T. Petersen's 'Writing about Response.'" *College English* 46 (1984): 306–08.

——— . "Dear Peter Elbow." *Pre/Text* 4 (1983): 95–101.

——— . "Getting It Together in the English Department." *ADE Bulletin* 55 (1977): 28–31.

——— . "Post-Structuralism and Composition." *Pre/Text* 4 (1983): 79–92.

——— . "The Realms of Meaning: Text Centered Criticism." *College Composition and Communication* 23 (1972): 399–405.

——— . "The Three R's: Reading, Reading, and Rhetoric." *College Composition and Communication* (1976): 51–63.

Witte, Stephen P., and Lester Faigley. "Coherence, Cohesion, and Writing Quality." *College Composition and Communication* 32 (1981): 189–204.

Wotring, Ann Miller, and Robert Tierney. *Two Studies of Writing in High School Science*. Classroom Research Study 5. Berkeley: Bay Area Writing Project, U of California, 1981.

Wresch, William, ed. *The Computer in Composition Instruction: A Writer's Tool*. Urbana: NCTE, 1984.

Writing Achievement, 1969–79: Results from the Third National Writing Assessment. Denver: National Assessment of Educational Progress, 1980.

Writing Mechanics, 1969–1974: A Capsule Description of Changes in Writing Mechanics. Washington: GPO, 1975.

Young, Art. "Rebuilding Community in the English Department." *ADE Bulletin* 77 (1984): 13–21.

Young, Richard E. "Paradigms and Problems: Needed Research in Rhetorical Invention." Cooper and Odell, *Research* 29–48.

Young, Richard E., and Alton L. Becker. "Toward a Modern Theory of Rhetoric: A Tagememic Contribution." *Harvard Educational Review* 35 (1965): 450–68.

Young, Richard E., Alton L. Becker, and Kenneth L. Pike. *Rhetoric: Discovery and*

Change. New York: Harcourt, 1970.

Zehm, S. J. "Educational Misfits: A Study of Poor Performers in the English Class 1825–1925." Diss. Stanford U, 1973.

Ziv, Nina D. "The Effect of Teacher Comments on the Writing of Four College Freshmen." Beach and Bridwell 362–80.

Notes on the Contributors

Nancie Atwell is an eighth-grade teacher in the Boothbay Region Elementary School, Boothbay Harbor, Maine. She holds a BA in English from the State University of New York, Buffalo. She directs the Boothbay Writing Project, consults on writing at schools and colleges throughout the United States and Canada, and sits on the Executive Committee of the National Council of Teachers of English. The author of articles on reading, writing, and research, she is coeditor of *Understanding Writing: Ways of Observing, Learning, and Teaching* (Chelmsford: NEREX, 1982).

Lil Brannon, who holds an EdD in composition and literature from East Texas State University, is assistant professor of English and education at New York University. She is also codirector of the Expository Writing Program, founder and director of the Writing Center, and founder and coeditor of the *Writing Center Journal*. She has published widely in professional journals and has coauthored two books: *Writers Writing* (Montclair: Boynton, 1982) and *Rhetorical Traditions and the Teaching of Writing* (Montclair: Boynton, 1984).

Hugh Burns, a lieutenant colonel in the United States Air Force, works on the artificial-intelligence research program at the Air Force Human Resources Laboratory. He received a PhD from the University of Texas, where he studied English education and rhetoric, specializing in computer-assisted invention and creativity. He has taught at the Air Force Academy as associate professor of English and has written extensively on computers and English education. He is best known for designing three invention programs—Topoi, Burke, and Tagi—all open-ended computer-assisted composition software.

Lucy Calkins is associate professor of English education at Teachers College, Columbia University, where she also directs the Writing Project, a large-scale teacher-training effort in the New York City schools that employs naturalistic research on how teachers change. She earned her PhD in English education from New York University. She is the author of numerous publications on teaching reading and writing, including *Lessons from a Child: On the Teaching and Learning of Writing* (Exeter: Heinemann, 1983) and *Teaching Writing* (Exeter: Heinemann, forthcoming).

John Clifford is associate professor of English at the University of North Carolina, Wilmington, where he also directs the composition program. His PhD from New York University is in composition, literature, and language. His publications in professional journals include articles on teaching literature, reading and writing theory, and collaborative learning. He is coauthor of *Modern American Prose: A Reader for Writers* (New York: Random, 1983), *Sentence Combining: Shaping Ideas for Better Style* (Indianapolis: Bobbs, 1983), and *Writing, Reading, and Research* (Indianapolis: Bobbs, 1984).

Timothy R. Donovan holds a PhD in English from the University of Wisconsin. He is associate professor of English at Northeastern University, where he directed the freshman English program for many years and now coordinates upper-division writing. He is also a fellow of the Iowa Institute on Writing and supervisor of the Martha's Vineyard Summer Institute on Teaching Writing. He has published numerous articles on writing pedagogy, teacher training, and program administration, and he is coeditor of *Eight Approaches to Teaching Composition* (Urbana: NCTE, 1980).

Anne Ruggles Gere, associate professor of English at the University of Washington, received her PhD from the University of Michigan. She is the director of the Puget Sound Writing Program. A consultant and workshop leader at schools and colleges, she has also published widely in the profession's journals. In addition to coauthoring *Attitudes, Language, and Change* (Urbana: NCTE, 1979), she has written *Writing and Learning* (New York: Macmillan, 1985) and *Roots in the Sawdust: Writing to Learn across the Disciplines* (Urbana: NCTE, 1985).

Glynda Hull, who received her PhD in English from the University of Pittsburgh, is a postdoctoral fellow at the university's Learning Research and Development Center. She is the recipient of the 1984 Outstanding Dissertation Award for Empirical Research from the American Educational Research Association. She has written several articles and contributions to books on composition research and pedagogy. Currently she is engaged in research on computer-assisted editing.

Michael L. Keene, associate professor of English at the University of Tennessee, specializes in teaching technical writing. He earned his PhD in English from the University of Texas. He has published articles on logic, second-language instruction, and teaching technical writing. A senior member of the Society for Technical Communication, he is also a freelance technical editor, specializing in proposals. He authored the revised eighth edition of W. Paul Jones's *Writing Scientific Papers and Reports* (Dubuque: Brown, 1981.)

C. H. Knoblauch received his PhD in English from Brown University. He is associate professor of English at the State University of New York, Albany, where he also directs the writing program. He has published numerous articles on rhetorical theory, composition theory and teaching, and eighteenth-century English literature. He is coauthor of *The Process of Writing: Discovery and Control* (Boston: Houghton, 1982) and *Rhetorical Traditions and the Teaching of Writing* (Montclair: Boynton, 1984). In addition, he has just completed a book-length manuscript on eighteenth-century British discourse theory.

Andrea Lunsford is associate professor of English at the University of British Columbia. She holds a PhD from Ohio State University. She has a distinguished record of service to professional associations and has published widely on history and theory of rhetoric, composition theory, reading theory, and eighteenth- and nineteenth-century nonfiction prose. Her books include *The Thinking Writer* (New York: Harper, 1986), *The Rhetorical Works of Alexander Bain* (Carbondale: Southern Illinois UP, 1986), and the coedited *Essays on Classical Rhetoric and Modern Discourse* (Carbondale: Southern Illinois UP, 1984).

Ben W. McClelland is professor of English at Rhode Island College, where he was the founding director of the Writing Center and chairman of the English department. He holds a PhD in English from Indiana University. A consultant on writing-program administration, he has conducted workshops at schools and colleges. He is coeditor of *Eight Approaches to Teaching English* (Urbana: NCTE, 1980) and author of *Writing Practice: A Rhetoric of the Writing Process* (New York: Longman, 1984).

Thomas Newkirk, associate professor of English at the University of New Hampshire, earned his PhD in English education at the University of Texas. He is director of the New Hampshire Writing Program, a teacher training institute. He has published several articles and contributions to books on reading, writing, and literacy. He is coeditor of *Understanding Writing: Ways of Observing, Learning, and Teaching* (Chelmsford: NEREX, 1982).

John Schilb, vice-president of the Associated Colleges of the Midwest, holds a PhD in English from the State University of New York, Binghamton. He was director of the Cape Fear Writing Project and has delivered numerous conference papers, authored articles, and contributed chapters to books on topics ranging from American literature, women's studies, and film to technical writing and composition.

William Strong is professor of secondary education at Utah State University, where he also directs the Utah Writing Project and edits the *Utah English Journal*. His PhD in English is from the University of Illinois. A ubiquitous presenter on sentence combining, he is also well-published in professional journals. Among his books are *Crafting Cumulative Sentences* (New York: Random, 1984), *Practicing Sentence Options* (New York: Random, 1984), and the coauthored *Facing Value Decisions: Rationale Building for Teachers* (New York: Wadsworth, 1976; New York: Teachers Coll. P, 1982).

John Trimbur, who received his PhD in English from the State University of New York, Buffalo, is a veteran writing-program administrator, who now teaches at the College of Basic Studies, Boston University. A participating fellow in the Brooklyn College Peer Tutoring Institute, he has published on peer tutoring, writing-program administration, and contemporary poetry.

Index